ITALIAN
AT A GLANCE

PHRASE BOOK & DICTIONARY FOR TRAVELERS

BY MARIO COSTANTINO
Assistant Principal, M.A.
Foreign Languages and Bilingual Education
Samuel J. Tilden High School
New York

HEYWOOD WALD, Coordinating Editor
Chairman, Department of Foreign Languages
Martin Van Buren High School
New York

BARRON'S EDUCATIONAL SERIES, INC.
New York ■ London ■ Toronto ■ Sydney

Cover and Book Design   Milton Glaser, Inc.

Illustrations   Juan Suarez

All inquiries should be addressed to:
Barron's Educational Series, Inc.
250 Wireless Boulevard
Hauppauge, New York 11788

Library of Congress Catalog Card No. 84-2871

Paper Edition
International Standard Book No. 0-8120-2713-2

Library of Congress Cataloging in Publication Data
Costantino, Mario.
    Italian at a glance.

    Includes index.
    1. Italian language—Conversation and phrase books—
English. I. Wald, Heywood. II. Title.
PC1121.C73   1984   458.3'421   84-2871
ISBN 0-8120-2713-2

PRINTED IN THE UNITED STATES OF AMERICA
901   880   16 15 14 13 12 11 10

CONTENTS

PREFACE

So you're taking a trip to one of the many fascinating countries of the world. That's exciting! In more ways than one, this new phrase book will prove an invaluable companion that will make your stay far more interesting and truly unforgettable.

This phrase book is part of a new series being launched by Barron's Educational Series, Inc. In these books we present the phrases and words that a traveler most often needs for a brief visit to a foreign country, where the customs and language are often different. Each of the phrase books highlights the terms particular to that country, in situations that the tourist is most likely to encounter. With a specially developed key to pronunciation, this book will enable you to communicate quickly and confidently in colloquial terms. It is intended not only for beginners with no knowledge of the language, but also for those who have already studied it and have some familiarity with it.

Some of the unique features and highlights of the Barron's series are:

■ Easy-to-follow *pronunciation keys* and complete phonetic transcriptions for all words and phrases in the book.

■ Compact *dictionary* of commonly used words and phrases—built right into this phrase book so there's no need to carry a separate dictionary.

■ Useful phrases for the *tourist*, grouped together by subject matter in a logical way so that the appropriate phrase is easy to locate when you need it.

■ Special phrases for the *business traveler*, including banking terms, trade and contract negotiations, and secretarial services.

■ Thorough section on *food and drink*, with comprehensive food terms you will find on menus; these terms are often difficult or impossible to locate in dictionaries, but our section gives you a description of the preparation as well as a definition of what it is.

■ *Emergency phrases* and terms you hope you won't need: legal complications, medical problems, theft or loss of valuables, replacement or repair of watches, camera, and the like.

■ *Sightseeing itineraries*, shopping tips, practical travel tips, and regional food specialties to help you get off the beaten path and into the countryside, to the small towns and cities, and to the neighboring areas.

■ A *reference section* providing: important signs, conversion tables, holidays, abbreviations, telling time, days of week and months of year.

■ A brief *grammar section*, with the basic elements of the language quickly explained.

Enjoy your vacation and travel with confidence. You have a friend by your side.

ACKNOWLEDGMENTS

We would like to thank the following individuals and organizations for their assistance on this project: Giuseppe Abbatangelo, Italian Government Travel Office, New York, New York; Professor Alvino Fantini, School for International Training, Brattleboro, Vermont; Jim Ferri, managing editor, *Travel-Holiday* magazine; Robert Fisher, Fisher Travel Guides, New York, New York; George Lang, George Lang, Inc., New York, New York; Professor Joseph Tursi, SUNY Stony Brook, New York; Professor Henry Urbanski, chairman, Department of Foreign Languages, SUC New Paltz, New York; Robert Brainerd; and Hedy Giusti-Lanham.

Also Alitalia, the Association of American Travel Writers, the Italian Cultural Council, the Italian Government Travel Office, the New York *Times, Signature* magazine, *Travel-Holiday* magazine, *Travel and Leisure* magazine, U.S. Tour Operators, and U.S. Travel Data Center.

Also I wish to thank Biagio Colucci, M.D. and Padre Saverio Corradino S.J. (Istituto Biblico Roma) for their suggestions and reviewing of various stages of manuscript.

QUICK PRONUNCIATION GUIDE

Although all the phrases in this book are presented with an easy-to-use key to pronunciation, you will find speaking Italian quite a bit easier if you learn a few simple rules. Many vowels and consonants in Italian are pronounced as they would be in English. There are some exceptions, however, which are given below. Since these sounds don't usually vary, you can follow these guidelines in pronouncing all Italian words. Note: When pronouncing the words in the following examples, stress the vowels that appear in CAPITAL letters.

ITALIAN LETTER(S)	SOUND IN ENGLISH	EXAMPLE
	VOWELS	
a	ah (yacht)	**casa** *(kAH-sah)*, house
è	eh (net)	**lèggere** *(lEH-jeh-reh)*, to read
e	ay (hay)	**mela** *(mAY-lah)*, apple
i	ee (feet)	**libri** *(lEE-bree)*, books
o	oh (rope)	**boccone** *(boh-kOH-neh)*, mouthful
u	oo (cool)	**tutto** *(tOOt-toh)*, everything
	CONSONANT SOUNDS	
ci	chee (cheese)	**cinema** *(chEE-nay-mah)*, movies
ce	chay (chair)	**piacere** *(pee-ah-chAY-reh)*, pleasure
ca	kah (cot)	**casa** *(kAH-sah)*, house
co	koh (cold)	**cotto** *(kOHt-toh)*, cooked
che	kay (kent)	**perché** *(pehr-kAY)*, because
chi	key (key)	**pochi** *(pOH-key)*, few
gi	jee (jeep)	**giro** *(jEE-roh)*, turn
ge	jay (general)	**generale** *(jay-nay-rAH-leh)*, general
gh	gh (spaghetti)	**spaghetti** *(spah-ghAYt-tee)*

ITALIAN LETTER(S)	SOUND IN ENGLISH	EXAMPLE
CONSONANT SOUNDS		
gli	ll (mi**ll**ion)	**egli** *(AY-ly-ee)*, he **bottiglia** *(boht-tEE-ly-ee-ah)*, bottle
gn	ny (ca**ny**on)	**magnifico** *(mah-ny-EE-fee-koh)*, magnificent
qu	koo (**qu**iet)	**àquila** *(AH-koo-ee-lah)*, eagle
sce	sh (fi**sh**)	**pesce** *(pAY-sheh)*, fish
sci		**sciòpero** *(shee-OH-peh-roh)*, strike
z or zz	ts (ea**ts**)	**pizza** *(pEE-tsah)*, pizza **zero** *(tsEH-roh)*, zero

---

TRAVEL TIP

It is possible, through diet and habit, to ease the transition to a new time zone, commonly referred to as "jet lag." Up to four days prior to your departure, begin accustoming your body to its future schedule by gradually changing the times you eat until they more closely match that of your destination. Eat lightly and avoid carbohydrates. If you are taking a night flight, eat very little the day of your departure and avoid alcohol and even dinner on the plane if it is offered. Instead, ask to have your breakfast earlier, then rest until it is served. When you arrive, you will have had your breakfast about the same time as people in that country, and be ready for your next meal at the appropriate time. When you do have your next meal, try to eat a lot of protein, followed in the next meal by a high-carbohydrate diet. Avoid taking a nap during your first day, and instead go to bed a little earlier than usual.

THE BASICS FOR GETTING BY

MOST FREQUENTLY USED EXPRESSIONS

The following are expressions you'll use over and over—the fundamentals of polite conversation, the way to express what you want or need, and some simple question tags that you can use to construct all sorts of questions. We suggest you become very familiar with these phrases.

Yes	**Sì**	*see*
No	**No**	*noh*
Maybe	**Forse**	*fOHr-seh*
Please	**Per piacere**	*pEHr pee-ah-chAY-reh*
Thank-you (very much)	**(Mille) grazie**	*(mEEl-leh) grAH-tsee-eh*
You're welcome	**Prego**	*prEh-goh*
Excuse me	**Mi scusi**	*mee skOO-see*
I'm sorry	**Mi dispiace**	*mee dee-spee-AH-cheh*
Just a second	**Un momento**	*OOn-moh-mEHn-toh*
That's all right, okay	**Va bene**	*vah bEH-neh*
It doesn't matter	**Non importa**	*nohn eem-pOHr-tah*
*Good morning (afternoon)	**Buon giorno**	*boo-OHn jee-OHr-noh*

*NOTE: Generally, **buon giorno** is used throughout the day until about 4–6 p.m. The expression **buon pomeriggio** ("good afternoon") is generally not used in conversation but might be heard on radio.

*Good evening (night)	**Buona sera (notte)**	*boo-Oh-nah sAY-rah (nOHt-teh)*
Sir	**Signore**	*see-ny-OH-reh*
Madame	**Signora**	*see-ny-OH-rah*
Miss	**Signorina**	*see-ny-oh-rEE-nah*
Good-bye	**Arrivederci**	*ahr-ree-veh-dAYr-chee*
*See you later (so long)	**A più tardi (ciao)**	*ah pee-OO tAHr-dee (chee-AH-oh)*
See you tomorrow	**A domani**	*ah doh-mAH-nee*

COMMUNICATING

Do you speak English?	**Parla inglese?** *pAHr-lah een-glAY-seh*
I don't speak Italian.	**Io non parlo italiano.** *EE-oh nohn pAHr-loh ee-tah-lee-AH-noh*
I speak a little Italian.	**Parlo poco l'italiano.** *pAHr-loh pOH-koh lee-tah-lee-AH-noh*
Is there anyone here who speaks English?	**C'è qualcuno qui che parla inglese?** *chEH koo-ahl-kOO-noh koo-EE kay pAHr-lah een-glAY-seh*
Do you understand?	**Capisce? (ha capito)?** *kah-pEE-sheh (ah kah-pEE-toh)*
I understand.	**Capisco (ho capito).** *kah-pEE-skoh (oh kah-pEE-toh*
I don't understand.	**Non capisco (non ho capito).** *nohn kah-pEE-skoh (nohn oh kah-pEE-toh)*
What does that mean?	**Che cosa significa (quello)?** *kay kOH-sah see-ny-EE-fee-kah (koo-AYl-loh)*

*NOTE: **Buona sera** is used when meeting people in the late afternoon and throughout the evening. **Buona notte** is used when leaving at the end of the evening. The casual expression **ciao** ("hello," "bye," "so long") is used only with friends and family.

What? What did you say?	**Che? Che cosa ha detto?** *kAY kay KOH-sah ah dAYt-toh*
What do you call this (that) in Italian?	**Come si chiama questo (quello) in italiano?** *kOH-meh see key-AH-mah koo-AYs-toh (koo-AYl-loh) een ee-tah-lee-AH-noh*
Please speak slowly.	**Per piacere parli lentamente.** *pehr pee-ah-chAY-reh pAHr-lee lehn-tah-mEHn-teh*
Please repeat that.	**Lo ripeta per favore.** *loh ree-pEH-tah pehr fah-vOH-reh*

INTRODUCTIONS

I'm American (English) (Australian) (Canadian).	**Sono americano(a) (inglese) (australiano) (canadese).** *sOH-noh ah-meh-ree-kAH-noh (nah) (een-glAY-seh) (ah-oos-trah-lee-AH-noh) (kah-nah-dAY-seh)*
My name is ____.	**Mi chiamo ____.** *mee kee-AH-moh*
What's your name?	**Lei, scusi, come si chiama?** *lEH-ee, skOO-see, kOH-meh see key-AH-mah*
How are you?	**Come sta?** *kOH-meh stAH*
How's everything?	**Come va?** *kOH-meh vAH*
Very well, thanks. And you?	**Molto bene, grazie. E lei?** *mOHl-toh bEH-neh, grAH-tsee-eh. Ay lEH-ee*

LOCATIONS

Where is ____?	**Dove si trova ____?** *dOH-veh see trOH-vah*
◼ the bathroom	**un gabinetto (una toilette)** *oon gah-bee-nAYt-toh (oo-nah too-ah-lEHt)*
◼ the dining room (restaurant)	**un ristorante** *oon rees-toh-rAHn-teh*
◼ the entrance	**l'ingresso** *leen-grEHs-soh*
◼ the exit	**l'uscita** *loo-shEE-tah*
◼ the telephone	**un telefono** *oon teh-lEH-phoh-noh*

I'm lost.	**Non so dove mi trovo.** *nohn sOH dOH-veh mee trOH-voh*
We are lost.	**Non sappiamo dove ci troviamo.** *nohn sahp-pee-AH-moh dOH-veh chee troh-vee-AH-moh*
Where are ____?	**Dove sono ____?** *dOH-veh sOH-noh*
I am looking for ____.	**Sto cercando ____.** *stOH chehr-kAHn-doh*
Which way do I go?	**In che direzione devo andare?** *een-kAY dee-reh-tsee-OH-neh dAY-voh ahn-dAH-reh*
■ to the left	**a sinistra** *ah see-nEE-strah*
■ to the right	**a destra** *ah dEH-strah*
■ straight ahead	**sempre diritto** *sehm-preh dee-rEEt-toh*
■ around the corner	**all'angolo (della via)** *ahl-lAHn-goh-loh (dAYl-lah vEE-ah)*
■ the first street on the right	**la prima strada a destra** *lah prEE-mah strAH-dah ah dEH-strah*
■ after (before) the second traffic light	**dopo il (prima del) secondo semaforo** *dOH-poh eel (prEE-mah dAYl) say-kOHn-doh say-mAH-foh-roh*

SHOPPING

How much is it?	**Quanto costa?**	*koo-AHn-toh kOH-stah*
I'd like ____.	**Vorrei ____.**	*vohr-rEH-ee*
Please bring me ____.	**Per piacere mi porti ____.**	*pehr pee-ah-chAY-reh mee pOHr-tee*
Please show me (please let me see) ____.	**Per piacere mi mostri (per piacere mi fa vedere) ____.**	*pehr pee-ah-chAY-reh mee mOH-stree (mee fah veh-dEH-reh)*
Here it is.	**Eccolo(a).**	*EH-koh-loh(ah)*

MISCELLANEOUS

I'm hungry.	**Ho fame.**	*oh fAH-meh*
I'm thirsty.	**Vorrei bere (ho sete).**	*vohr-rEH-ee bAY-reh (oh sAY-teh)*
I'm tired.	**Mi sento stanco(a).**	*mee sEHn-toh stAHn-koh(ah)*
What's that?	**Che cos'è quello(a)?**	*kay ko-sEH koo-AYl-loh (lah)*
What's up?	**(Che) cosa succede?**	*(kay) kOH-sah soo-chEH-deh*
I (don't) know.	**(Non) lo so.**	*(nohn) loh sOH*

QUESTIONS

Where is ____?	**Dov'è ____?**	*doh-vEH*
When?	**Quando?**	*koo AHn-doh*
How?	**Come?**	*kOH-meh*
How much?	**Quanto?**	*koo-AHn-toh*
Who?	**Chi?**	*key*
Why?	**Perchè?**	*pehr-kAY*
Which?	**Quale?**	*koo-AH-leh*

EXCLAMATIONS, SLANG, COLLOQUIALISMS

Ouch!	**Ahi!** *AH-ee*
Wow! Gosh! (expressing surprise)	**Eh! Càspita!** *AYh kAH-spee-tah*
Darn it! (expressing annoyance)	**Maledizione!** *mah-leh-dee-tsee-OH-neh*
How beautiful!	**Che bellezza! (che bello!)** *kay behl-lEH-tsah (kay bEHl-loh)*
Ugh!	**Uh!** *OOh*
Phew!	**Uff!** *OOf-f*
That's awful!	**Non va! Non si fa così!** *nohn vAH nohn see fAH koh-sEE*
Great! Wonderful!	**Magnifico! Splendido!** *mah-ny-EE-fee-koh splEHn-dee-doh*
That's it!	**Proprio così!** *prOH-pree-oh ko-sEE*
My goodness!	**Per l'amor del cielo!** *pehr lah-mOHr dayl chee-AY-loh*
Good Heavens!	**Grazie a Dio!** *grAH-tsee-eh ah DEE-oh*
Bottoms up, cheers.	**(Alla) salute! Cin-cin!** *(AHl-lah) sah-lOO-teh cheen-chEEn*
Quiet!	**Silenzio!** *see-lEHn-tsee-oh*
Shut up!	**Zitto(a)(i)(e)!** *tsEEt-toh(tah)(teeh)(teh)*
That's enough!	**Basta!** *bAH-stah*
Never mind!	**Non importa!** *nohn eem-pOHr-tah*
Of course!	**Naturalmente!** *nah-too-rahl-mEHn-teh*
With pleasure!	**Con piacere!** *kohn pee-ah-chAY-reh*
Let's go!	**Andiamo!** *ahn-dee-AH-moh*
What a shame (pity)!	**Peccato!** *pehk-kAH-toh*

What a nuisance (showing annoyance)!	**Che seccatura!** *kay sayk-ah-tOO-rah*
Nonsense! No way!	**Ma che! Impossibile!** *mah kay eem-pohs-sEE-bee-leh*
Don't be stupid.	**Non faccia lo stupido (la stupida).** *nohn fAH-chee-ah loh stOO-pee-doh (lah stOO-pee-dah)*
Are you crazy?	**È pazzo(a)?!?** *EH pAH-tsoh(ah)*
What a fool!	**Che sciocco(a)!** *kay shee-OH-koh(ah)*
Good luck.	**Buona fortuna. (In bocca al lupo!)** *boo-OH-nah fohr-tOO-nah (een bOHk-ah ahl lOO-poh)*

God bless you!

■ (sneeze)   **Salute!** *sah-lOO-teh*

■ (congratulations)   **Dio ti(vi) benedica!** *dEE-oh tee(vee) beh-neh-dEE-cah*

PROBLEMS, PROBLEMS, PROBLEMS (EMERGENCIES)

Watch out! Be careful!	**Attenzione! Stia attento(a)!** *ah-tehn-tsee-OH-neh stEE-ah aht-tEHn-toh(ah)*
Hurry up!	**Si sbrighi!** *see sbrEE-ghee*
Look!	**Guardi!** *goo-AHr-dee*
Wait!	**Aspetti un momento!** *ah-spEHt-tee oon moh-mEHn-toh*
Fire!	**Al fuoco!** *AHl foo-OH-koh*

ANNOYANCES

What's the matter with you?	**Ma che cosa ha?** *mah kay kOH-sah ah*

What (the devil) do you want?	**Ma che (diavolo) vuole?** *mah kay (dee-AH-voh-loh) voo-OH-leh*
Stop bothering me!	**Non mi stia a seccare!** *nohn mee stEE-ah ah sayk-kAH-reh*
Go away!	**Se ne vada!** *say nay vAH-dah*
Scram! Beat it!	**Si tolga dai piedi!** *see tOHl-gah dah-ee pee-EH-dee*
Leave me alone!	**Mi lasci in pace!** *mee lAH-shee een pAH-cheh*
Help, police!	**Aiuto, polizia!** *ah-ee-OO-toh poh-lee-tsEE-ah*
I'm going to call a cop!	**Adesso chiamo un poliziotto!** *ah-dEHs-soh key-AH-moh oon poh-lee-tsee-OHt-toh*
Get out!	**Via! Se ne vada!** *vEE-ah say nay vAH-dah*
That (one) is a thief!	**Quello è un ladro!** *koo-AYl-loh EH oon lAH-droh*
He has snatched my bag!	**Mi ha scippato la borsa!** *mee ah sheep-pAH-toh lah bOHr-sah*

He has stolen _____.	**Mi ha rubato _____.** *mee ah roo-bAH-toh*
I have lost _____.	**Ho perduto _____.** *OH pehr-dOO-toh*
■ my car	**la (mia) auto** *lah (mEE-ah) AH-oo-toh*
■ my passport	**il (mio) passaporto** *eel (mEE-oh) pahs-sah-pOHr-toh*
■ my purse	**la (mia) borsa** *lah (mEE-ah) bOHr-sah*
■ my suitcase	**la (mia) valigia** *lah (mEE-ah) vah-lEE-jee-ah*
■ my wallet	**il (mio) portafoglio** *eel (mEE-oh) pohr-tah-fOH-ly-ee-oh*
■ my watch	**l'orologio (il mio orologio)** *loh-roh-lOH-jee-oh (eel mEE-oh oh-roh-lOH-jee-oh)*
This young man is annoying me.	**Questo giovanotto mi sta disturbando.** *Koo-AY-stoh jee-oh-vah-nOHt-toh mee stah dee-stoor-bAHn-doh*
He keeps following me.	**Sta continuando a seguirmi.** *stah kohn-tee-noo-AHn-doh ah say-goo-EEr-mee*
Stop that boy!	**Fermate quel ragazzo!** *fayr-mAH-teh koo-AYl rak-gAH-tsoh*

TROUBLE

I haven't done anything.	**Non ho fatto niente.** *nohn oh fAHt-toh nee-AYn-teh*
It's a lie!	**È una bugia!** *EH oo-nah boo-jEE-ah*
It's not true.	**Non è vero.** *nohn EH vEH-roh*
I'm innocent.	**Sono innocente.** *sOH-noh een-noh-chEHn-teh*
I want a lawyer.	**Voglio un avvocato.** *vOH-ly-ee-oh oon ahv-voh-kAH-toh*

| I want to go ____. | **Voglio andare ____.** *vOH-ly-ee-oh ahn-dAH-reh* |

■ to the American (British) (Australian) (Canadian) Consulate.

al Consolato Americano (Inglese) (Australiano) (Canadese). *ahl kohn-soh-lAH-toh ah-meh-ree-kAH-noh (een-glAY-seh) (ah-oo-strah-lee-ah-noh) (kah-nah-dAY-seh)*

■ *to the police station

all'ufficio di polizia (al Commissariato) *ahl-loof-fEE-chee-oh dee poh-lee-tsEE-ah (ahl kohm-mees-sah-ree-AH-toh)*

I need help, quick!

Ho bisogno d'aiuto, subito! *oh bee-sOH-ny-oh dah-ee-OO-toh, sOO-bee-toh*

Can you help me, please?

Può aiutarmi, per favore? *poo-OH ah-ee-oo-tAHr-mee pehr fah-vOH-reh*

Does anyone here speak English?

Qui c'è qualcuno che parla inglese? *Koo-EE chEH koo-ahl-kOO-noh kay pAHr-lah een-glAY-seh*

I need an interpreter.

Ho bisogno di un interprete. *oh bee-sOH-ny-oh dee oon een-TEHR-preh-teh*

NUMBERS

You will use numbers the moment you land in Italy, whether it be to exchange money at the airport, purchase a bus ticket for a ride into town, or describe the length of your stay to a customs official. We list here first the cardinal numbers, then follow with ordinal numbers, fractions, and other useful numbers.

CARDINAL NUMBERS

0	**zero** *tsEH-roh*
1	**uno** *OO-noh*
2	**due** *dOO-eh*

*NOTE: In small towns and villages without a local police force, ask to go to **la caserma dei carabinieri.**

3	**tre** *trEH*
4	**quattro** *koo-AHt-troh*
5	**cinque** *chEEn-koo-eh*
6	**sei** *sEH-ee*
7	**sette** *sEHt-teh*
8	**otto** *OHt-toh*
9	**nove** *nOH-veh*
10	**dieci** *dee-EH-chee*
11	**undici** *OOn-dee-chee*
12	**dodici** *dOH-dee-chee*
13	**tredici** *trEH-dee-chee*
14	**quattordici** *koo-aht-tOHr-dee-chee*
15	**quindici** *koo-EEn-dee-chee*
16	**sedici** *sAY-dee-chee*
17	**diciassette** *dee-chee-ahs-sEHt-teh*
18	**diciotto** *dee-chee-OHt-toh*
19	**diciannove** *dee-chee-ahn-nOH-veh*
20	**venti** *vAYn-tee*
▪ 21	**ventuno** *vayn-tOO-noh*
▪ 22	**ventidue** *vayn-tee-dOO-eh*
▪ 23	**ventitrè** *vayn-tee-trEH*
▪ 24	**ventiquattro** *vayn-tee-koo-AHt-troh*
▪ 25	**venticinque** *vayn-tee-chEEn-koo-eh*
▪ 26	**ventisei** *vayn-tee-sEH-ee*
▪ 27	**ventisette** *vayn-tee-sEHt-teh*
▪ 28	**ventotto** *vayn-tOHt-toh*
▪ 29	**ventinove** *vayn-tee-nOH-veh*
30	**trenta** *trEHn-tah*

40	**quaranta**	*koo-ah-rAHn-tah*
50	**cinquanta**	*cheen-koo-AHn-tah*
60	**sessanta**	*sehs-sAHn-tah*
70	**settanta**	*seht-tAHn-tah*
80	**ottanta**	*oht-tAHn-tah*
90	**novanta**	*noh-vAHn-tah*
100	**cento**	*chEHn-toh*
■ 101	**centouno**	*chEHn-toh OO-noh*
■ 102	**centodue**	*chEHn-toh dOO-eh*
200	**duecento**	*doo-eh-chEHn-toh*
300	**trecento**	*treh-chEHn-toh*
400	**quattrocento**	*koo-aht-troh-chEHn-toh*
500	**cinquecento**	*cheen-koo-eh-chEHn-toh*
600	**seicento**	*seh-ee-chEHn-toh*
700	**settecento**	*seht-teh-chEHn-toh*
800	**ottocento**	*oht-toh-chEHn-toh*
900	**novecento**	*noh-veh-chEHn-toh*
1.000	**mille**	*mEEl-leh*
2.000	**duemila**	*dOO-eh mEE-lah*
1.000.000	**un milione**	*OOn mee-lee-OH-neh*
2.000.000	**due milioni**	*dOO-eh mee-lee-OH-nee*

ORDINAL NUMBERS

first	**primo**	*prEE-moh*
second	**secondo**	*seh-kOHn-doh*
third	**terzo**	*tEHr-tsoh*
fourth	**quarto**	*koo-AHr-toh*
fifth	**quinto**	*koo-EEn-toh*

sixth	**sesto**	*sEHs-toh*
seventh	**settimo**	*sEHt-tee-moh*
eighth	**ottavo**	*oht-tAH-voh*
ninth	**nono**	*nOH-noh*
tenth	**decimo**	*dEH-chee-moh*
the last one	**l'ultimo**	*lOOl-tee-moh*
once	**una volta**	*oo-nah vOHl-tah*
twice	**due volte**	*dOO-eh vOHl-teh*
three times	**tre volte**	*trEH vOHl-teh*

FRACTIONS

half of ____.	**la metà di ____.**	*lah meh-tAH dee*
■ half of the money	**la metà dei soldi**	*lah meh-tAH day-ee sOHl-dee*
half a ____.	**mezzo**	*mEH-tsoh*
■ half a kilo	**mezzo chilo**	*mEH-tsoh kEE-loh*
a fourth (quarter)	**un quarto**	*oon koo-AHr-toh*
a dozen	**una dozzina**	*oo-nah doh-tsEE-nah*
■ a dozen oranges	**una dozzina d'arance**	*oo-nah doh-tsEE-nah dah-rAHn-cheh*
100 grams	**un etto**	*oon EHt-toh*
200 grams	**due etti**	*dOO-eh EHt-tee*
350 grams	**tre etti e mezzo**	*treh EHt-tee ay mEH-tsoh*
a pair (of)	**un paio (di)**	*oon pAH-ee-oh (dee)*
■ a pair of shoes	**un paio di scarpe**	*oon pAH-ee-oh dee skAHr-peh*

WHEN YOU ARRIVE

PASSPORT AND CUSTOMS

Italian passport control is a very simple process. If the visitor's passport is in order (up to date), questions are hardly ever asked. In the event of difficulties, the following information will be useful.

My name is _____.	**Mi chiamo _____.**	*mee key-AH-moh*
I'm American (British) (Australian) (Canadian).	**Sono americano(a) (inglese) (australiano-a) (canadese).**	*sOH-noh ah-meh-ree-kAH-noh(ah) (een-glAY-seh) (ah-oo-strah-lee-AH-noh-ah) (kah-nah-dAY-seh)*
My address is _____.	**Il mio indirizzo è _____.**	*eel mEE-oh een-dee-rEE-tsoh EH*
I'm staying at _____.	**Starò a _____.**	*stah-rOH ah*
Here is (are) _____.	**Ecco _____.**	*EHk-oh*
■ my documents	**i (miei) documenti**	*ee (mee-EH-ee) doh-koo-mEHn-tee*
■ my passport	**il (mio) passaporto**	*eel (mEE-oh) pahs-sah-pOHr-toh*
■ my I.D. card	**la (mia) carta d'identità**	*lah (mEE-ah) kAHr-tah dee-dehn-tee-tAH*
I'm _____.	**Sono _____.**	*sOH-noh*
■ on a business trip	**in viaggio d'affari**	*een vee-AH-jee-oh dahf-fAH-ree*
■ on vacation	**in vacanza**	*een vah-kAHn-tsah*
■ visiting relatives (friends)	**venuto(a) a trovare i parenti (gli amici)**	*sOH-noh vay-nOO-toh(ah) ah troh-vAH-reh ee pah-rEHn-tee (ly-ee ah-mEE-chee)*
■ just passing through	**solo di passaggio**	*sOH-loh dee pahs-sAH-jee-oh*

I'll be staying here for ____.	**Resterò qui ____.** *ray-steh-rOH koo-EE pehr*
■ a few days	**alcuni giorni** *ahl-kOO-nee jee-OHr-nee*
■ a few weeks	**alcune settimane** *ahl-kOO-neh seht-tee-mAH-neh*
■ a week	**una settimana** *oo-nah seht-tee-mAH-nah*
■ a month	**un mese** *oon mAY-seh*
I'm traveling ____.	**Sto viaggiando.** *stOH vee-ah-jee-AHn-doh*
■ alone	**da solo(a)** *dah sOH-loh(ah)*
■ with my husband	**con mio marito** *kOHn mEE-oh mah-rEE-toh*
■ with my wife	**con mia moglie** *kOHn mEE-ah mOH-ly-ee-eh*
■ with my family	**con la mia famiglia** *kOHn lah mEE-ah fah-mEE-ly-ee-ah*
■ with my friend	**con il mio amico (la mia amica)** *kOHn eel mEE-oh ah-mEE-koh (lah mEE-ah ah-mEE-kah)*

Customs (**la dogana**—*lah doh-gAH-nah*) in the major port-of-entry airports in Italy is divided into two sections: one, indicated by a red arrow, is for passengers with goods to declare (**merci da dichiarare**); another, marked with a green arrow, is for those with nothing to declare (**nulla da dichiarare**).

The following can be brought into Italy duty-free: 300 (15 packs) of cigarettes, 75 cigars, 1 fifth of liquor (spirits) or 3 bottles of wine. Generally all items for personal use enter the country duty-free.

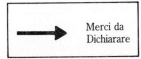

Merci da Dichiarare

Nulla da Dichiarare

These are my bags.	**Queste sono le mie valigie.** *koo-AYs-teh sOH-noh leh mEE-eh vah-lEE-jee-eh*
I have nothing to declare.	**Non ho nulla da dichiarare.** *nohn oh nOOl-lah dah dee-key-ah-rAH-reh*
I only have _____.	**Ho solo _____.** *oh sOH-loh*
■ a carton of cigarettes	**una stecca di sigarette** *oo-nah stAYk-kah dee see-gah-rAYt-teh*
■ a bottle of whisky	**una bottiglia di whisky** *oo-nah boht-tEE-ly-ee-ah dee oo-EE-skey*
They're gifts.	**Sono regali.** *sOH-noh reh-gAH-lee*
They're for my personal use.	**Sono cose di uso personale.** *sOH-noh kOH-seh dee OO-soh pehr-soh-nAH-leh*
Do I have to pay duty?	**Devo pagare dogana?** *dAY-voh pah-gAH-reh doh-gAH-nah*
May I close the bag now?	**Posso chiudere la valigia adesso?** *pOHs-soh key-OO-deh-reh lah vah-lEE-jee-ah ah-dEHs-soh*

IDENTITY CARD

Upon entering the country (or on your flight into the country), you will be required to complete an identity card, usually with the following information.

Cognome: _____	Last name: _____
Nome: _____	First name: _____
Nazionalità: _____	Nationality: _____
Data di nascita: _____	Date of birth: _____
Professione: _____	Profession: _____
Indirizzo: _____	Address: _____
Passaporto da: _____	Passport from: _____

BAGGAGE AND PORTERS

Porters are scarce at European airports. You may be able to locate one, but you'll find it easier and faster to simply use the baggage carts provided at the baggage claim. You can usually wheel your bags right through customs out to the street.

Where can I find a baggage cart?	**Dove posso trovare un carrello portabagagli?** *dOH-veh pOHs-soh troh-vAH-reh oon kahr-rEHl-loh (pohr-tah-bah-gAH-ly-ee)*
I need a porter.	**Ho bisogno di un portabagagli.** *oh bee-sOH-ny-oh dee oon pohr-tah-bah-gAH-ly-ee*
Porter!	**Portabagagli!** *pohr-tah-bah-gAH-ly-ee*
These are our (my) bags.	**Queste sono le nostre (mie) valigie.** *koo-AYs-teh sOH-noh leh nOH-streh (mEE-eh) vah-lEE-jee-eh*
That big (little) one.	**Quella grande (piccola).** *koo-AYl-lah grAHn-deh (pEEk-koh-lah)*

These two black (green) ones.	**Queste due nere (verdi).** *koo-AYs-teh dOO-eh nAY-reh (vAYr-dee)*
Put them here (there).	**Le metta qui (lì).** *leh mAYt-tah koo-EE (lEE)*
Be careful with that one!	**Stia attento a quella lì!** *stEE-ah aht-tEHn-toh ah koo-AYl-lah lEE*
I'll carry this one myself.	**Questa la porto io.** *koo-AYs-tah lah pOHr-toh ee-oh*
I'm missing a suit-case.	**Mi manca una valigia.** *mee mAHn-cah oo-nah vah-lEE-jee-ah*
How much do I owe you?	**Quanto le devo?** *koo-AHn-toh leh dAY-voh*
Thank-you (very much). This is for you.	**(Molte) grazie. Questo è per Lei.** *(mOHl-teh) grAH-tsee-eh Koo-AYs-toh EH pehr lEH-ee*
Where can I get a bus (taxi) to the city?	**Dove posso prendere l'autobus (il tassì) per andare in città?** *dOH-veh pOHs-soh prAYn-deh-reh lAH-oo-toh-boos (eel tahs-sEE) pehr ahn-dAH-reh een cheet-tAH*

TRAVEL TIP

Tired of waiting for your suitcase to come off the plane? You can avoid this delay by packing all your belongings into a small carry-on bag. Especially for those who travel light, the carry-on bag is sufficient to hold a week or two's clothing and personal goods. Avoid bags that are too large to fit under your seat on the plane, however, since not all airlines use planes with overhead bins capable of holding such bags. Some airlines have limits on the dimensions of carry-on bags, and if your bag exceeds those limits, you must check the item.

BANKING AND MONEY MATTERS

Italy's money is based on the **lira** *(lEE-rah)*. Although 100 **centesimi** make up 1 **lira,** these represent an infinitesimal amount and are not exchanged.

Banks in Italy are open five days a week from 8:30 a.m. to 1:30 p.m. They are closed on public holidays (see page 179) and Saturdays. Exchange offices in major airports and railroad stations keep longer hours. A passport is required to exchange cash and checks at a bank. Many hotels will exchange money for you but you will get a better exchange at a bank.

Italian money, the **lira** *(lEE-rah),* is issued in the following denominations: notes—500, 1000, 2000, 5000, 10.000, 20.000, 50.000, and 100.000; coins—5, 10, 20, 50, 100, 200, and 500 lira.

EXCHANGING MONEY

Where is the currency exchange (bank)?	**Dov'è l'ufficio di cambio (la banca)?** *doh-vEH loof-fEE-chee-oh dee kAHm-bee-oh (lah bAHn-kah)*
I wish to change _____.	**Desidero cambiare _____.** *day-sEE-deh-roh kahm-bee-AH-reh*
■money	**il denaro** *eel deh-nAH-roh*
■dollars (pounds)	**i dollari (le sterline)** *ee-dOHl-lah-ree (le stehr-lEE-neh)*
■traveler's checks	**traveler's checks (assegni da viaggiatori)** *(ahs-sEH-ny dah vee-ah jee-ah tOH-ree)*
May I cash a personal check?	**Posso cambiare un assegno personale?** *pOHs-soh kahm-bee-AH-reh oon ahs-sEH-ny-ee-oh pehr-soh-nAH-leh*
What time do they open (close)?	**A che ora aprono (chiudono)?** *ah kay OH-rah AH-proh-noh (key-OO-doh-noh)*

Where is the cashier's window?	**Dov'è lo sportello del cassiere?**
	doh-vEH loh spohr-tEHl-loh dayl kahs-see-AY-reh

The current exchange rates are posted in banks that exchange money and are also published daily in the city newspapers. Since the rates fluctuate from day to day, it may be useful to convert the following lira amounts into their values in your own currency so that you can readily compare prices and determine values.

LIRE	YOUR OWN CURRENCY	LIRE	YOUR OWN CURRENCY
500		50.000	
1.000		75.000	
10.000		100.000	
25.000			

BUSINESS BANKING TERMS • 23

What's the current exchange rate for dollars (pounds)?	**Qual è il cambio corrente del dollaro (della sterlina)?** *koo-ahl-EH eel kAHm-bee-oh kohr-rEHn-teh dayl dOHl-lah-roh (dAYl-lah stehr-lEE-nah)*
What commission do you charge?	**Quale percentuale vi fate pagare?** *koo-AH-leh pehr-chehn-too-AH-leh vee fAH-teh pah-gAH-reh*
Where do I sign?	**Dove debbo firmare?** *dOH-veh dAYb-boh feer-mAH-reh*
I'd like the money _____.	**Vorrei i soldi _____.** *vohr-rEH-ee ee sOHl-dee*
■ in large (small) bills	**in grosse (piccole) banconote** *een grOHs-seh (pEEk-oh-leh) bahn-koh-nOH-teh*
■ in small change	**in spiccioli** *een spee-chee-oh-lee*
Give me two twenty (thousand)-lire bills.	**Mi dia due biglietti da ventimila lire.** *mee dEE-ah dOO-eh bee-ly-ee-AYt-tee dah vayn-tee mEE-lah lEE-reh*
■ fifty thousand lire	**cinquanta mila lire** *cheen-koo-AHn-tah mEE-lah lEE-reh*
■ one hundred thousand lire	**centomila lire** *chehn-toh-mEE-lah lEE-reh*
Do you accept credit cards?	**Si accettano carte di credito?** *see ah-chEHt-tah-noh kAHr-teh dee-krEH-dee-toh*

BUSINESS BANKING TERMS

amount	**ammontare** *ahm-mohn-tAH-reh*
bad check	**assegno scoperto** *ahs-sAY-ny-oh skoh-pEHr-toh*
banker	**banchiere** *bahn-key-EH-reh*
bill	**banconota, biglietto di banca** *bahn-koh-nOH-tah, bee-ly-AYt-toh dee bAHn-kah*

borrow (to)	**prendere a prestito** *prAYn-deh-reh ah prEHs-tee-toh*
cashier	**cassiere** *kahs-see-AY-reh*
capital	**capitale** *kah-pee-tAH-leh*
cashier's office	**cassa** *kAHs-sah*
checkbook	**libretto d'assegni** *lee-brAYt-toh dahs-sEH-ny-ee*
endorse (to)	**firmare** *feer-mAH-reh*
income	**reddito, entrata** *rEHd-dee-toh, ehn-trAH-tah*
interest rate	**tasso d'interesse** *tAHs-soh deen-teh-rEHs-seh*
investment	**investimento** *een-vehs-tee-mEHn-toh*
loss	**perdita** *pEHr-dee-tah*
make change (to)	**cambiare la moneta (i soldi)** *kahm-bee-AH-reh lah moh-nAY-tah (ee sOHl-dee)*
mortgage	**ipoteca** *ee-poh-tEH-kah*
open an account (to)	**aprire un conto in banca** *ah-prEE-reh oon kOHn-toh*
poster	**affisso, avviso** *ahf-fEEs-soh, ahv-vEE-soh*
premium	**premio, compenso** *prEH-mee-oh, kohm-pEHn-soh*
profit	**guadagno, reddito, profitto** *goo-ah-dAH-ny-oh, rEHd-dee-toh, proh-fEEt-toh*
secretary	**secretario(a)** *seh-kreh-tAH-ree-oh(ah)*
safe	**cassaforte** *kahs-sah-fOHr-teh*
signature	**firma** *fEEr-mah*
window	**sportello** *spohr-tEHl-loh*

TIPPING

In many instances, a service charge is included in the price of the service rendered. The added-on service charge usually comes to about 15 to 20 percent, most times indicated on the bill. It is customary, however, to leave some small change in addition to the service included on the bill. This usually consists of 300 to 500 lire, or whatever small change you receive from paying the bill.

It is customary, particularly at the large, deluxe hotels, to leave a tip for the maid and to tip the bellhop, desk attendant, and doorman as well. If you take a tour, the guide will expect a tip, as will taxi drivers, theater ushers, and other service personnel. The following is a table of the most appropriate amounts.

SERVICE	TIP
Waiter	12–15% (included in bill)
Bellhop, porter	1000 lire or 500 lira per bag
Maid	5000 lire per week
Theater usher	500 lire
Taxi driver	15% of fare
Guide	10% of tour cost, also depending on the helpfulness and quality of his/her talk
Barber, hairdresser	15% of the total bill
Shoeshine	500 lire
Bathroom attendant	500 lire

TRAVEL TIP

Always carry traveler's checks, never cash. You'll get a better exchange for your traveler's checks at a bank than at your hotel.

AT THE HOTEL

If you are unfamiliar with the city to which you are going, you'll probably find it best to make a hotel reservation in advance from home. You'll also find that some terminals have reservation desks, at which you may be able to reserve a room. Lastly, if you are unable to locate a hotel once you arrive, go to the tourist information office; someone there will be able to speak English and will help you in locating a suitable hotel. The following is a listing of the major types of hotels you will encounter. By law, the official price of the room must be posted in the room (usually found on the inside of a closet door). The final bill, however, will also include the value-added tax (**I.V.A.**).

albergo	Hotels are classified as deluxe, first, second, third, or fourth class. The extent of the services and luxuriousness of the furnishings will vary with the class.
motel	Situated near the autostrada, these are mostly new and getting better all the time.
locanda	These are lovely, small country inns.
pensione	Usually pretty casual, most of the time these are small residences similar to boardinghouses, in which you are customarily offered meals as well. **Pensione completa** refers to 3 meals a day, **mezza pensione** to 2 meals. Pensiones are also classed and vary in quality, but almost always are a good value.
albergo diurno	These are daytime hotels; that is, they are open during the day to travelers seeking showers, bathrooms, and other facilities. They do not offer beds, and they usually close at night.

GETTING TO YOUR HOTEL

I'd like to go to the ___ Hotel.	**Vorrei andare all'Hotel (Albergo) ___.** *vohr-rEH-ee ahn-dAH-reh ahl-loh-tEHl (ahl-lahl-bEHr-goh)*
Is it near (far)?	**È vicino (lontano)?** *EH vee-chEE-noh (lohn-tAH-noh)*
Where can I get a taxi?	**Dove posso prendere un taxi?** *dOH-veh pOHs-soh prAYn-deh-reh oon tahs-sEE*
What buses go into town?	**Quali autobus vanno in città?** *koo-AH-lee AH-oo-toh-boos vAHn-noh een cheet-tAH*
Where is the bus stop?	**Dov'è la fermata dell'autobus?** *doh-vEH lah fehr-mAH-tah dayl-lAH-oo-toh-boos*
How much is the fare?	**Quant'è la corsa? (il biglietto?)** *koo-ahn-tEH lah kOHr-sah (eel bee-ly-ee-AYt-toh)*

CHECKING IN

Most first-class or deluxe hotels will have personnel who speak English. If you are checking into a smaller hotel, you might find these phrases useful in getting what you want. A room for two persons with a double bed is called **una camera matrimoniale** *(oo-nah kAH-meh-rah mah-tree-moh-nee-AH-leh)* and a room with twin beds is **una camera con due letti** *(oo-nah kAH-meh-rah kohn dOO-eh lEHt-tee)*.

I'd like a single (double) room for tonight.	**Vorrei una camera singola (doppia) per stanotte.** *vohr-rEH-ee oo-nah kAH-meh-rah sEEn-goh-lah (dOHp-pee-ah) pehr stah-nOHt-teh*
How much is the room ___?	**Quant'è la camera ___?** *koo-ahn-tEH lah kAH-meh-rah*
■ with a shower	**con doccia** *kohn dOH-chee-ah*

■ with a private bath	**con bagno proprio (privato)** *kohn bAH-ny-oh prOH-pree-oh (pree-vAH-toh)*
■ with a balcony	**con terrazzino** *kohn tehr-rah-tsEE-noh*
■ facing the sea	**che dia sul mare** *kay dEE-ah sool mAH-reh*
■ facing (away from) the street	**che (non) dia sulla strada** *kay (nohn) dEE-ah sOOl-lah strAH-dah*
■ facing the courtyard	**che dia sul cortile** *kay dEE-ah sOOl kohr-tEE-leh*
Does it have ____?	**Ha ____?** *AH*
■ air-conditioning	**l'aria condizionata** *lAH-ree-ah kohn-dee-tsee-oh-nAH-tah*
■ hot water	**l'acqua calda** *lAH-koo-ah kAHl-dah*
■ television	**la televisione** *lah teh-leh-vee-see-OH-neh*

I (don't) have a reservation.	**(Non) ho prenotazione.** *(nohn) OH preh-noh-tah-tsee-OH-neh*
Could you call another hotel to see if they have something?	**Potrebbe telefonare a un altro hotel per vedere se hanno qualcosa?** *poh-trAYb-beh teh-leh-foh-nAH-reh ah oon AHl-troh oh-tEHl pehr vay-dAY-reh say AHn-noh koo-ahl-kOH-sah*
May I see the room?	**Potrei vedere la camera?** *poh-trEH-ee veh-dAY-reh lah kAH-meh-rah*
I (don't) like it.	**(Non) mi piace.** *(nohn) mee pee-AH-cheh*
Do you have something ____?	**Ha qualche cosa ____?** *ah koo-AHl-keh kOH-sah*
■ better	**di meglio** *dee mEH-ly-ee-oh*
■ larger	**più grande** *pee-OO grAHn-deh*
■ smaller	**più piccolo** *pee-OO pEEk-koh-loh*
■ cheaper	**meno costoso** *mAY-noh koh-stOH-soh*
■ quieter	**più quieto (tranquillo)** *pee-OO quee-EH-toh (trahn-hoo-EEl-loh)*
What floor is it on?	**A che piano è?** *ah kay pee-AH-noh EH*
Is there an elevator (lift)?	**C'è l'ascensore?** *chEH lah-shehn-sOH-reh*
How much is the room ____?	**Quanto si paga per una camera ____?** *koo-AHn-toh see pAH-gah pehr OO-nah kAH-meh-rah*
■ with the American plan (three meals a day)	**con pensione completa** *kohn pehn-see-OH-neh kohm-plEH-tah*
■ with breakfast	**con colazione** *kohn koh-lah-tsee-OH-neh*
■ with no meals	**senza i pasti** *sEHn-tsah ee pAH-stee*

Is everything included?	**È tutto compreso?** *EH tOOt-toh kohm-prAY-soh*
The room is very nice. I'll take it. ·	**La camera è molto bella. La prendo.** *lah kAH-meh-rah EH mOHl-toh bEHl-lah lah prAYn-doh*
We'll be staying ____.	**Resteremo ____.** *rehs-teh-rAY-moh*
■ one night	**una notte** *OO-nah nOHt-teh*
■ a few nights	**alcune notti** *ahl-kOO-neh nOHt-tee*
■ one week	**una settimana** *OO-nah sayt-tee-mAH-nah*
How much do you charge for children?	**Quanto fanno pagare per i bambini?** *koo-AHn-toh fAHn-noh pah-gAH-reh pehr ee bahm-bEE-nee*
Could you put another bed in the room?	**Si potrebbe avere un altro letto nella camera?** *see poh-trAYb-beh ah-vAY-reh oon-AHl-troh lEHt-toh nAYl-lah kAH-meh-rah*
Is there a charge? How much?	**C'è da pagare? Quanto?** *chEH dah pah-gAH-reh koo-AHn-toh*

OTHER ACCOMMODATIONS

I'm looking for ____.	**Sto cercando ____.** *stOH chehr-kAHn-doh*
■ a boardinghouse	**una pensione** *oo-nah pehn-see-OH-neh*
■ a private house	**una casa privata (un villino)** *oo-nah kAH-sah pree-vAH-tah (oon veel-lEE-noh)*
I want to rent an apartment.	**Voglio affittare un appartamento.** *vOH-ly-ee-oh ahf-feet-tAH-reh oon ahp-pahr-tah-mEHn-toh*
I need a living room, bedroom, and kitchen.	**Ho bisogno di salotto, camera da letto, e cucina.** *oh bee-sOH-ny-oh dee sah-lOHt-toh, kAH-meh-rah dah lEHt-toh, ay koo-chEE-nah*

Do you have a furnished room?	**Ha una camera ammobiliata?** *AH oo-nah kAH-meh-rah ahm-moh-bee-lee-AH-tah*
How much is the rent?	**Quant'è d'affitto?** *koo-ahn-tEH dahf-fEEt-toh*
I'll be staying here for _____.	**Resterò qui _____.** *rehs-teh-rOH koo-EE*
■ two weeks	**due settimane** *dOO-eh seht-tee-mAH-neh*
■ one month	**un mese** *oon mAY-seh*
■ the whole summer	**tutta l'estate** *tOOt-tah leh-stAH-teh*
I want a place _____.	**Voglio abitare _____.** *vOH-ly-ee-oh ah-bee-tAH-reh*
■ that's centrally located	**al centro** *ahl chAYn-troh*
■ near public transportation	**vicino ai servizi di trasporti pubblici** *vee-chEE-noh AH-ee sayr-vEE-tsee dee trah-spOHr-tee pOOb-blee-chee*
Is there a youth hostel around here?	**C'è un ostello per la gioventù qui vicino?** *chEH oon oh-stAYl-loh pehr lah jee-oh-vehn-tOO koo-EE vee-chEE-noh*

ORDERING BREAKFAST

Larger hotels will offer breakfast. The Italian breakfast is a simple one—coffee and a sweet roll or brioche, sometimes **focaccia,** and jam or marmalade. At hotels that cater to American or British tourists, you will also be able to order an English breakfast (juice, eggs, bacon, and toast). Larger hotels will have a dining room where you can eat breakfast, but the usual procedure is to have breakfast sent up to your room.

We'll have breakfast in the room.	**Faremo colazione in camera.** *fah-rAY-moh koh-lah-tsee-OH-neh een kAH-meh-rah*

Please send up _____.	**Per favore mandino** _____. *pehr fah-vOH-reh mAHn-dee-noh*
■ one (two) coffee(s)	**un (due) caffè** *oon (dOO-eh) kahf-fEH*
■ tea	**un tè** *oon tEH*
■ hot chocolate	**una cioccolata calda** *OO-nah chee-oh-koh-lAH-tah kAHl-dah*
■ a sweet roll (brioche)	**un berlingozzo (brioche)** *oon behr-leen-gOH-tsoh (brEE-osh)*
■ fruit (juice)	**un (succo di) frutta** *oon (sOO-koh-dee) frOOt-tah*
I'll eat breakfast downstairs.	**Mangerò la colazione giù.** *mahn-jeh-rOH lah koh-lah-tsee-OH-neh jee-OO*
We'd both like _____.	**Noi due desideriamo** _____. *nOH-ee dOO-eh deh-see-deh-ree-AH-moh*
■ bacon and eggs	**uova al tegamino con pancetta** *oo-OH-vah ahl teh-gah-mEE-noh kohn pahn-chAYt-tah*
■ scrambled (fried, boiled) eggs	**uova al tegamino strapazzate (fritte, alla coque)** *oo-OH-vah ahl teh-gah-mEE-noh strah-pah-tsAH-teh (frEEt-teh) (ahl-lah kOHk)*
■ toast	**pan tostato** *pAHn toh-stAH-toh*
■ jam (marmalade)	**marmellata** *mahr-mehl-lAH-tah*

NOTE: See the food section (pages 71–100) for more phrases dealing with ordering meals.

HOTEL SERVICES

Where is _____?	**Dov'è** _____? *doh-vEH*
■ the dining room	**la sala da pranzo** *lah sAH-lah dah prAHn-tsoh*

■ the bathroom   **il bagno? (la toilette)** *eel bAH-ny-oh (lah too-ah-lEHt)*

■ the elevator (lift)   **l'ascensore** *lah-shehn-sOH-reh*

■ the phone   **il telefono** *eel teh-lEH-foh-noh*

What is my room number?   **Qual è il numero della mia camera?** *koo-ah-lEH eel nOO-meh-roh dAYl-lah mEE-ah kAH-meh-rah*

May I please have my key?   **Può darmi la chiave, per favore?** *poo-OH dAHr-mee lah key-AH-veh pehr fah-vOH-reh*

I've lost my key.   **Ho perduto la chiave.** *oh pehr-dOO-toh lah key-AH-veh*

GETTING WHAT YOU NEED

I need ＿＿.   **Ho bisogno di ＿＿.** *oh bee-sOH-ny-oh dee*

■ a bellhop   **un fattorino** *oon faht-toh-rEE-noh*

■ a chambermaid   **una cameriera** *oo-nah kah-meh-ree-EH-rah*

Please send ＿＿ to my room.   **Per piacere mi mandi ＿＿ in camera.** *pehr pee-ah-chAY-reh mee mAHn-dee ＿＿ een kAH-meh-rah*

■ a towel   **un asciugamano** *oon ah-shoo-gah-mAH-noh*

■ a bar of soap   **una saponetta** *oo-nah sah-poh-nAYt-tah*

■ some hangers   **delle grucce (degli attaccapanni)** *dAYl-lay grOO-cheh (dAY-ly-ee aht-AHk-kah-pAHn-nee)*

■ a pillow   **un cuscino** *oon koo-shEE-noh*

■ a blanket   **una coperta** *oo-nah koh-pEHr-tah*

■ some ice cubes   **dei cubetti di ghiaccio** *day-ee koo-bAYt-tee dee ghee-AH-chee-oh*

■ some ice water **dell'acqua ghiacciata** *dayl-lAH-koo-ah ghee-ah-chee-AH-tah*

■ a bottle of mineral water **una bottiglia d'acqua minerale** *OO-nah boht-tEE-ly-ee-ah dAH-koo-ah mee-neh-rAH-leh*

■ an ashtray **un portacenere** *oon pohr-tah-chAY-nay-reh*

■ toilet paper **della carta igienica** *dayl-lah kAHr-tah ee-jee-EH-nee-kah*

■ a reading lamp **una lampada per la lettura** *OO-nah lAHm-pah-dah pehr lah leht-tOO-rah*

■ an electric adaptor* **un trasformatore elettrico** *oon trahs-fohr-mah-tOH-reh ay-lEHt-tree-koh*

AT THE DOOR

Who is (was) it? **Chi è (era)?** *key-EH (EH-rah)*

Just a minute. **Un momento.** *oon moh-mEHn-toh*

Come in. **Entri (venga).** *AYn-tree (vEHn-gah)*

Put it on the table. **Lo metta sul tavolo.** *loh mAYt-tah sool tAH-voh-loh*

Please wake me tomorrow at ___. **Per favore mi svegli domani alle ___.** *pehr fah-vOH-reh mee svAY-ly-ee doh-mAH-nee AHl-leh*

COMPLAINTS

There is no ___. **Manca ___.** *mAHn-kah*

■ running water **l'acqua corrente** *lAH-koo-ah kohr-rEHn-teh*

*NOTE: If you bring electric appliances with you from the U.S. (electric shaver, for example), you may need to have an adaptor so that the voltage corresponds with that in the hotel. Newer hotels have 110-volt systems and an adaptor isn't necessary.

■ hot water	**l'acqua calda** *lAH-koo-ah kAHl-dah*
■ electricity	**la luce elettrica** *lah lOO-cheh eh-lEHt-tree-kah*
The ____ doesn't work.	**____ non funziona.** *nohn foont-see-OH-nah*
■ air-conditioning	**l'aria condizionata** *lAH-ree-ah kohn-dee-tsee-oh-nAH-tah*
■ fan	**il ventilatore** *eel vehn-tee-lah-tOH-reh*
■ faucet	**il rubinetto** *eel roo-bee-nAYt-toh*
■ light	**la luce** *lah lOO-cheh*
■ radio	**la radio** *lah rAH-dee-oh*
■ electric socket	**la presa della corrente** *lah prAY-sa dehl-lah kohr-rEHn-teh*
■ light switch	**l'interruttore** *leen-tehr-root-tOH-reh*
■ television	**la televisione** *lah teh-leh-vee-see-OH-neh*
Can you fix it?	**Può farlo(la) riparare?** *poo-OH fAHr-loh(ah) ree-pah-rAH-reh*
The room is dirty.	**La camera è sporca.** *lah kAH-meh-rah EH spOHr-kah*
Can you clean it ____?	**Può farla pulire ____?** *poo-OH fAHr-lah poo-lEE-reh*
■ now	**subito** *sOO-bee-toh*
■ as soon as possible	**il più presto possibile** *eel pee-OO prEH-stoh pohs-sEE-bee-leh*

AT THE DESK

Are there (any) ____ for me?	**Ci sono ____ per me?** *chee sOH-noh ____ payr mAY*
■ letters	**(delle) lettere** *(dAYl-leh) lAYt-teh-reh*

■ messages	**(dei) messaggi** *(day-ee) mehs-sAH-jee*
■ packages	**(dei) pacchi** *(day-ee) pAH-key*
■ postcards	**(delle) cartoline postali** *(dAYl-leh) kahr-toh-lEE-neh poh-stAH-lee*
Did anyone call for me?	**Mi ha cercato qualcuno?** *mee-AH chehr-kAH-toh koo-ahl-kOO-noh*
I'd like to leave this in your safe.	**Vorrei lasciare questo nella sua cassaforte.** *vohr-rEH-ee lah-shee-AH-reh koo-AYs-toh nAYl-lah sOO-ah kahs-sah-fOHr-teh*
Will you make this call for me?	**Può farmi questa telefonata?** *poo-OH fAHr-mee koo-AYs-tah teh-leh-foh-nAH-tah*

CHECKING OUT

I'd like the bill, please.	**Vorrei il conto per favore.** *vohr-rEH-ee eel kOHn-toh pehr fah-vOH-reh*
I'll be checking out today (tomorrow).	**Pagherò e partirò oggi (domani).** *pah-gheh-rOH ay pahr-tee-rOH OH-jee (doh-mAH-nee)*
Please send someone up for our baggage.	**Per favore mandi qualcuno a prendere le valigie.** *pehr fah-vOH-reh mAHn-dee koo-ahl-kOO-noh ah prAYn-deh-reh leh vah-lEE-jee-eh*

TRAVEL TIP

When you are packing to leave home, leave a little space in your suitcase to hold the small purchases you will make while you are away. If you can't manage this, then pack a collapsible tote bag in your suitcase, to be filled up and carried separately on your return trip.

GETTING AROUND TOWN

In smaller towns, you can walk to most places you want to visit, catching the flavor and color of the area at the same time. In the larger cities, you might want to get about using public transportation—another wonderful way to sample a country's way of life. For information on train or plane travel, see pages 49–54.

TRAM (TRANVAI)	Trolley cars
FILOBUS	Trackless trolley (streetcar)
METROPOLITANA	Subway (underground)
AUTOCORRIERA **AUTOPULLMAN** **EUROWAYS** **EUROPABUS**	Bus services
ALISCAFO	Hydrofoil
NAVE TRAGHETTO	Ferryboat

THE SUBWAY (UNDERGROUND)

Getting about Rome is made easier because of its **metro-politana.** You'll find maps posted in every station, as well as in every train. The stops are clearly marked, and you should have no problem reaching your destination. On the street, the station entrances have a large **M** posted. Fares are low, with one fare taking you through the entire system. Milan has a subway that functions similarly.

Is there a subway (underground) in this city?	**C'è una metropolitana in questa città?** *chEH oo-na meh-troh-poh-lee-tAH-nah een koo-AYs-tah cheet-tAH*
Do you have a map showing the stops?	**Ha una cartina che indica le fermate della metropolitana?** *ah oo-nah kahr-tEE-nah kay EEn-dee-kah lay fayr-mAH-teh dAYl-lah meh-troh-poh-lee-tAH-nah*

Where is the closest subway (underground) station?	**Dov'è la stazione più vicina della metropolitana?** *doh-vEH lah stah-tsee-OH-neh pee-OO vee-chEE-nah dAYl-lah meh-troh-poh-lee-tAH-nah*
How much is the fare?	**Quanto costa il biglietto?** *koo-AHn-toh kOHs-tah eel bee-ly-ee-AYt-toh*
Where can I buy a token (a ticket)?	**Dove posso comprare un gettone (un biglietto)?** *dOH-veh pOHs-soh kohm-prAH-reh oon jee-eht-tOH-neh (oon bee-ly-ee-AYt-toh)*
Which is the train that goes to _____?	**Qual è il treno che va a _____?** *koo-ah-lEH eel trEH-noh keh vah ah*
Does this train go to _____?	**Questo treno va a _____?** *koo-AYs-toh trEH-noh vAH ah*
How many more stops?	**Quante fermate ancora?** *koo-AHn-teh fehr-mAH-teh ahn-kOH-rah*
What's the next station?	**Qual è la prossima stazione?** *koo-ah-lEH lah prOHs-see-mah stah-tsee-OH-neh*
Where should I get off?	**Dove dovrei scendere?** *dOH-vay doh-vrEH-ee shAYn-deh-reh*
Do I have to change trains?	**Devo cambiare treno?** *dAY-voh kahm-bee-AH-reh trEH-noh*
Please tell me when we get there.	**Può farmi sapere quando siamo arrivati(e).** *poo-OH fAHr-mee sah-pAY-reh koo-AHn-doh see-AH-moh ahr-rEE-vah-tee(eh)*

THE BUS (STREETCAR, TRAM)

Oftentimes you can purchase a book of tickets, saving you the trouble of purchasing them each time you take the bus. Fares are charged by destination, and on less-traveled routes the driver also collects the fares.

Where is the bus stop (bus terminal)?	**Dov'è la fermata dell'autobus (il capolinea)?** *doh-vEH lah fehr-mAH-tah dayl-lAH-oo-toh-boos (eel kah-poh-lEE-neh-ah)*
Which bus (trolley) do I take to get to _____?	**Quale autobus (tram) devo prendere per andare a _____?** *koo-AH-leh AH-oo-toh-boos (trAH-m) dAY-voh prAYn-deh-reh pehr ahn-dAH-reh ah*
In which direction do I have to go?	**In quale direzione devo andare?** *een koo-AH-leh dee-reh-tsee-OH-neh dAY-voh ahn-dAH-reh*
How often do the buses run?	**Ogni quanto tempo passano gli autobus?** *OH-ny-ee koo-AHn-toh tEHm-poh pAHs-sah-noh ly-ee AH-oo-toh-boos*
Do you go to _____?	**Va a _____?** *vAH ah*
I want to go to _____.	**Voglio andare a _____.** *vOH-ly-ee-oh ahn-dAH-reh ah*
Is it far from here?	**È lontano da qui?** *EH lohn-tAH-noh dah koo-EE*
How many stops are there?	**Quante fermate ci sono?** *koo-AHn-teh fehr-mAH-teh chee sOH-noh*
Do I have to change buses?	**Devo cambiare autobus?** *dAY-voh kahm-bee-AH-reh AH-oo-toh-boos*
How much is the fare?	**Quanto costa il biglietto?** *koo-AHn-toh kOH-stah eel bee-ly-ee-AYt-toh*
Where do I get off?	**Dove devo scendere?** *dOH-vay dAY-voh shAYn-deh-reh*
Please tell me where to get off.	**Può dirmi dove devo scendere?** *poo-OH dEEr-mee dOH-veh dAY-voh shAYn-deh-reh*

TAXIS

Taxis are metered, but it is still a good idea to ask the driver about how much it will cost to get to your destination. Most cabs add a supplement for travel after 10 p.m.

Is there a taxi stand near here?	**C'è un posteggio dei taxi qui vicino?** *chEH oon poh-stAY-jee-oh dAY-ee tahs-sEE koo-EE vee-chEE-noh*
Please get me a taxi.	**Per favore mi chiami un taxi.** *pehr fah-vOH-reh mee key-AH-mee oon tahs-sEE*
Taxi! Are you free?	**Taxí! È libero?** *tahs-sEE EH lEE-beh-roh*
Take me (I want to go) _____.	**Mi porti (voglio andare) _____.** *mee pOHr-tee (vOH-ly-ee-oh ahn-dAH-reh)*
■ to the airport	**all'aeroporto** *ahl-lah-eh-roh-pOHr-toh*
■ to this address	**a questo indirizzo** *ah koo-AYs-toh een-dee-rEE-tsoh*
■ to the station	**alla stazione** *AHl-lah stah-tsee-OH-neh*
■ to _____ Street	**in via _____** *een vEE-ah*
Do you know where it is?	**Sa dove si trova?** *sah dOH-veh see trOH-vah*
How much is it to _____?	**Qual è la tariffa per _____?** *koo-ah-lEH lah tah-rEEf-fah pehr*
Faster! I'm in a hurry.	**Più presto (veloce)! Ho fretta.** *pee-OO prEH-stoh (veh-lOH-cheh) oh frAYt-tah*
Please drive slower.	**Per cortesia guidi più piano.** *pehr kohr-tay-sEE-ah goo-EE-dee pee-OO pee-AH-noh*

Stop here at the corner.	**Si fermi qui all'angolo.** *see fAYr-mee koo-EE ahl-lAHn-goh-loh*
Stop at the next block.	**Si fermi alla prossima via.** *see fAYr-mee AHl-lah prOHs-see-mah vEE-ah*
Wait for me. I'll be right back.	**Mi aspetti. Torno subito.** *mee ah-spEHt-tee tOHr-noh sOO-bee-toh*
I think you are going the wrong way.	**Penso che lei stia andando nella direzione sbagliata.** *pEHn-soh kay lEH-ee stEE-ah ahn-dAHn-doh nAYl-lah dee-reh-tsee-OH-neh sbah-ly-ee-AH-tah*
How much do I owe you?	**Quanto le devo?** *koo-AHn-toh leh dAY-voh*
This is for you.	**Questo è per lei.** *koo-AYs-toh EH pehr lEH-ee*

SIGHTSEEING AND TOURS

You'll want to visit a variety of sights—cathedrals, fountains and plazas, parks, and museums—and we give you here some phrases to help you locate the English-language tours, when available. In larger cities, you'll find facilities equipped for English-speaking tourists; in smaller towns, you may have to get along more on your own.

Where is the Tourist Information Office?	**Dov'è l'Ente Locale (Nazionale) per il Turismo?** *doh-vEH lEHn-teh loh-kAH-leh (nah-tsee-oh-nAH-leh) pehr eel too-rEEs-moh*
Where can I buy an English guidebook?	**Dove posso comprare una guida turistica in inglese?** *dOH-veh pOHs-soh kohm-prAH-reh OO-nah goo-EE-dah too-rEEs-tee-kah een een-glAY-seh*
I need an English-speaking guide.	**Ho bisogno di una guida che parli inglese.** *oh bee-sOH-ny-oh dee oo-nah goo-EE-dah kay pAHr-lee een-glAY-seh*
How much does he charge ____?	**Quanto si fa pagare ____?** *koo-AHn-toh see fah pah-gAH-reh*
■ per hour	**all'ora** *ahl-lOH-rah*
■ per day	**al giorno** *ahl jee-OHr-noh*
When does the tour begin?	**Quando inizia il tour (la gita)?** *koo-AHn-doh ee-nEE-tsee-ah eel tOOr (lah jEE-tah)*
How long is the tour?	**Quanto dura il tour (la gita)?** *koo-AHn-toh dOO-rah eel tOOr (lah jEE-tah)*
There are two (four, six) of us.	**Siamo in due (quattro, sei).** *see-AH-moh een-dOO-eh (koo-AHt-troh, sEH-ee)*
What are the main attractions?	**Quali sono le principali attrazioni?** *koo-AH-lee sOH-noh leh preen-cee-pAH-lee aht-trah-tsee-OH-nee*

We are here for one (two) day(s) only.	**Saremo qui un giorno (due giorni) soltanto.** *sah-rAY-moh koo-EE oon gee-OHr-noh (dOO-eh jee-OHr-nee) sohl-tAHn-toh*
Are there trips through the city?	**Si fanno (dei tour) delle gite turistiche della città?** *see fAHn-noh (day tOOr) dAYl-leh jEE-teh too-rEE-stee-keh dAYl-lah cheet-tAH*
Where do they leave from?	**Da dove iniziano i tour (le gite)?** *dah dOH-veh ee-nEE-tsee-ah-noh ee tOOr (leh jEE-teh)*
We want to see _____.	**Vogliamo vedere _____.** *voh-ly-ee-AH-moh vay-dAY-reh*
■ the botanical garden	**il giardino botanico** *eel jee-ahr-dEE-noh boh-tAH-nee-koh*
■ the business center	**il centro commerciale** *eel chAYn-troh kohm-mehr-chee-AH-leh*
■ the castle	**il castello** *eel kahs-tEHl-loh*
■ the cathedral	**la cattedrale** *lah kaht-teh-drAH-leh*
■ the church	**la chiesa** *lah key-EH-sah*
■ the concert hall	**la sala dei concerti** *lah sAH-lah dAY-ee kohn-chEHr-tee*
■ the downtown area	**la zona del centro** *lah tsOH-nah dayl chAYn-troh*
■ the fountains	**le fontane** *leh fohn-tAH-neh*
■ the library	**la biblioteca** *lah bee-blee-oh-tEH-kah*
■ the main park	**il parco principale** *eel pAHr-koh preen-chee-pAH-leh*
■ the main square	**la piazza principale** *lah pee-AH-tsah preen-chee-pAH-leh*
■ the market	**il mercato** *eel mehr-kAH-toh*
■ the mosque	**la moschea** *lah moh-skEH-ah*

■the museum (of fine arts) **il museo (delle belle arti)** *eel moo-sEH-oh (dAYl-leh bEHl-leh AHr-tee)*

■a nightclub **un night (locale notturno)** *oon nAH-eet (loh-kAH-leh noht-tOOr-noh)*

■the old part of town **la parte vecchia della città** *lah pAHr-teh vEHk-key-ah dAYl-la cheet-tAH*

■the opera **il teatro dell'opera** *eel teh-AH-troh dayl-lOH-peh-rah*

■the palace **il palazzo** *eel pah-lAH-tsoh*

■the stadium **lo stadio** *loh stAH-dee-oh*

■the synagogue **la sinagoga** *lah see-nah-gOH-gah*

■the university **l'università** *loo-nee-vehr-see-tAH*

■the zoo **il giardino zoologico (lo zoo)** *eel jee-ahr-dEE-no tsoh-oh-lOH-jee-koh (loh tsOH-oh)*

Is it all right to go in now? **Si può entrare adesso?** *see poo-OH ehn-trAH-reh ah-dEHs-soh*

Is it open (closed)? **È aperto (chiuso)?** *EH ah-pEHr-toh (key-OO-soh)*

At what time does it open (close)? **A che ora aprono (chiudono)?** *ah kay OH-rah AH-proh-noh (key-OO-doh-noh)*

What's the admission price? **Quant'è l'entrata?** *koo-ahn-tEH lehn-trAH-tah*

How much do children pay? **Quanto pagano i bambini?** *koo-AHn-toh pAH-gah-noh ee bahm-bEE-nee*

Can they go in free? Until what age? **Possono entrare gratis? Fino a quale età?** *pOHs-soh-noh ehn-trAH-reh grAH-tees fEE-noh ah koo-AH-leh eh-tAH*

Is it all right to take pictures?	**Si possono fare fotografie?** *see pOHs-soh-noh fAH-reh foh-toh-grah-fEE-eh*
How much extra does it cost to take pictures?	**Quanto costa in più per fare delle fotografie?** *koo-AHn-toh kOHs-tah een pee-OO pehr fAH-reh dAYl-leh foh-toh-grah-fEE-eh*
I do (not) use a flash attachment.	**Io (non) uso il flash.** *EE-oh (nohn) OO-soh eel flEH-sh*

A SIGHTSEEING ITINERARY

Italy has long attracted foreigners for its natural beauties and its visible reminders of a continuous history, a history that reaches back through the ages to the heights of Roman and Greek civilizations and beyond. Its rugged mountains, rolling plains, clear lakes, blue seas, flowery gardens, picturesque castles, imposing palaces and villas, great cathedrals and churches, busy city squares, and narrow, winding streets, ancient ruins and excavations—all these give pleasure to both the eye and the mind. Italy remains one of the world's richest treasuries of Western history, art, and civilization.

While retaining a strong sense of the past, present-day Italy is a thoroughly modern country, offering the tourist a vast and efficient network of super highways and public transportation systems as well as the most advanced facilities for everyday comfort.

Even today, the visitor to Italy would need a lifetime to know the country, since there are thousands of places and things to see, each with its own flavor and history. The following is only a limited itinerary of principal points of interest to help the traveler become acquainted with this fascinating and seductive land.

ROME

Rome is the heart of Italy. For unforgettable views of ancient Rome, its temples and monuments, see the Colosseum, the Roman Forum, the Capitol **(Campidoglio),** and the Pantheon, the most perfectly preserved ancient building. Visit St. Peter's, the Vatican Museums, and the Sistine Chapel. Stroll along the Via Veneto, renowned as the center of the *dolce vita* ("sweet life") of film celebrities and the international jet set in the 1950s and 1960s. Descend the Spanish Steps to Via Condotti, Via del Babuino, Via Margutta (once an artists' quarter), and Piazza del Popolo. Smart boutiques, cafés, jewelry shops, and art galleries makes this area very fashionable. Make a wish while tossing a coin in the famous Trevi Fountain. Piazza Navona, the old district of Trastevere, and the Sunday flea market at Porta Portese offer a glimpse of Roman daily life.

Near Rome, the gardens of Villa d'Este, with their water cascades and fountains, and the ruins of the Roman emperor Hadrian's Villa, both in Tivoli, are a must.

FLORENCE

Florence is the seat of the Italian Renaissance. Visit the Cathedral of Santa Maria del Fiore and the Academia Museum to see Michelangelo's renowned *David*. Stroll through the Piazza della Signoria to the Uffizi, one of the world's most famous art museums. Cross the Ponte Vecchio, glancing in the gold- and silversmiths' shops lined up on the sides of the bridge, and from there walk to the Pitti Palace and through the Boboli Gardens. Ride to Piazzale Michelangelo for a bird's-eye view of the city with which such illustrious names as Dante, Michelangelo, Leonardo da Vinci, Giotto, Machiavelli, and Galileo are associated. Be sure to take a sidetrip to nearby Pisa to see the Leaning Tower and the Baptistry with its echo.

MILAN

Italy's business and financial capital, Milan is also a historical city. Visit the Duomo, the dazzling Gothic cathedral with its hundred pinnacles; La Scala, the world-famous opera house; the Castello Sforzesco; and the Church of Santa Maria delle

Grazie, to see Leonardo da Vinci's *Last Supper* in the refectory of the adjoining Dominican monastery. The shops in Via Montenapoleone are among the most elegant in Europe.

MILAN TO VENICE

The route from Milan to Venice passes through the Po Valley, Italy's richest agricultural region. Stop off at Lake Garda, which can probably be best viewed from the lovely little town of Sirmione near the southern end of the lake. On the way to Venice, stop in Verona to see "the house of Juliet," the Roman Arena (where operas are performed in the summer), and the well-preserved historical center of the city, especially Piazza dei Signori and Piazza delle Erbe (the old market square).

VENICE

With its lagoons, canals, and palaces built on water, Venice inevitably enchants the visitor. Visit St. Mark's Square (Piazza San Marco) to see St. Mark's Church, its freestanding bell tower *(Campanile)*, and the Palace of the Doges. Take a stroll through the narrow streets to the Rialto Bridge, which arches over the Grand Canal. A boat trip to the picturesque island towns of Murano and Burano, famous centers of glass and lace making, will prove fascinating.

VENICE TO RAVENNA, SAN MARINO, AND ASSISI

Ravenna, on the coast south of Venice, is most famous for the magnificent mosaics in the Churches of San Vitale and Sant' Apollinare Nuovo and in the Mausoleum of Galla Placidia. A visit to the tomb of Dante, the father of Italian literature, will be interesting.

San Marino is an independent republic perched on a rocky pinnacle not far south of Ravenna. Tourists are attracted by its castles and picturesque old houses. This is an excellent place to buy stamps, coins, medieval armor, and gold jewelry.

The route from San Marino to Assisi passes through the Apennines, the rugged mountain chain which is called the backbone of Italy as it runs north-south down the Italian peninsula.

The town of Assisi is a very important pilgrimage center and tourist attraction. The old town is well preserved, with its medieval houses and narrow streets. Visit the magnificent Basilica of San Francesco, which contains celebrated frescoes by Giotto and Cimabue.

ROME TO NAPLES

On the way to Naples, stop in Cassino to visit the Abbey of Montecassino, destroyed in World War II and rebuilt as a monument to faith, the arts, and culture.

Italy's third largest city, Naples is the gateway to the largely unspoiled beauties of southern Italy. Visit the Cathedral of San Gennaro (the city's patron saint), the steep, narrow staired streets of the old quarter (Spaccanapoli), and the opera house of San Carlo. In the vicinity of Naples, discover the excavated Roman cities of Pompeii and Herculaneum in the shadow of Mt. Vesuvius. Take a ride on the breathtaking serpentine Amalfi Drive, or go out to the island of Capri.

SICILY

From Naples there are direct airplane and boat connections to Palermo, Sicily. The island of Sicily is fascinating for its landscapes and the relics of its long, complex history. Visit the ancient Greek temples at Agrigento and Siracusa, reminders of the Greek foundations of Sicilian culture.

RELIGIOUS SERVICES

In addition to viewing the churches and cathedrals throughout Italy, you may wish to attend services.

Is there a _____ near here?	**C'è qui vicino una _____?**	*chEH koo-EE vee-chEE-noh OO-nah*
■ Catholic church	**chiesa cattolica**	*key-EH-sah kaht-tOH-lee-kah*
■ Protestant church	**chiesa protestante**	*key-EH-sah proh-teh-stAHn-teh*
■ synagogue	**sinagoga**	*see-nah-gOH-gah*
■ mosque	**moschea**	*moh-skEH-ah*

PLANNING A TRIP

During your stay you may want to plan some excursions into the country or to other Italian cities. Visitors to Italy can move about the country by airplane, train, bus, boat, and car (see Driving a Car). For air travel within Italy, look for signs to the domestic terminal (sometimes separate from the international terminal).

AIR SERVICES

ALITALIA	The Italian national airline offers domestic and international flights.
ATI	The national domestic airline linking major cities.
ALISARDA	Flights to the island of Sardinia.

When is there a flight to _____?	**Quando c'è un volo per _____?** *koo-AHn-doh chEH oon vOH-loh pehr*
I would like _____.	**Vorrei _____.** *vohr-rEH-ee*
■ a round-trip (one-way) ticket_____.	**un biglietto di andata e ritorno (di andata)** *oon bee-ly-ee-AYt-toh dee ahn-dAH-tah ay ree-tOHr-noh (dee ahn-dAH-tah)*
■ in tourist class	**in classe turistica** *een klAHs-seh too-rEE-stee-kah*
■ in first class	**in prima classe** *een prEE-mah klAHs-seh*
I would like a seat _____.	**Vorrei un posto_____.** *vohr-rEH-ee OOn pOH-stoh*
■ in the (non)smoking section	**tra i (non)fumatori** *trAH ee (nohn)foo-mah-tOH-ree*
■ next to the window	**accanto al finestrino** *ah-kAHn-toh ahl fee-neh-strEE-noh*
■ on the aisle	**vicino al corridoio** *vee-chEE-noh ahl kohr-ree-dOH-ee-oh*

What is the fare?	**Qual è il prezzo del biglietto?** *koo-ah-lEH eel prEH-tsoh dAYl bee-ly-ee-EHt-toh*
Are meals served?	**Sono inclusi i pasti?** *sOH-noh een-klOO-see ee pAH-stee*
When does the plane leave (arrive)?	**A che ora parte (arriva) l'aereo?** *ah kay OH-rah pAHr-teh (ahr-ree-vAH) lah-EH-reh-oh*
When must I be at the airport?	**Quando dovrò trovarmi all'aeroporto?** *koo-AHn-doh doh-vrOH troh-vAHr-mee ahl-lah-eh-roh-pOHr-toh*
What is my flight number?	**Qual è il (mio) numero di volo?** *koo-AH-lEH eel (mEE-oh) nOO-meh-roh dee vOH-loh*
What gate do we leave from?	**Qual è la nostra porta d'uscita?** *koo-ah-lEH lah nOH-strah pOHr-tah doo-shEE-tah*
I want to confirm (cancel) my reservation for flight ____.	**Desidero confermare (cancellare) la mia prenotazione per il volo ____.** *day-sEE-deh-roh kohn-fayr-mAH-reh (kahn-chehl-lAH-reh) lah mEE-ah preh-noh-tah-tsee-OH-neh pehr eel vOH-loh*
I'd like to check my bags.	**Vorrei consegnare le valigie.** *vohr-rEH-ee kohn-say-ny-AH-reh leh vah-lEE-jee-eh*
I have only carry-on baggage.	**Ho soltano bagagli a mano.** *oh sohl-tAHn-toh bah-gAH-ly-ee ah MAH-noh*
Please pass my film (camera) through by hand.*	**Per piacere mi passi il rollino.(la macchina fotografica) a mano** *pehr pee-ah-chAY-reh, mee pAHs-see eel rohl-lEE-noh (lah mAH-kee-nah foh-toh-grAH-fee-koh) ah MAH-noh*

NOTE: Some high-speed film can be damaged by airport security X-rays. It is best to pack film in your suitcase, protected in a lead insulated bag. If you have film in your camera or carry-on baggage, avoid problems and ask the guard to pass it through by hand instead. If the guard refuses, bow to his wishes.

TRAIN SERVICE

The major train lines are fast and comfortable, although all service slows a bit during the tourist season. Trains have two classes—first and second—with first class being the advisable one to choose. People often disregard the signs distinguishing the classes, thus you are apt to find second-class passengers sitting in first-class seats. Just politely ask the person to move. The following is a brief description of the varieties of Italian trains.

R	**Rapido**	High-speed luxury train between major cities (supplementary fare required)
DD	**Direttissimo**	Fast train, stopping only at main stations between large cities
D	**Diretto**	Shorter-distance train, stopping only at major stations
L	**Locale**	Local train, making all stops (also called an **accelerato**)
TEE	**Trans Europa Express**	International luxury train linking Italy and other western European countries (with additional fare and reservations)
TEN	**Trans Europa Notte**	International overnight train with sleeping cars, with berths (**cuccette,** *koo-chEHt-teh*), which can be reserved from two months to four hours in advance.

Where is the train station?	**Dov'è la stazione ferroviaria?** *doh-vEH lah stah-tsee-OH-neh fehr-roh-vee-AH-ree-ah*
When does the train for (from) _____ leave (arrive)?	**Quando parte (arriva) il treno per (da) _____.** *koo-AHn-doh pAHr-teh (ahr-rEE-vah) eel trEH-noh pehr (dah)*
Does this train stop at _____?	**Questo treno si ferma a _____?** *koo-AYs-toh trEH-noh see fAYr-mah ah*

BUYING A TICKET

I would like _____.	**Vorrei _____.** *vohr-rEH-ee*
■ a first (second)-class ticket for _____.	**un biglietto di prima (seconda) classe per _____.** *oon bee-ly-ee-AYt-toh dee prEE-mah (say-kOHn-dah) klAHs-seh pehr*
■ a half-price ticket	**un biglietto a tariffa ridotta** *oon bee-ly-ee-AYt-toh ah tah-rEEf-fah ree-dOHt-tah*
■ a one-way (round-trip) ticket	**un biglietto di andata (andata e ritorno)** *oon bee-ly-ee-AYt-toh dee ahn-dAH-tah (ahn-dAH-tah ay ree-tOHr-noh)*
■ with supplement (for the rapid train)	**con supplemento rapido** *kohn soop-pleh-MEN-toh rAH-pee-doh*
■ with reserved seat	**con prenotazione** *kohn prey-noh-tAH-tzee-oh-neh*
Is the train late?	**Il treno è in ritardo?** *eel trEH-noh EH een ree-tAHr-doh*
How long does it stop?	**Quanto tempo si ferma?** *koo-AHn-toh tEHm-poh see fAYr-mah*

ON THE TRAIN

Is there time to get a bite?	**C'è tempo per comprare un boccone?** *chEH tEHm-poh pehr kohm-prAH-reh oon boh-kOH-neh*
Is there a dining car (a sleeping car)?	**C'è un vagone ristorante (un vagone letto)?** *chEH oon vah-gOH-neh ree-stoh-rAHn-teh (oon vah-gOH-neh lEHt-toh)*
Is this an express (local) train?	**È questo un (treno) rapido (locale)?** *EH koo-AYs-toh oon (trEH-noh) rAH-pee-doh (loh-kAH-leh)*
Do I have to change trains?	**Debbo cambiar treno?** *dAYb-boh kahm-bee-AHr trEH-noh*

Is this seat taken?	**È occupato questo posto?** *EH oh-koo-pAH-toh koo-AYs-toh pOH-stoh*
Excuse me, but you are in my seat.	**Mi scusi ma lei ha occupato il mio posto.** *mee skOO-see mah lEH-ee ah oh-koo-pAH-toh eel mEE-oh pOHs-toh*
Where is the train station?	**Dov'è la stazione ferroviaria?** *doh-vEH lah stah-tsee-OH-neh fehr-roh-vee-AH-ree-ah*
When does the train for (from) _____ leave (arrive)?	**Quando parte (arriva) il treno per (da) _____.** *koo-AHn-doh pAHr-teh (ahr-rEE-vah) eel trEH-noh pehr (dah)*
Does this train stop at _____?	**Questo treno si ferma a _____?** *koo-AYs-toh trEH-noh see fAYr-mah ah*

SHIPBOARD TRAVEL

If you want to visit some of the islands (Capri, Sicily, Sardinia), then you'll want to arrange to take the boat there.

Where is the port (dock)?	**Dov'è il porto (molo)?** *doh-vEH eel pOHr-toh (mOH-loh)*

When does the next boat leave for ____?	**Quando parte il prossimo battello per ____?** *koo-AHn-doh pAHr-teh eel prOHs-see-moh baht-tEHl-loh*
How long does the crossing take?	**Quanto dura la traversata?** *koo-AHn-toh dOO-rah lah trah-vehr-sAH-tah*
Do we stop at any other ports?	**Ci fermiamo in qualche altro porto?** *chee fayr-mee-AH-moh een koo-AHl-keh AHl-troh pOHr-toh*
How long will we remain in the port?	**Quanto tempo resteremo in porto?** *koo-AHn-toh tEHm-poh reh-stay-rEH-moh een pOHr-toh*
When do we land?	**Quando sbarcheremo?** *koo-AHn-do sbahr-keh-rAY-moh*
At what time do we have to go back on board?	**A che ora ritorniamo a bordo?** *ah kay OH-rah ree-tohr-nee-AH-moh ah bOHr-doh*

TRAVEL TIP

Now that many airlines allow you to reserve your seat in advance, you can ensure that you have the place you want without arriving at the airport well in advance. But what a good seat is depends on the type of aircraft and your personal preferences. Familiarize yourself with the layouts of the major types of planes, especially the wide-bodies, so you know what to ask for. If you prefer nonsmoking, you may wish to avoid the seats in that section which are immediately in front of or behind the smoking section. Also, some overseas airlines divide the plane lengthwise, so nonsmokers are only across the aisle from smokers. If you want to see the movie, avoid the bulkhead seats; if you want to walk around and stretch your legs frequently, choose an aisle seat. If you wish to sleep, avoid a seat near the galley.

ENTERTAINMENTS AND DIVERSIONS

MOVIES, THEATER, CONCERTS, OPERA, BALLET

In Italy, foreign language films shown in commercial theaters are dubbed rather than subtitled. Cinema houses are classified first run **(prima visione),** second run **(seconda visione),** and so on. All films are interrupted by an intermission **(intervallo),** during which refreshments are sold. No smoking is allowed by law. Not all cinemas are open at a given time in the summer, as each closes for a period (usually a month).

Most theater presentations are performed by repertory companies, some of which go on tour to smaller towns. Musical comedies are rare in Italy. In recent years, cabaret theater has become popular. Theaters are closed in the summer.

The opera season varies from place to place; however, most of the major opera houses offer out-of-season events (concerts, ballets).

Theater and opera tickets are easily purchased at the box office.

Ushers in cinemas, theaters, and opera houses expect to be tipped (see page 25). You also must buy a program; you will not be given one.

Let's go to the _____.	**Andiamo al _____.**	*ahn-dee-AH-moh ahl*
■ movies (cinema)	**cinema**	*chEE-neh-mah*
■ theater	**teatro**	*teh-AH-troh*
What are they showing today?	**Che spettacoli ci sono oggi?**	*kay speht-tAH-koh-lee chee sOH-noh OH-jee*
Is it a _____?	**È _____?**	*EH*
■ mystery	**un giallo**	*oon jee-AHl-loh*
■ comedy	**una commedia**	*OO-na kohm-mEH-dee-ah*
■ drama	**un dramma**	*oon drAHm-mah*

■ musical	**un'operetta** *oo-noh-peh-rAYt-tah*
■ romance	**un romanzo** *oon roh-mAHn-tsoh*
■ Western	**un western** *oon oo-EH-stehrn*
■ war film	**un film di guerra** *oon fEElm dee goo-EHr-ra*
■ science fiction film	**un film di fantascienza** *oon fEElm dee fahn-tah-shee-EHn-tsah*
Is it in English?	**È parlato in inglese?** *EH pahr-lAH-toh een een-glAY-seh*
Has it been dubbed?	**È stato doppiato?** *EH stAH-toh dohp-pee-AH-toh*
Where is the box office?	**Dov'è il botteghino?** *doh-vEH eel boht-tay-ghEE-noh*
What time does the (first) show begin?	**A che ora comincia lo (il primo) spettacolo?** *ah kay OH-rah koh-mEEn-chee-ah loh (eel prEE-moh) speht-tAH-koh-loh*
What time does the (last) show end?	**A che ora finisce lo (l'ultimo) spettacolo?** *ah kay OH-rah fee-nEE-sheh loh (lOOl-tee-moh) speht-tAH-koh-loh*

I want a seat near the middle (front, rear).	**Desidero un posto al centro (davanti, dietro).** *day-sEE-deh-roh oon-pOHs-toh ahl chAYn-troh (dah-vAHn-tee, dee-EH-troh)*
Can I check my coat?	**Posso consegnare (lasciare) il mio cappotto?** *pOHs-soh kohn-seh-ny-ee-AH-reh (lah-shee-AH-reh) eel mEE-oh kahp-pOHt-toh*

BUYING A TICKET

I need ___ tickets for tonight (tomorrow night).	**Mi occorrono ___ biglietti per stasera (domani sera).** *mee oh-kOHr-roh-noh dOO-eh bee-ly-ee-AYt-tee pehr stah-sAY-rah (doh-mAH-nee sAY-rah)*
■ two orchestra seats	**due poltrone d'orchestra** *doo-eh pohl-trOH-neh dohr-kEHs-trah*
■ two box seats	**due poltrone nei palchi** *doo-eh pohl-trOH-neh nAY-ee pAHl-kee*
■ two mezzanine seats	**due poltrone** *doo-eh pohl-trOH-neh*
■ two gallery seats	**due posti in galleria** *doo-eh pOHs-tee een gahl-leh-rEE-ah*

MORE ABOUT MUSIC

How much are the front-row seats?	**Qual è il prezzo dei posti di prima fila?** *koo-ah-lEH eel prEH-tsoh dAY-ee pOH-stee dee prEE-mah fEE-lah*
What are the least expensive seats?	**Quali sono i posti meno costosi?** *koo-AH-lee sOH-noh ee pOH-stee mAY-noh koh-stOH-see*
Are there any seats for tonight's performance?	**Ci sono posti per lo spettacolo di stasera?** *chee sOH-noh pOH-stee pehr loh speht-tAH-koh-loh dee stah-sEH-rah*

We would like to attend ____.	**Vorremmo assistere ad ____.** *vohr-rEHm-moh ahs-sEE-steh-reh ahd*
■ a ballet	**un balletto** *oon bahl-lAYt-toh*
■ a concert	**un concerto** *oon kohn-chEHr-toh*
■ an opera	**un'opera** *oo-nOH-peh-rah*
What are they playing (singing)?	**Che cosa recitano (cantano)?** *kay kOH-sah rEH-chee-tah-noh (kAHn-tah-noh)*
Who is the conductor?	**Chi è il direttore d'orchestra?** *key-EH eel dee-reht-tOH-reh dohr-kEH-strah*
I prefer ____.	**Preferisco ____.** *preh-feh-rEE-skoh*
■ classical music	**la musica classica** *lah mOO-see-kah clAHs-see-kah*
■ popular music	**la musica popolare** *lah mOO-see-kah poh-poh-lAH-reh*
■ folk dance	**la danza folcloristica** *lah dAHn-tsah fohl-kloh-rEE-stee-kah*
■ ballet	**il balletto** *eel bahl-lAYt-toh*
When does the season begin (end)?	**Quando cominicia (finisce) la stagione (lirica)?** *koo-AHn-doh koh-mEEn-chee-ah (fee-nEE-sheh) lah stah-jee-OH-neh (lEE-ree-kah)*
Should I get the tickets in advance?	**Debbo comprare i biglietti in anticipo?** *dAYb-boh kohm-prAH-reh ee bee-ly-ee-AYt-tee een ahn-tEE-chee-poh*
Do I have to dress formally?	**È prescritto l'abito da sera?** *EH preh-skrEEt-toh lAH-bee-toh dah sAY-rah*
May I buy a program?	**Posso comprare il programma di sala?** *pOHs-soh kohm-prAH-reh eel proh-grAHm-mah dee sAH-lah*
What opera (ballet) are they performing?	**Quale opera (balletto) danno?** *koo-AH-leh OH-peh-rah (bahl-lAYt-toh) dAHn-noh*

Who's singing (tenor, soprano, baritone, contralto)?	**Chi sta cantando (il tenore, il soprano, il baritono, il contralto)?** *key stah kahn-tAHn-doh (eel teh-nOH-reh, eel soh-prAH-noh eel bah-rEE-toh-noh, eel kohn-trAHl-toh)*

NIGHTCLUBS, DANCING

Let's go to a nightclub.	**Andiamo al night.** *ahn-dee-AH-moh ahl nAH-eet*
Is a reservation necessary?	**È necessaria la prenotazione?** *EH neh-chehs-sAH-ree-ah lah preh-noh-tah-tsee-OH-neh*
We haven't gotten a reservation.	**Non abbiamo la prenotazione.** *nohn ahb-bee-AH-moh lah preh-noh-tah-tsee-OH-neh*
Is there a good discotheque here?	**C'è una buona discoteca qui?** *chEH OO-nah boo-OH-nah dee-skoh-tEH-kah koo-EE*
Is there dancing at the hotel?	**Si balla in albergo (all'hotel)?** *see bAHl-lah een ahl-bEHr-goh (ahl-loh-tEHl)*
We'd like a table near the dance floor.	**Vorremmo un tavolo vicino alla pista (di ballo).** *vohr-rEHm-moh oon tAH-voh-loh vee-chEE-noh AHl-lah pEE-stah (dee bAHl-loh)*
Is there a minimum (cover charge)?	**C'è un prezzo minimo (per il tavolo)?** *chEH oon prEH-tsoh mEE-nee-moh (pehr eel tAH-voh-loh)*
Where is the checkroom?	**Dov'è il guardaroba?** *doh-vEH eel goo-ahr-dah-rOH-bah*
At what time does the floor show go on?	**A che ora comincia lo spettacolo (di varietà)?** *ah kay OH-rah koh-mEEn-chee-ah loh speht-tAH-koh-loh dee vah-ree-eh-tAH*

QUIET RELAXATION

Italians have been world champions of bridge, and you'll find playing bridge or any other card game an excellent way to meet people and learn the language.

Where can I get a deck of cards?	**Dove posso trovare un mazzo di carte?** *dOH-veh pOHs-soh troh-vAH-reh oon mAH-tsoh dee kAHr-teh*
Let's play a game!	**Facciamoci una partita!** *fah-chee-AH-moh-chee OO-nah pahr-tEE-tah*
Do you want to play ____?	**Vuole giocare ____?** *voo-OH-leh jee-oh-kAH-reh*
■ cards	**a carte** *ah kAHr-teh*
■ bridge	**a bridge** *ah bree-dge*
■ blackjack	**a sette e mezzo** *ah sEHt-teh ay mEH-tsoh*
■ poker	**a poker** *ah pOH-kehr*
I have the highest card.	**Io ho la carta più alta.** *EE-oh OH lah kAHr-tah pee-OO AHl-tah*
■ an ace	**un asso** *oon AHs-soh*
■ a king	**un re** *oon rAY*
■ a queen	**una donna** *OO-nah dOHn-nah*
■ a jack	**un cavallo (un fante)** *oon kah-vAHl-loh (oon fAHn-teh)*
Do you want to cut?	**Vuole tagliare il mazzo?** *voo-OH-leh tah-ly-ee-AH-reh eel mAH-tsoh*
Do you want to shuffle?	**Vuole mischiare?** *voo-OH-leh mee-skey-AH-reh*
I pass.	**Io passo.** *EE-oh pAHs-soh*
Do you have clubs (hearts, spades, diamonds)?	**Ha fiori (cuori, picche, quadri)?** *AH fee-OH-ree, koo-OH-ree, pEEk-keh, koo-AH-dree*

It's your turn (to deal).	**Tocca a lei (dare le carte).**	*tOHk-kah ah lEH-ee (dAH-reh leh kAHr-teh)*
Who opens?	**Chi apre?** *key AH-preh*	
What's your score?	**Qual è il suo punteggio?**	*koo-ah-lEH eel sOO-oh poon-tAY-jee-oh*
I am winning (losing).	**Ho vinto (perduto).**	*oh vEEn-toh (pehr-dOO-toh)*
I win (lose).	**Vinco (perdo) io.**	*vEEn-koh (pehr-doh) EE-oh*

BOARD GAMES

Do you want to play _____?	**Vuole giocare _____?**	*voo-OH-leh jee-oh-kAH-reh*
■ checkers (draughts)	**a dama** *ah dAH-mah*	
■ chess	**a scacchi** *ah skAHk-key*	
■ dominoes	**a domino** *ah dOH-mee-noh*	
We need _____.	**Abbiamo bisogno _____.**	*ahb-bee-AH-moh bee-sOH-ny-oh*
■ a board	**di una scacchiera**	*dee OO-nah skahk-key-EH-rah*
■ dice	**dei dadi** *dAY-ee dAH-dee*	
■ the pieces	**dei pezzi** *dAY-ee pEH-tsee*	
■ the king	**del re** *dayl rAY*	
■ the queen	**della regina** *dayl-lah reh-jEE-nah*	
■ the rook (castle)	**della torre** *dayl-lah tOHr-reh*	
■ the bishop	**dell'alfiere** *dayl lahl-fee-EH-reh*	
■ the knight	**del cavallo** *dayl kah-vAHl-loh*	
■ the pawn	**del pedone** *dayl peh-dOH-neh*	
Check.	**Scacco.** *skAHk-koh*	
Checkmate.	**Scaccomatto.** *skahk-koh-mAHt-toh*	

SPECTATOR SPORTS

I'd like to watch a soccer game. **Vorrei vedere una partita di calcio.** *vohr-rEH-ee veh-dAY-reh OO-nah pahr-tEE-tah dee kAHl-chee-oh*

Where's the stadium? **Dov'è lo stadio?** *doh-vEH loh stAH-dee-oh*

When does the first half begin? **Quando inizia il primo tempo?** *koo-AHn-doh ee-nEE-tsee-ah eel prEE-moh tEHm-poh*

What teams are going to play? **Quali squadre giocheranno?** *koo-AH-lee skoo-AH-dreh jee-oh-keh-rAHn-noh*

Who is playing _____? **Chi è _____?** *key EH*

■ center **il centroavanti** *eel chehn-troh-ah-vAHn-tee*

■ fullback **il terzino** *eel tehr-tsEE-noh*

■ halfback **il libero** *eel lEE-beh-roh*

Who is playing wing? **Chi sta all'ala?** *key stAH ahl-lAH-lah*

Go! **Forza!** *fOHr-tsah*

What was the score? **Qual è stato il punteggio?** *koo-ah-lEH stAH-toh eel poon-tAY-jee-oh*

Is there a racetrack here? **C'è un ippodromo qui?** *chEH oon eep-pOH-droh-moh koo-EE*

ACTIVE SPORTS

Do you play tennis? **Gioca a tennis?** *jee-OH-kah ah tEHn-nees*

I (don't) play very well. **(Non) gioco molto bene.** *(nohn) jee-OH-koh mOHl-toh bEH-neh*

Do you play singles (doubles)?	**Gioca il singolo (in doppio)?** *jee-OH-kah eel sEEn-goh-loh (een dOHp-pee-oh)*
Do you know where there is a court?	**Sa dove c'è un campo da tennis?** *sAH doh-veh-chEH oon kAHm-poh dah tEHn-nees*
Is it a private club? I'm not a member.	**È un club privato? Io non sono socio.** *EH oon clEHb pree-vAH-toh? EE-oh nohn sOH-noh sOH-chee-oh*
How much do they charge per hour?	**Quanto si paga all'ora?** *koo-AHn-toh see pAH-gah ahl-lOH-rah*
Can I rent a racquet?	**Posso affittare una racchetta?** *pOHs-soh ahf-feet-tAH-reh OO-nah rahk-kAYt-tah*
Do you sell balls for a hard (soft) surface?	**Vendono palle per fondo duro (morbido)?** *vAYn-doh-noh pAHl-leh pehr fOHn-doh dOO-roh (mOHr-bee-doh)*
Let's rally first to warm up.	**Prima scambiamo qualche battuta per riscaldarci.** *prEE-mah skahm-bee-AH-moh koo-AHl-keh baht-tOO-tah pehr rees-kahl-dAHr-chee*
I serve (you serve) first.	**Io servo (lei serve) per primo.** *EE-oh sEHr-voh (lEH-ee sEHr-veh) pehr prEE-moh*
You play very well.	**Lei gioca molto bene.** *lEH-ee jee-OH-kah mOHl-toh bEH-neh*
You've won. Let's play another set.	**Lei ha vinto. Giochiamo un altro set.** *lEH-ee ah vEEn-toh jee-oh-key-AH-moh oon-AHl-troh seht*
Let's play another set.	**Giochiamo un altro set.** *jee-oh-key-AH-moh oon-AHl-troh seht*
Do you know where there is a handball (squash) court?*	**Sa dov'è un campo cintato per giocare a palla a muro (squash)?** *sah doh-vEH oon kAHm-poh cheen-tAH-toh pehr jee-oh-kAH-reh ah pAHl-lah ah mOO-roh (squash)*

Are there racquetball courts?*	**Ci sono campi per giocare a palla a muro con la racchetta?** *chee sOH-noh kAHm-pee pehr jee-oh-kAH-reh ah pAHl-lah ah mOO-roh kohn lah rah-kAYt-tah*
Where is a safe place to run (to jog)?	**Dov'è un posto buono dove si può correre (fare del footing)?** *doh-vEH oon pOHs-toh boo-OH-noh dOH-veh see poo-OH kOHr-reh-reh (fAH-reh dayl fOO-teeng)*
Where is there a health club?	**Dove si può trovare un centro fitness?** *doh-veh see poo-OH troh-vAH-reh oon chAYn-tro feet-nEHs*
Where can I play bocci?	**Dove posso giocare alle bocce?** *dOH-veh pOHs-soh jee-oh-kAH-reh AHl-leh bOH-cheh*

NOTE: These are not popular sports in Italy, so you will have great difficulty locating facilities.

AT THE BEACH/POOL

Let's go to the beach (to the pool).	**Andiamo alla spiaggia (in piscina).** *ahn-dee-AH-moh AHl-lah spee-AH-jee-ah (een pee-shEE-nah)*
Which bus will take us to the beach?	**Quale autobus ci porterà alla spiaggia?** *koo-AH-leh AH-oo-toh-boos chee pohr-teh-rAH AHl-lah spee-AH-jee-ah*
Is there an indoor (outdoor) pool in the hotel?	**C'è una piscina coperta (scoperta) nell'hotel?** *chEH OO-nah pee-shEE-nah koh-pEHr-tah (skoh-pEHr-tah) nayl-loh-tEHl*
I (don't) know how to swim well.	**(Non) so nuotare bene.** *(nohn) soh noo-oh-tAH-reh bEH-neh*

I just want to stretch out in the sand.	**Voglio solo stendermi sulla sabbia.** *vOH-ly-ee-oh sOH-loh stEHn-dehr-mee sOOl-lah sAHb-bee-ah*
Is it safe to swim here?	**Si può nuotare qui senza pericolo?** *see poo-OH noo-oh-tAH-reh koo-EE sEHn-tsah peh-rEE-koh-loh*
Is it dangerous for children?	**È pericoloso per i bambini?** *EH peh-ree-koh-lOH-soh pehr ee bahm-bEE-nee*
Is there a lifeguard?	**C'è un bagnino?** *chEH oon bah-ny-EE-noh*
Where can I get ____?	**Dove posso trovare ____?** *dOH-vey pOHs-soh troh-vAH-reh*

- an air mattress

  un materassino pneumatico *oon mah-teh-rahs-sEE-noh p-neh-oo-mAH-tee-koh*

- a bathing suit

  un costume da bagno *oon koh-stOO-meh dah bAH-ny-oh*

- a beach ball

  un pallone per la spiaggia *oon pahl-lOH-neh pehr lah spee-AH-jee-ah*

- a beach chair

  una sedia per la spiaggia *OO-nah sEH-dee-ah pehr lah spee-AH-jee-ah*

- a beach towel

  una tovaglia da spiaggia *OO-nah toh-vAH-ly-ee-ah dah spee-AH-jee-ah*

- diving equipment

  un equipaggiamento subacqueo *oon ay-koo-ee-pah-jee-ah-mEHn-toh soob-AH-koo-eh-oh*

- sunglasses

  degli occhiali da sole *dAY-ly-ee oh-key-AH-lee dah sOH-leh*

- suntan lotion

  una lozione per l'abbronzatura *OO-nah loh-tsee-OH-neh pehr lahb-brohn-tsah-tOO-rah*

- water skis

  degli sci acquatici? *dAY-ly-ee shEE ah-koo-AH-tee-chee*

ON THE SLOPES

Which ski area do you recommend?	**Quali campi di sci consiglia?** *koo-AH-lee kAHm-pee dee shee kohn-sEE-ly-ee-ah*
I am a novice (intermediate, expert) skier.	**Sono uno sciatore (una sciatrice) principiante, dilettante, esperto(a).** *sOH-noh oo-noh shee-ah-tOH-reh (oo-nah shee-ah-trEE-ceh) preen-chee-pee-AHn-teh, dee-leht-tAHn-teh, ehs-pEHr-toh(ah)*
What kind of lifts are there?	**Come sono le sciovie?** *kOH-meh sOH-noh leh shee-oh-vEE-eh*
How much does the lift cost?	**Quant'è il biglietto per la sciovia?** *koo-ahn-tEH eel bee-ly-ee-AYt-toh pehr lah shee-oh-vEE-ah*
Do they give lessons?	**Danno lezioni?** *dAHn-noh leh-tsee-OH-nee*

Is there enough snow this time of the year?	**C'è abbastanza neve in questo periodo dell'anno?** *chEH ahb-bah-stAHn-tsah nAY-veh een koo-AY-stoh peh-rEE-oh-doh dayl-lAHn-noh*
Is there any cross-country skiing?	**C'è anche lo sci di fondo?** *chEH AHn-keh loh shee dee fOHn-doh*
Where can I stay at the summit?	**Sulla cima dove posso trovare alloggio?** *sool-lah chEE-mah dOH-veh pOHs-soh troh-vAH-reh ahl-lOH-jee-oh*
Can I rent _____ there?	**Posso affittare _____ sul posto?** *pOHs-soh ahf-feet-tAH-reh sOOl pOH-stoh*
■ equipment	**l'attrezzatura** *laht-treh-tsah-tOO-rah*
■ poles	**le racchette da sci** *leh rah-kAYt-teh dah shEE*
■ skis	**gli sci** *ly-ee shEE*
■ ski boots	**gli scarponi da sci** *ly-ee skahr-pOH-nee dah shEE*

ON THE LINKS

Is there a golf course here?	**C'è un campo di golf (qui)?** *chEH oon kAHm-poh dee gOHlf (koo-EE)*
Can one rent clubs?	**Si possono affittare le mazze?** *see pOHs-soh-noh ahf-feet-tAH-reh leh mAH-tseh*

CAMPING

Is there a camping area near here?	**C'è un campeggio qui vicino?** *chEH oon kahm-pAY-jee-oh koo-EE vee-chEE-noh*
Do we pick our own site?	**Possiamo scegliere il posto che ci piace?** *pohs-see-AH-moh shay-ly-ee-EH-reh eel pOHs-toh kay chee pee-AH-cheh*

We only have a tent. **Noi abbiamo solo una tenta.** *nOH-ee ahb-bee-AH-moh sOH-loh OO-nah tEHn-tah*

Where is it on this map? **Dov'è su questa cartina?** *doh-vEH soo koo-AY-stah kahr-tEE-nah*

Can we park our trailer (caravan)? **Possiamo posteggiare la nostra roulotte?** *pohs-see-AH-moh poh-steh-jee-AH-reh lah nOH-strah roo-lOH-te*

Can we camp for one night only? **Possiamo accamparci per una notte solamente?** *pohs-see-AH-moh ahk-kahm-pAHr-chee pehr OO-nah nOHt-teh soh-lah-mEHn-teh*

Is (are) there _____? **C'è (ci sono) _____?** *cheh (chee sOH-noh)*

■ drinking water **acqua potabile** *AH-koo-ah poh-tAH-bee-leh*

■ showers **docce?** *dOH-cheh*

■ fireplaces **caminetti** *kah-mee-nAYt-tee*

■ picnic tables **tavoli per il pic-nic** *tAH-voh-lee pehr eel peek-nEEk*

■ electricity **l'elettricità** *leh-leh-tree-chee-tAH*

■ a grocery store **un negozio di generi alimentari** *oon nay-gOH-tsee-oh dee jEH-neh-ree ah-lee-mehn-tAH-ree*

■ a children's play-ground **un posto dove far giocare i bambini** *oon pOH-stoh dOH-veh fahr jee-oh-kAH-reh ee bahm-bEE-nee*

■ flush toilets **gabinetti** *gah-bee-nAYt-tee*

How much do they charge per person? (per car)? **Quanto si paga a persona? (per macchina)?** *koo-AHn-toh see pAH-gah ah pehr-sOH-nah (pehr mAHk-key-nah)*

We intend to stay _____ days (weeks). **Pensiamo di stare _____ giorni (settimane).** *pehn-see-AH-moh dee stAH-reh jee-OHr-nee (seyt-tee-mAH-neh)*

IN THE COUNTRYSIDE

Are there tours to the countryside?	**Si organizzano gite in campagna?** *see ohr-gah-nEE-tsah-noh jEE-teh een kahm-pAH-ny-ah*
What a beautiful landscape!	**Che bel panorama!** *kay bEHl pah-noh-rAH-mah*
Look at ____.	**Osserva (guarda) ____.** *ohs-sAYr-vah (goo-AHr-dah)*
■ the barn	**la stalla** *lah stAHl-lah*
■ the birds	**gli uccelli** *ly-ee oo-chEHl-lee*
■ the bridge	**il ponte** *eel pOHn-teh*
■ the castle	**il castello** *eel kah-stEHl-loh*
■ the cottages (small houses)	**i villini** *ee veel-lEE-nee*
■ the farm	**la fattoria** *lah faht-toh-rEE-ah*
■ the fields	**i campi** *ee kAHm-pee*
■ the flowers	**i fiori** *ee fee-OH-ree*
■ the forest	**il bosco** *eel bOH-skoh*
■ the hill	**la collina** *lah kohl-lEE-nah*
■ the lake	**il lago** *eel lAH-goh*
■ the mountains	**le montagne** *leh mohn-tAH-ny-eh*
■ the sea	**il mare** *eel mAH-reh*
■ the plants	**le piante** *leh pee-AHn-teh*
■ the pond	**lo stagno** *loh stAH-ny-oh*
■ the river	**il fiume** *eel fee-OO-meh*
■ the stream	**il ruscello** *eel roo-shEHl-loh*
■ the trees	**gli alberi** *ly-ee AHl-beh-ree*
■ the valley	**la valle** *lah vAHl-leh*

■ the village   **il paese (il villaggio)**   *eel pah-AY-seh (eel veel-lAH-jee-oh)*

■ the waterfall   **la cascata**   *lah kah-skAH-tah*

Where does this path lead to?   **Dove porta questo sentiero?**   *dOH-veh pOHr-tah koo-AY-stoh sehn-tee-EH-roh*

What kind of a tree is this?   **Che pianta è questa?**   *kay pee-AHn-tah EH koo-AYs-tah*

These gardens are beautiful.   **Questi giardini sono belli.**   *koo-AYs-tee jee-ahr-dEE-nee sOH-noh bEHl-lee*

TRAVEL TIP

Touring on the cheap? You'll find that keeping travel costs under control is a lot easier if you watch your daily expenses on such items as breakfast. Just how important is it for you to have that scrambled egg every morning? If you have the more native "continental breakfast," you'll have the money leftover to enjoy a theater performance or buy that special gift you saw in the shop window. Another way to save money and have more fun is to take public transportation. Sure, taxis are easier, but you'll get to the heart of the country a lot faster when you take the bus or metro. You'll observe how everyday people get around town, and you're likely to have some interesting adventures too. Exercise caution, however, and do not travel crowded trains or buses with valuables easily within view. Pickpockets are everywhere and, as a tourist, you are usually paying more attention to the sights than to riders nearby. Women should keep a firm grasp on their purses.

FOOD AND DRINK

How wonderful it is when a tourist can not only appreciate the sights and sounds of a country, but also enjoy its wonderful flavors. The food of Italy is world famous, justifiably so. To savor the great range of culinary delights, you must first understand the differences among places that serve food and drink and the customs of the country. Always ask for **un posto dove si mangia bene,** a place where you can eat well.

Bar or Snack Bar	Ice cream, coffee, pastries, and drinks are served. This is also a favorite place for a quick breakfast consisting of a hot, foamy **cappuccino** and a **mottino,** or a **maritozzo,** a **cornetto,** a **tramezzino,** or other pastry.
Trattoria or Osteria	Small, family-operated inn serving simple but delicious local dishes prepared while you wait.
Tavola Calda	Small, self-service cafeteria with simple, hot dishes that you choose from a hot table. In some places local specialties and dishes from other countries are prepared.
Rosticceria	Generally a take-out place for grilled meats.
Pizzeria	Small, family-operated pizza parlor. Local pizza specialties and other simple dishes are served. In some places they are called **pizzeria-rosticceria,** where you can sit and enjoy a nice meal.
Autogrill	A self-service cafeteria or snack area on the **autostrade** (motorway, turnpike) with bar, restaurant, tourist market, souvenirs, telephones, and bedrooms.
Ristorante	Elegant place classified by stars (some restaurants are rated according to their decor, others by the quality of their cuisine). *Often closed on Mondays.*

Most tourists will have their breakfast in the hotel, so much of the information that follows applies to lunch and dinner. Breakfast, **la prima colazione**, for an Italian consists of **caffelatte** (coffee with milk) and a **croissant**, **panini** (rolls) with butter (**burro**) and jam or marmalade (**marmellata**) or cheese (**formaggio**). If your hotel doesn't serve breakfast, or you prefer to go out, you'll find a suitable Italian breakfast at a caffé or bar.

LUNCH—IL PRANZO

Lunch is served from about noon or 12:30 to 3 p.m. (Usually siesta time is after **il pranzo**.) A regular **pranzo** includes:

antipasto	*ahn-tee-pAH-stoh*	appetizer
primo	*prEE-moh*	pasta or soup (**minestra in brodo**)
secondo	*say-kOHn-doh*	a meat or fish dish with vegetable, wine, and water
formaggi	*fohr-mAH-jee*	cheese course
dolci o frutta	*dOHl-chee oh frOOT-ta*	fruit or a sweet dessert
caffé	*kahf-fEH*	coffee

DINNER—LA CENA

Dinner follows the same general arrangement as lunch. It is served from around 7 p.m. to 10 p.m. In Northern Italy, dinner is served earlier than in Southern Italy.

THE MENU

Many restaurants offer a special plate of the day (**il piatto del giorno**) or have a tourist menu at a set price (**il menù turistico a prezzo fisso**). These are usually very good values. You should also watch for the specialty of the chef or of the restaurant (**la specialità del cuoco o del ristorante**). Often the local wine is included in the price of a meal (**vino incluso**).

The bill may or may not include a service charge (**servizio**), which is usually 12 to 15 percent of the bill. Other items that may appear on the bill are the tip **(mancia)**, bread and cover charge **(pane e coperto)**, and a surcharge **(supplemento)**. Even if the service and tip are included, you should leave some remaining change; it is a token of your appreciation for good service and excellent food.

EATING OUT

Do you know a good restaurant?	**Scusi, conosce un buon ristorante?** *skOO-see koh-nOH-sheh oon boo-OHn ree-stoh-rAHn-teh*
Is it very expensive (dressy)?	**È molto costoso (elegante)?** *eh mohl-toh koh-stOH-soh (eh-leh-gAHn-teh)*
Do you know a restaurant that serves typical dishes?	**Conosce un ristorante tipico (del luogo)?** *koh-nOH-sheh oon res-toh-rAHn-teh tEE-pee-koh (dAYl loo-OH-goh)*
Waiter!	**Cameriere!** *kah-meh-ree-EH-reh*
A table for two please.	**Un tavolo per due, per favore.** *oon tAH-voh-loh pehr dOO-eh peh fah-vOH-reh*
■ in the corner	**all'angolo** *ahl-lAHn-goh-loh*
■ near the window	**vicino alla finestra** *vee-chee-noh AHl-lah fee-nEHs-trah*
■ on the terrace	**sul terrazzo** *sOOl tehr-rAH-tsoh*
I'd like to make a reservation ___.	**Vorrei fare una prenotazione ___.** *vohr-rEH-ee fAH-reh oon-ah preh-noh-tah-tsee-OH-neh*
■ for tonight	**per stasera** *pehr stah-sAY-rah*
■ for tomorrow evening	**per domani sera** *pehr doh-mAH-nee sAY-rah*
■ for two (four) persons	**per due (quattro) persone** *pehr dOO-eh (koo-AHt-troh) pehr-SOH-neh*

■ at 8 p.m.	**per le venti** *pehr leh vAYn-tee*
■ at 8:30 p.m.	**per le venti e trenta** *pehr leh vAYn-tee ay trEHn-tah*
We'd like to have lunch (dinner) now.	**Vorremmo pranzare adesso.** *vohr-rAYm-moh prahn-tsAH-reh ah-dEHs-soh*
The menu, please.	**Il menù, per piacere.** *eel may-noo pehr pee-ah-chAY-reh*
I'd like the set menu.	**Vorrei il menù turistico. (Il menù a prezzo fisso.)** *vohr-rEH-ee eel meh-nOO too-rEEs-tee-koh (eel meh-nOO ah prEH-tsoh fEEs-soh)*
What's today's special?	**Qual è il piatto del giorno?** *koo-ah-lEH eel pee-AHt-toh dayl jee-OHr-noh*
What do you recommend?	**Che cosa mi consiglia lei?** *kay kOH-sah mee kohn-sEE-ly-ee-ah lEH-ee*
What's the house specialty?	**Qual è la specialità della casa?** *koo-ah-lEH lah speh-chee-ah-lee-tAH dayl-lah kAH-sah*
Do you serve children's portions?	**Si servono porzioni per bambini?** *see sEHr-voh-noh pohr-tsee-OH-nee pehr bahm-bEE-nee*
I'm (not) very hungry.	**(Non) ho molta fame.** *(nohn) oh mOHl-tah fAH-meh*
Are the portions small (large)?	**Le porzioni sono piccole (grandi)?** *leh pohr-tsee-OH-nee sOH-noh pEE-koh-leh (grAHn-dee)*
To begin with, please bring us ____.	**Per cominciare, ci porti ____.** *pehr koh-meen-chee-AH-reh chee pOHr-tee*
■ an aperitif	**un aperitivo** *oon ah-peh-ree-tEE-voh*
■ a cocktail	**un cocktail** *oon kOHk-tayl*
■ some white (red) wine	**del vino bianco (rosso)** *dayl vEE-noh bee-AHn-koh (rOHs-soh)*

■ some water	**dell'acqua** *dayl-LAH-koo-ah*
■ a bottle of mineral water, with (without) gas	**una bottiglia d'acqua minerale gassata (naturale)** *oo-nah boht-tEE-ly-ee-ah dAH-koo-ah mee-neh-rAH-leh gahs-sAH-tah (nah-too-rAH-leh)*
■ a beer	**una birra** *OO-nah bEEr-rah*
I'd like to order now.	**Vorrei ordinare adesso** *vohr-rEH-ee ohr-dee-nAH-reh ah-dEHs-soh*
I'd like _____.	**Vorrei _____.** *vohr-rEH-ee*

(See the listings that follow for individual dishes, and also the regional specialties noted on pages 89–97)

Do you have a house wine?	**Hanno il vino della casa?** *AHn-noh eel VEE-noh dAYl-lah kAH-sah*
Is it dry (mellow, sweet)?	**È vino secco (amabile, dolce)?** *EH vEE-noh sAY-koh (ah-mAH-bee-leh, dOHl-cheh)*
Please also bring us _____.	**Per piacere ci porti anche _____.** *pehr pee-ah-chAY-reh chee pOHr-tee AHn-keh*
■ a roll	**un panino** *oon pah-nEE-noh*
■ bread	**il pane** *eel pAH-neh*
■ bread and butter	**pane e burro** *pAH-neh ay bOOr-roh*
Waiter, we need _____.	**Cameriere(a), abbiamo bisogno di _____.** *kah-meh-ree-EH-reh(ah) ahb-bee-AH-moh bee-sOH-ny-oh dee*
■ a knife	**un coltello** *oon kohl-tEHl-loh*
■ a fork	**una forchetta** *oo-nah fohr-kAYt-tah*
■ a spoon	**un cucchiaio** *oon koo-key-AH-ee-oh*
■ a teaspoon	**un cucchiaino** *oon koo-key-ah-EE-noh*

■ a soup spoon	**un cucchiaio per la minestra (il brodo)** *oon koo-key-AH-ee-oh pehr lah mee-nEHs-trah (eel brOH-doh)*
■ a glass	**un bicchiere** *oon bee-key-EH-reh*
■ a cup	**una tazza** *oo-nah tAH-tsah*
■ a saucer	**un piattino** *oon pee-aht-tEE-noh*
■ a plate	**un piatto** *oon pee-AHt-toh*
■ a napkin	**un tovagliolo** *oon toh-vah-ly-ee-OH-loh*
■ toothpicks	**gli stuzzicadenti** *ly-ee stOO-tsee-kah-dEHn-tee*

APPETIZERS (STARTERS)

Antipasti mostly consist of raw salads, cooked chilled vegetables dressed with a vinaigrette, and massive varieties of sausages and salamis. Some key terms are:

acciughe	*ah-chee-OH-gheh*	anchovies
antipasto misto	*ahn-tee-pAHs-toh mEEs-toh*	assorted appetizers
carciofi	*kahr-chee-OH-fee*	artichoke
mortadella	*mohr-tah-dEHl-lah*	cold sausage, similar to bologna
prosciutto crudo	*proh-shee-OOt-toh krOO-doh*	raw cured ham
tartufi	*tahr-tOO-fee*	truffles (white)

SOUPS

Soups can be either thick or thin, and thus are given different names. **Brodi** are generally broths, while **zuppe** are thick and hearty. .

brodo di manzo	*brOH-doh dee mAHn-tsoh*	broth, generally meat-based
brodo di pollo	*brOH-hod dee pOHl-loh*	chicken broth
brodo magro di vegetali	*brOH-doh mAH-groh dee veh-jeh-tAH-lee*	vegetable broth
crema di ____	*krEH-mah dee*	creamed ____ soup
buridda	*boo-rEEd-dah*	fish stew
cacciucco	*kah-chee-OO-koh*	seafood chowder
minestra in brodo	*mee-nEHs-trah een brOH-doh*	pasta in broth
minestrone	*mee-nehs-trOH-neh*	thick vegetable soup
zuppa di ____	*tsOOp-pah dee*	thick soup

PASTA OR RICE COURSE

A pasta course usually precedes your entree, so it is usually a small serving offered as in special presentation. Since the varieties of pasta are almost endless, you'll find them offered on menus as **agnellotti, cappelletti, fettuccine, lasagne, tagliatelle, tortellini,** and many more. It will be sauced, perhaps with a cream and cheese mixture or served with tomato sauce. It may also be stuffed or baked, or served in a soup.

In parts of northern Italy, rice is often substituted for pasta. These dishes are generally less well known, but are no less tasty. Generally you'll find on a menu a plain rice dish (**riso**) or as a **risotto,** a creamy rice mixture often combined with cheese, fruit, vegetables, or meat.

A few other "pasta" dishes you will find on some menus are **polenta** *(poh-lEHn-tah)*—a cornmeal mush often sliced and served with sausages or chicken—and **gnocchi** *(ny-OH-*

key)—dumplings made from potatoes and often mixed with spinach, cheese, or cornmeal. Egg dishes are also often offered for this course. A **frittata** *(free-tAH-tah)* is an omelet, often filled with vegetables.

ENTREES (MEAT AND FISH DISHES)

The "main course" of an Italian meal is usually somewhat plain, either a sautéed or grilled meat or a baked fish or chicken. Along the coast and in Sicily and Sardinia, you'll find unusual and exciting varieties of seafood.

acciughe	*ah-chee-OO-gheh*	anchovies
anguille	*ahn-goo-EEl-leh*	eel
aragosta	*ah-rah-gOHs-tah*	lobster (spiny)
aringa	*ah-rEEn-gah*	herring
■ **affumicata**	*ahf-foo-mee-kAH-tah*	smoked
baccalà	*bah-kah-lAH*	dried salt cod
branzino (nasello)	*brahn-tsEE-noh (nah-sEHl-loh)*	bass (hake)
calamari (seppie)	*kah-lah-mAH-ree (sAYp-pee-eh)*	squid
cozze	*kOH-tseh*	mussels
gamberetti	*gAHm-beh-rAY-tee*	prawns
granchi	*grAHn-key*	crabs
lumache	*loo-mAH-keh*	snails
merluzzo	*mayr-lOOt-tsoh*	cod
ostriche	*OHs-tree-keh*	oysters
polipo	*pOH-lee-poh*	octopus
salmone	*sahl-mOH-neh*	salmon
sardine	*sahr-dEE-neh*	sardines

scampi	*skAHm-pee*	shrimps
sogliola	*sOH-ly-ee-oh-lah*	flounder (sole)
trota	*trOH-tah*	trout
tonno	*tOHn-noh*	tuna
vongole	*vOHn-goh-leh*	clams
trance di pesce alla griglia	*trAHn-cheh dee pAY-sheh AHl-lah grEE-ly-ee-ah*	grilled fish steaks
fritto misto di pesce	*frEEt-toh mEEs-toh dee pAY-sheh*	mised fried fish

Meat dishes are often sauced or served with some type of gravy. Here are some basic terms you'll encounter on Italian menus.

agnello (abbacchio)	*ah-ny-EHl-loh (ahb-bAH-key-oh)*	lamb
capretto	*kah-prAHy-toh)*	goat
maiale	*mah-ee-AH-leh*	pork
manzo	*mAHn-tsoh*	beef
montone	*mohn-tOH-neh*	mutton
vitello	*vee-tEHl-loh*	veal

And some common cuts of meat, plus other terms you'll find on a menu:

affettati	*ahf-fayt-tAH-tee*	cold cuts
costate	*kohs-tAH-teh*	chops
animelle	*ah-nee-mEHl-leh*	sweetbreads
cervello	*chehr-vEHl-loh*	brains
fegato	*fAY-gah-toh*	liver
bistecca	*bees-tAY-kah*	steak
lingua	*lEEn-goo-ah*	tongue

pancetta	*pahn-chAYt-tah*	bacon
polpette	*pohl-pAYt-teh*	meatballs
prosciutto cotto	*proh-shee-OOt-toh kOHt-toh*	ham (cooked)
rognoni	*roh-ny-OH-nee*	kidneys

And some terms for fowl and game:

anitra	*AH-nee-trah*	duck
beccaccia	*bay-kAH-chee-ah*	woodcock
cappone	*kahp-pOH-neh*	capon
carne di cervo	*kAHr-neh dee chEHr-voh*	venison
coniglio	*koh-nEE-ly-ee-oh*	rabbit
fagiano	*fah-jee-AH-noh*	pheasant
faraona	*fah-rah-OH-nah*	guinea fowl
lepre	*lEH-preh*	hare

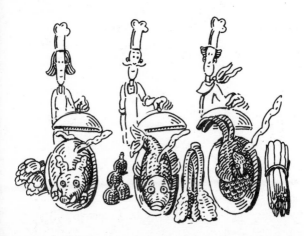

oca	*OH-kah*	goose
pernice	*pehr-nEE-cheh*	partridge
piccioncino	*pEE-chee-ohn-chEE-noh*	squab (pigeon)
pollo	*pOHl-loh*	chicken
porcellino di latte	*pohr-chehl-lEE-noh dee lAHz-teh*	suckling pig
quaglia	*koo-AH-ly-ee-ah*	quail
tacchino	*tah-kEY-noh*	turkey

Is it ____?	**È____?** *eh*
■ baked	**cotta al forno** *kOHt-tah ahl fOHr-noh*
■ boiled	**lessa** *lAYs-sah*
■ braised (stewed)	**brasata** *brah-sAH-tah*
■ broiled (grilled)	**ai ferri** *AH-ee fEHr-ree*
■ roasted	**arrosto** *ahr-rOH-stoh*
■ grilled	**alla griglia** *AHl-lah grEE-ly-ee-ah*
■ poached	**bollita** *bohl-lEE-tah*
I like the meat ____.	**La carne mi piace ____.** *lah kAHr-neh mee pee-AH-cheh*
■ well done	**ben cotta** *bEHn kOHt-tah*
■ medium	**cotta a puntino** *kOHt-tah ah poon-tEE-noh*
■ rare	**al sangue** *ahl sAHn-goo-eh*
■ tender	**tenera** *tEH-neh-rah*

VEGETABLES

Italians love vegetables, so you will find many types, prepared in a variety of ways.

asparagi	*ahs-pAH-rah-jee*	asparagus

carciofi	*kahr-chee-OH-fee*	artichoke
carote	*kah-rOH-teh*	carrots
cavoli	*kAH-voh-lee*	cabbage
cavolfiori	*kah-vohl-fee-OH-ree*	cauliflower
cetriolo	*cheh-tree-OO-loh*	cucumber
ceci	*chay-chee*	chick-peas
fagioli	*fah-jee-oh-lEE*	beans (dried)
fagiolini	*fah-jee-oh-lEE-nee*	green beans
fave	*fAH-veh*	broad beans
finocchi	*fee-nOH-key*	fennel
funghi	*fOOn-ghee*	mushrooms
lattuga	*laht-tOO-gah*	lettuce
lenticchie	*len-tEE-key-eh*	lentils
granturco	*grahn-tOO-rkoh*	corn (maize)
melanzana	*meh-lAHn-tsah-nah*	eggplant (aubergine)
peperoni	*peh-peh-rOH-nee*	pepper
patate	*pah-tAH-teh*	potatoes
■ **patatine fritte**	*pah-tah-tEE-neh frEEt-teh*	French fries (chips)
piselli	*pee-sEHl-lee*	peas
pomodoro	*poh-moh-dOH-roh*	tomato
porcini	*pohr-chee-nee*	wild mushroom, similar to cepes
sedano	*sAY-dah-noh*	celery
spinaci	*spee-nAH-chee*	spinach
zucchini	*tsoo-key-nee*	green squash (courgettes)

SEASONINGS

Although Italians season their food well, personal preferences sometimes intercede. Here's how to ask for what you want.

I'd like ____.	**Vorrei ____.**	*vohr-rEH-ee*
■ butter	**burro**	*bOOr-roh*
■ horseradish	**rafano**	*rAH-fah-noh*
■ ketchup	**ketchup**	*keh-chOHp*
■ margarine	**margarina**	*mahr-gah-rEE-nah*
■ mayonnaise	**maionese**	*mah-ee-oh-nAY-seh*
■ mustard	**senape, mostarda**	*sEH-nah-peh, moh-stAHr-dah*
■ olive oil	**olio d'oliva**	*OH-lee-oh doh-lEE-vah*
■ pepper (black)	**pepe (nero)**	*pAY-peh (nAY-roh)*
■ pepper (red)	**pepe (rosso)**	*pAY-peh (rOHs-soh)*
■ salt	**sale**	*sAH-leh*
■ sugar	**zucchero**	*tsOO-keh-roh*
■ saccharin	**saccarina, dolcificante (Sweet and Low)**	*sah-kah-rEE-nah, dohl-chee-fee-kAHn-teh*
■ vinegar	**aceto**	*ah-chAY-toh*

CHEESE COURSE

There are many, many varieties of Italian cheeses, and if you order a cheese course you will have the opportunity to try some that never get exported. Rather than give you the names of all the types, we offer a few useful words you can use in discussing your choices with the waiter.

Is the cheese ____?	**È il formaggio ____?**	*eh eel fohr-mAH-jee-oh*
■ mild	**dolce**	*dOHl-cheh*

■ sharp	**piccante**	*pee-kAHn-teh*
■ hard	**duro**	*dOO-roh*
■ soft	**molle**	*mOHl-leh*

FRUITS AND NUTS

Since the Italian meal is a filling one, often Italians will conclude their meal with a piece of fruit. Here are the names of some.

What kind of fruit do you have?	**Che frutta c'è?**	*kay frOOt-tah chEH*
albicocca	*ahl-bee-kOH-kah*	apricot
ananasso	*ah-nah-nAHs-soh*	pineapple
anguria	*ahn-gOO-ree-ah*	watermelon
arancia	*ah-rAHn-chee-ah*	orange
castagne	*kahs-tAH-ny-eh*	chestnuts
cedro	*chAY-droh*	lime
ciliege	*chee-lee-EH-jee-eh*	cherries
datteri	*dAHt-teh-ree*	dates
fichi	*fEE-key*	figs
fragole	*frAH-goh-leh*	strawberries
lampone	*lahm-pOH-neh*	raspberry
limone	*lee-mOH-neh*	lemon
mandarini	*mahn-dah-rEE-nee*	tangerines
mandorle	*mAHn-dohr-leh*	almonds
mela	*mAY-lah*	apple
more	*mOH-reh*	mulberries
noci	*nOH-chee*	nuts
nocciole	*noh-chee-OH-leh*	hazelnuts (filberts)
melone	*meh-lOH-neh*	melon

pera	*pAY-rah*	pear
pesca	*pAYs-kah*	peach
pompelmo	*pohm-pEHl-moh*	grapefruit
prugne	*prOO-ny-eh*	plum
uva	*OO-vah*	grape

DESSERT—SWEETS

Many restaurants do not serve elaborate desserts, since Italians don't generally eat pastries after a meal. We list below a few things you are likely to find on a menu. In particular, Italian ice cream is something not to be missed. Since it is not beaten with air, it is very rich and creamy.

torta	*tOHr-tah*	cake
dolci	*dOHl-chee*	sweets
macedonia di frutta	*mah-cheh-dOH-nee-ah dee frOOt-tah*	fresh fruit salad
mousse al cioccolato	*mOOs ahl chee-oh-koh lAH-toh*	chocolate mousse
crema inglese	*krEH-mah een-glAY-seh*	custard
crostata	*kroh-stAH-tah*	pie
budino	*boo-dEE-noh*	pudding
■ di pane	*dee pAH-neh*	bread
■ di crema	*dee krEH-mah*	cream
■ di riso	*dee rEE-soh*	rice
crema di caramello	*crEH-mah dee kah-rah-mEHl-loh*	caramel custard
gelato	*jeh-lAH-toh*	ice cream
■ al cioccolato	*ahl chee-oh-koh-lAH-toh*	chocolate

■ alla vaniglia	*AHl-lah vah-nEE-ly-ee-ah*	vanilla
■ alla fragola	*AHl-lah frAH-goh-lah*	strawberry
■ di caffè (con panna)	*dee kahf-fEH (kOHn pAHn-nah)*	coffee (with whipped cream)

SPECIAL CIRCUMSTANCES

Many travelers have special dietary requirements, so here are a few phrases that might help you get what you need or avoid what does you wrong.

I don't want anything fried (salted).	**Non posso mangiare cose fritte (salate).** *nohn pOHs-soh mahn-jee-AH-reh kOH-seh frEEt-teh (sah-lAH-teh)*
I cannot eat anything made with ____.	**Non posso mangiare niente fatto con ____.** *nohn pOHs-soh mahn-jee-AH-reh nee-EHn-teh fAHt-toh kohn*
Is this very spicy?	**Questo è molto piccante?** *koo-AY-stoh eh mohl-toh pee-kAHn-teh*
Do you have any dishes without meat?	**Hanna piatti (cibi) senza carne?** *AHn-noh pee-AHt-tee (chEE-bee) sEHn-tsah kAHr-neh*

BEVERAGES

See pages 97–100 for information on Italian wines. As for other beverages, we give you the following phrases to help you ask for exactly what you wish.

Waiter, please bring me ____.	**Cameriere(a), per piacere mi porti ____.**	*kah-meh-ree-EH-reh(ah), pehr pee-ah-chAY-reh mee pOHr-tee*

coffee (regular or American)	**caffè**	*kahf-fEH*
■ with milk	**caffelatte**	*kahf-fEH-lAHt-teh*
■ with sugar	**con zucchero**	*kOHn tsOO-keh-roh*
■ without sugar	**senza zucchero**	*sEHn-tsah tsOO-keh-roh*
■ with saccharin	**con saccarina**	*kohn sah-kah-rEE-nah*
■ with cream	**con panna**	*kOHn pAHn-nah*
Italian coffee	**espresso**	*ehs-prEHs-soh*
■ with anisette	**corretto all'an- isetta**	*kohr-rEHt-toh ahl-lah-nee-sAYt-tah*
iced (coffee)	**freddo**	*frAYd-doh*
tea	**tè**	*tEH*
■ with milk	**con latte**	*kOHn lAHt-teh*
■ with lemon	**con limone**	*kOHn lee-mOH-neh*
■ with sugar	**con zucchero**	*kOHn tsOO-keh-roh*
■ iced	**con ghiaccio**	*kOHn ghee-AH-chee-oh*
water	**acqua**	*AH-koo-ah*
■ cold	**fredda**	*frAYd-dah*
■ iced	**con ghiaccio**	*kOHn ghee-AH-chee-oh*
■ mineral	**minerale**	*mee-neh-rAH-leh*
(with gas)	**gassata**	*gahs-sAH-tah*
(without gas)	**naturale**	*nah-too-rAH-leh*

a glass of ____.	**un bicchiere di ____.**	*oon bee-key-EH-reh dee*
■ milk (cold)	**latte (fresco)**	*lAHt-teh (frAY-skoh)*
■ malted milk	**latte con malto**	*lAHt-teh kOHn mAHl-toh*
■ milk shake	**frullato di latte**	*frool-LAH-toh dee lAHt-teh*
■ orangeade	**aranciata**	*ah-rahn-chee-AH-tah*
■ punch	**punch**	*pOHn-ch*
■ soda	**bibita anal-colica (soda)**	*bEE-bee-tah ah-nahl-kOH-lee-kah*
■ (fruit) juice	**succo di (frutta)**	*sOO-koh dee (frOOt-tah)*
■ lemonade	**limonata**	*lee-moh-nAH-tah*

SETTLING UP

The bill normally includes a surcharge for service. Tips are never included in the bill and customers leave from 10 to 15 percent of the bill in appreciation of courteous service, only 10 percent if the service wasn't that good.

The check, please.	**Il conto, per favore.** *eel kOHn-toh, pehr fah-vOH-reh*
Separate checks.	**Conti separati.** *kOHn-tee seh-pah-rAH-tee*
Is the service included?	**È incluso il servizio?** *EH een-klOO-soh eel sehr-vEE-tsee-oh*
I haven't ordered this.	**Non ho ordinato questo.** *nohn oh ohr-dee-nAH-toh koo-AY-stoh*
I don't think the bill is right.	**Non penso che il conto sia corretto.** *nohn pEHn-soh kay eel kOHn-toh sEE-ah kor-rEHt-toh*

We're in a hurry. | **Abbiamo fretta.** *ahb-bee-AH-moh frAYt-tah*

This is for you. | **Questo è per lei.** *koo-AY-stoh EH pehr lEH-ee*

REGIONAL ITALIAN SPECIALTIES

We can give only a limited idea of the extensive and varied cuisines of Italy. In whatever part of the country you are, ask for the local specialties and regional dishes. Much of this information has been derived from *The Food of Italy* by Waverly Root (Vintage Books, 1971).

There is no "Italian" cuisine; Italy is divided into regions and each region has a cuisine based on its resources. Regions that border on the sea are often strong in seafood, while mountainous regions have wonderful meat dishes. Likewise, Italy can be divided somewhat gastronomically north and south, with favorites such as polenta and rice more to the north, while southern regions concentrate on pasta. Likewise, the lusher portions of Italy (mostly in the north) have a cuisine rich with meats and game, whereas the southern regions are poorer and consequently use more vegetables and fish in their dishes. The delicate pasta of the north is enriched with eggs, whereas in the south it is firmer and often factory-made.

There is another thing to note about Italian food, especially in contrast with French food. Italian food is basically from the home—that is, every good cook knows how to make a sauce at home, and the food you get in restaurants is founded on good home cooking. Just as every home has its favorite version of a sauce or soup, so Italian restaurants will differ greatly in their preparations of well-known Italian dishes, such as minestrone.

The following is a list of Italy's regions, along with some of the specialties you are likely to find there.

1. VALLE D'AOSTA (Aosta) This northernmost area of Italy is actually French-speaking, but the food is quite coarse with a lot of game, dark breads, and thick soups. Most famous is the **chamois,** a high mountain goat that is cooked in red wine and spiked with **grappa** (an *eau de vie*). **Motzetta** is the name for chamois when it is cured and sliced, served on bread. The sausages are also good here, mostly hard salami types. The **costoletta di vitello con fontina** is a veal chop stuffed with fontina cheese, coated with bread crumbs, and sautéed. Potatoes are usually served with these heavy game and meat dishes. The honey from this region is quite good, as is the butter.

2. PIEMONTE (Torino)   Turin is the center of this northern region of Italy. The area borders on Switzerland, so one of its famous dishes is **fonduta,** an Italian version of fondue, made with melted fontina cheese lightened with egg yolks and milk, and graced with slivers of white truffles. It is served like a soup, often poured over polenta. Also from this region is **bagna cauda,** a dipping sauce of oil and butter flavored with anchovies and sprinkled with white truffles. The mountain streams flow with trout, which these Italians prepare very simply—broiled or sautéed, sometimes with a touch of sage. **Riso alla piemontese** is stubby Italian rice with white truffles, topped with a meat sauce. For the pasta in this area, you'll most often be served **agnolotti,** small studded pillows. The **gnocchi** here are made with fontina cheese, and the polenta is often topped with melted fontina. For a sweet taste, the people in this region are fond of **gianduiotti,** chocolate drops from Turin.

3. LOMBARDIA (Milano)   This is a region very rich with good food. The inventiveness of Milanese cooks has made the cuisine famous throughout the world. It is also the region that produces the best-known cheeses, such as Bel Paese, Robiola, Gorgonzola (white), Mascarpone, and Stracchino. Some specialties you're likely to see on a menu are: **ossibuchi** (a veal shank braised in an herbed white wine and tomato sauce), **costoletta alla milanese** (a crisp-fried, breaded veal chop), **polenta** (a cornmeal mush, eaten as an accompaniment to stews and liver, or by itself with cheese or a sauce), **risotto** (a hearty rice dish in which rice is simmered in broth, often with butter, Parmesan cheese, and saffron), **ris con la luganega** (rice cooked with chopped Monza sausage and cheese), **busecca** (stewed tripe, served on French bread and covered with cheese), minestrone with rice, **lesso misto** (often called **bollito misto,** a boiled mixed meats dish in a rich broth), **stufato** (a tender and succulent beef stew), and **panettone** (a buttery yeast cake studded with raisins and candied fruits, usually enjoyed around Christmastime).

4. TRENTINO ALTO ADIGE (Bolzano)   This area of northern Italy borders on Austria and Switzerland, so don't be surprised to see sauerkraut (**crauti**) or Tirolean noodles. It is a German-speaking area, very mountainous with valleys where rye, corn, and wheat grow. They have what is called the Elephant Platter, an enormous quantity of food including at least 6 types of meats and 12 kinds of vegetables. There are also trout from the streams and much smoked pork. The **nockerln** are similar to gnocchi, offered as an accompaniment to meat dishes. There are also endless varieties of strudel, most of them involving fruits or cream wrapped in a paper-thin crust and sprinkled with chopped nuts.

5. VENETO (Venezia, Padova, Verona)   Early traders brought many unusual spices and seasonings to Venice, so the food from this area is very colorful. Saffron colors the polenta, while ginger and cloves accent the sweets. Seafood is prominent, with eels a favorite either fried or marinated. Sardines, mullet, mussels, cuttlefish, and salted cod (**baccalà**) are the foundations for soups (**brodeto**). **Fegato alla veneziana** is a famous fish—thin slices of calves liver lightly sautéed with onions and butter. Rice plays a prominent role, in **risi e bisi** (rise with peas), in **risotto nero** (rice with octopus), and in multiple other varieties. **Scampi** (shrimp) are served in a myriad of ways, sometimes fried, other times in a dish with rice, or in a soup. This is also an area for sweets, including **fritole di Venezia,** little fritters flavored with cinnamon, raisins, pignoli, and lemon peel. **Focaccia pasquale veneziana** is the traditional Easter cake in the shape of a dove, filled with eggs and sprinkled with kirsch and grappa.

6. FRIULI VENEZIA GIULIA (Trieste)   This is not a rich area, so the food of the region reflects that with an emphasis on poultry rather than meat, soups based on vegetables, and all of it served with a lot of bread. The prosciutto from San Daniele, however, is world famous. The **lujarnis** is their long and thin sausage, usually grilled. **Brovada** is a vegetable dish based on turnips. **Broeto** is a fish chowder, a variation of **brodetto.** In Trieste, the foods reflect some Austrian influences, with **liptauer** (a spreadable mixture of cheese and spices) made from Gorgonzola and Mascarpone instead. Trieste also has its own versions of calves liver, flavored with cloves and lemon juice and its own **risi e bisi,** more of a pea-and-rice puree served over pasta.

7. LIGURIA (Genova)   This is a small region, dominated by the city of Genova, but its foods are vast and varied. There is a lot of seafood, but not as much as you might expect from this seacoast region. From this area come some very famous Italian specialties, including **pesto,** that fragrant purée of basil leaves, olive oil, Parmesan cheese, and pignoli nuts. **Ravioli** is also from here, filled with minced meat and herbs. The minestrone is thick and creamy, varying as much among Ligurian cooks as it does throughout Italy. Also from this region are fish soups that are simply flavored with fennel and/or other herbs. The **focaccia** is a flatbread similar to a pizza without the topping. **Torta pasqualina** is their Easter cake made with many layers of puff pastry, filled with artichoke hearts, hard-cooked eggs, and cheese. For a sweet, **pandolce** is a yeast cake punctuated with grapes, raisins, and pignolis.

8. EMILIA ROMAGNA (Bologna, Ravenna)   This region of northern Italy extends across the country following the ancient Emilian way. The fertile farmland produces a lot of wheat for pasta, but the sausages from this region are also famous, as is its prosciutto from Parma. **Zampone di Mantova** is a very large sausage of chopped seasoned meats and pork skin that is simmered, then sliced and served with lentils and onions. **Cotechina,** from Modena, is another sausage, simmered in wine and served with a thick sauce. From Bologna comes **mortadella,** a smooth, heavily spiced sausage that has traveled round the world as "bologna," and **tortellini.** circles of pasta that are stuffed with meat and cheese, then folded into rings and served with a sauce. **Tortellini mantovani** are bite-sized pastas stuffed with puréed pumpkin. When a pasta is served **alla bolognese,** expect a meat sauce thick with tomatoes.

This region stretches to the Adriatic, and along the coast you'll find much seafood, particularly turbot (**rombo**), tuna (**tonno**), mackerel (**sgombero**), mullet (**barboni, triglie di scoglio**), angler fish (**rospo**), eel (**anguilla**), octopus (**seppia**), squid (**calamaro, totano**), spiny lobster (**agagosta**), crayfish (**gambero**), or scallops (**cappa santa**). For desserts, this area has to offer the **mandorlini,** an almond-flavored biscuit, and **crespelli,** strips of dough that are deep-fried, then dusted with sugar. But this is only a start of the wonderful foods of this region.

9. TOSCANA (Firenze, Pisa)   The food of Toscana is hearty and simple. This is the region that produces the best olive oil in Italy, from Lucca. It is also where the finest of beef is raised in Italy and so you will often see on a menu their Florentine steak, which is similar to a T-bone. It is served rare, unless you indicate otherwise. Chicken is served with a ginger sauce, **pollo alla diavola;** pork is slowly braised in broth and flavored with rosemary and garlic. **Stracotto alla fiorentina** is similar to pot roast, with carrots, celery, onions, and tomatoes. There aren't any exceptional fish dishes served here, although **baccalà** (salt cod) is popular, plumped in a tomato sauce. **Caciucco alla livornese** is a fish soup that comes from Leghorn, which is a brew very similar to bouillabaisse. In Pisa, you can eat **le cieche,** baby eels seared in hot oil. In contrast, **ribollita** is a dish of what is essentially leftovers, perked up with a helping of beans, which are a favorite ingredient in these parts. They can also be found in the minestrone, in their rice dishes, and served along with the steak. For dessert, these Italians like **castagnaccio,** a deep-fried chestnut cake.

10. MARCHE (Ancona)   This is actually several regions put together, so you won't find many unifying dishes; each area of the Marches has a proud cuisine of its own, mostly not known well outside of the area. Some of the famous foods from this region are the stuffed olives (**olive all'ascolana**) from Ascoli Piceno; the **brodetto** (fish chowder) which must always include the **scorfano** (hog fish); and the **porchetta** (roasted suckling pig). Also notable is **vincisgrassi,** a baked layered dish of lasagna, chicken livers, mushrooms, and onions, graced with a béchamel sauce.

11. UMBRIA (Perugia)   Saddled between the Marches and Lazio, Umbria has a cuisine that blends the heartiness of the mountains with the sophistication of the cities. The food is prepared fairly simply, but often includes some black truffles, which grow in this region. There are other wild mushrooms too, including the fleshy cèpes. Fennel flavors much of the cooking, including the **porchetta** (roast suckling pig). From here we also get **prosciutto di montagna,** a cured mountain ham, and some sheep's milk cheeses, **ravigiolo** and **caciotto.**

From Norcia comes a liver sausage, **mazzafegati.** The sweets likely to be found here are **mostaccioli,** a spiced cake, and **pinoccata,** a chocolate-flavored cake made with pignolis.

12. LAZIO (Roma)   The food of this region centers on Rome, and in Rome you will find many specialties. One common one is **porchetta,** a split-roasted suckling pig, and another is **abbacchio,** a baby lamb which is roasted with rosemary. **Saltimbocca** (slices of veal topped with prosciutto, then sautéed and sauced with Marsala) comes from Rome, although it appears on menus now in many parts of Italy. **Coda alla vaccinara** is oxtails in a tomato sauce, while **gnocchi alla romana** is that light dumpling, this time made without potatoes and instead with semolina and cheese. **Fettuccine all' Alfredo** is, of course, from Rome's infamous restaurant; this is the tagliatelle noodles in a butter and cheese (Parmesan) sauce. Another popular pasta dish is **spaghetti alla carbonara,** in which spaghetti are tossed with bacon, garlic, oil, and Parmesan cheese. The Romans make a **stracciatelle,** which is a chicken or beef broth into which is beaten strands of egg—sort of an egg-drop soup. On menus you'll see some robust fish soups, plus a lot of other seafood: sardines stuffed with spinach, **baccalà** in a tomato sauce, grilled clams (**vongole**). **Stufatino** is a beef stew, **coppa** is head cheese, **trippa alla romana** is tripe that has been simmered with vegetables in a tomato sauce, along with parsley and mint. Vegetables are varied and plentiful, with several preparations for artichokes (including fried in oil until they are black and opened out as a flower), eggplant, spinach, and peppers. For dessert, you'll probably be offered fruit or **budino di ricotta** (cheese pudding). At Christmastime, you'll see **pangiallo,** a fruit-studded cake, and at Easter, **quaresimali,** dry and crisp cookies. **Maritozzi** are soft breakfast buns with raisins.

13. ABRUZZO (Pescara, L'Aquila)   This is very rugged country, with a coastline that drops sharply to the Adriatic. Therefore, in the food you'll find an abundance of trout from mountain streams, and **scapece,** a pickled fish, flavored with saffron. **Polpi in purgatorio** is a highly spiced cuttlefish; **triglie ripiene** is red mullet, stuffed and baked. The area produces a **prosciutto aquilano** and also liver sausages (**fegati dolci, fegati pazzi**), one sweet and one hot. **Agnello con sottaceti**

is a stewed lamb, done up with rosemary and pickled vegetables. This area is famous for its **panarda,** which is a celebratory meal of at least 30 courses.

14. MOLISE (Campobasso)   This food follows Abruzzo in style, with a few additional specialties such as **capretti al forno** (roasted kid) and **maccheroni alla chitarra,** a homemade macaroni which is cut into slices with guitar strings. The mozzarella here is made from water buffalo milk. **Picellati** are round, crisp biscuits.

15. CAMPANIA (Napoli)   Much of the Italian food that has traveled to other countries comes originally from Naples. This is the home of the **pizza,** and also of the **calzoni,** basically a pizza that has been wrapped up and sealed around the edges. Mozzarella cheese comes from here, historically made from water buffalo milk but now more commonly from cow's milk; and also **provolone,** both smoked and fresh. Most of the pasta dishes are based on macaroni, made in factories, and in countless widths and lengths. Other dishes are **mozzarella in carrozza,** a simple sandwich of mozzarella cheese between two pieces of bread that is dipped in beaten egg and fried until crisp. There is little meat but a lot of fish on the menus, including **fritto di pesce,** any kind of seafood that has been breaded and deep-fried. **Zuppa alla marinara** is the fish soup from Naples, spiked with garlic and served over fried bread. Desserts here are plentiful, and include babas, **zeppole** (fritters), and, of course, **spumone** (ice cream).

16. PUGLIA (Bari)   Part of Apulia is the spur of Italy's boot, jutting into the Adriatic, so much of the food of this region is fish and shellfish. In particular, you'll find many preparations of black mussels (**cozze**), as well as **calamaretti in casseruola** (squid stew), baked anchovies, and fried fishes of many other types. The melons (**poponi**) from this area are wonderfully fragrant. Among the pastries, there are **scatagghiett,** honey-dipped bits of pastry; **castagnedi,** chocolate-iced pastries with almond filling; **fichi confettati,** sugar-coated figs; and **pettole,** fritters dusted with sugar.

17. BASILICATA (Potenza)   The food of this region follows that of Apulia, although the sausages and sauces here are more heavily spiced. The pasta often is a **fusilli** (corkscrew pasta), served with a meat sauce or ricotta. **Maccheroni alla train-**

iera is macaroni with capers, garlic, and ginger. On menus, you'll see lamb dishes, some goat, and also game. There are dishes based on beans and bean purées, others with artichokes.

18. CALABRIA (Reggio Calabria) This is a poor region, with many mountainous areas and little land in which to grow crops. Where there is land, fruit is grown, especially citrus fruits such as lemons and oranges, some of which are used to make perfume. Except for some sausages, the food is mostly vegetables and pasta. There is not even much cheese. Soups are very good, usually thick, and the pasta is often served with **soffritto** (usually a sauce base but here it is a sauce itself, made with liver, tripe, garlic, and tomatoes). Many pastas are stuffed and baked, as one would cannelloni. Tomatoes are also stuffed, as are eggplants and peppers. Sweets include **crocette** (roasted figs), **turiddu** (almond biscuits), and **cannariculi** (fritters soaked in honey).

19. SICILIA (Palermo) An island in the Mediterranean, Sicily has a vast array of seafood upon which to base its cuisine. In addition, the soil around Mount Etna is fertile, allowing the people to grow quantities of fruits. This is there the best oranges in Italy come from, and also where most of the almonds are grown. Among the vegetables, tomatoes, beans, peas, and artichokes are exceptional. Leading cheeses are **pecorino siciliano** (a hard romano type), **caciocaballo** (a spicy cow's milk cheese), and **ragusano** (varying in color, also as smoked). Sicily is a large region, and you'll find that each area has its own specialties. A typical dish for the island, however, is **caponata,** a hearty mixture of vegetables, including especially eggplant, in a pickled mixture with capers, olives, and anchovies. You're also likely to find **couscous,** an obvious import from Arabia, but here it is made with fish. Pasta with sardines (**pasta con sarde**) is popular, as it **farsumagru,** a beef roll, stuffed with spices and herbs, hard-cooked eggs, and sausage meat. **Arancine** are meat-and-rice balls, while **braciola** is a roast pork with a sweet stuffing of raisins and pignolis. But perhaps the best of Sicily's offerings is its desserts. Most well known are the **cannoli** (cylinders of pastry filled with sweetened ricotta cheese) and **cassata** (a highly variable cake of sponge layers and sweetened ricotta, studded with candied fruits). There are many pastries, but also notable are the **tor-**

rone (nougat) and **frutta candita** (candied fruits). And, of course, the ice cream in Sicily is unmatched.

20. SARDEGNA (Cagliari) Like Sicily, Sardinia is a rugged island. The small number of people who live there raise sheep and goats. It is noted for its **pecorino** (sheep's cheese) and its **fiore sardo** (a grating cheese). Their prosciutto from Ogliastra is highly respected, but they also make a **prosciutto di cinghiale,** from wild boar. There isn't much use made of the fish from the waters that surround the island, although the spiny lobster (**aragosta**) is popular. Rather than pasta, this island's people survive on coarse breads. But perhaps the most typical food of this region is the **cinghiale allo spiedo,** a spit-roasted wild boar.

SELECTING ITALIAN WINES

With the exception of some outstanding restaurants where they have a waiter who really knows wines, the waiter is not an expert. He is likely to ask "red wine or white?" as soon as you sit down and before you have decided what to eat. The rule of "red with dark meats and white with chicken, fish, and egg dishes" applies, of course. Wine is the Italian national drink, and if you want the most economical wine, ask for the local open wine (not in bottles but served from large flasks or pitchers) or **vino della casa.** Vintages also are not very important in Italy. The weather is usually good and, except for some dramatic disaster at harvest time, one year is as good as the other. White wines, however, are best when two years old at most; one year is even better.

TYPE OF WINE	SUGGESTED VARIETIES	REGION OF ORIGIN	MAJOR CITY
	White Wines		
Dry light-bodied whites	**Est! Est! Est! Frascati Marino**	Latium	Rome
	Lugana	Lombardy	Milan

TYPE OF WINE	SUGGESTED VARIETIES	REGION OF ORIGIN	MAJOR CITY
	Pinot Bianco Pinot Grigio	Veneto and Friuli-Venezia Giulia	Venice / Trieste
Dry medium-bodied whites	**Orvieto Secco**	Umbria	Perugia
	Soave	Veneto	Venezia
	Tocai	Friuli-Venezia Giulia	Trieste
	Trebbiano di Romagna	Emilia Romagna	Bologna
	Verdicchio	Marche	Ancona
Mellow whites	**Orvieto Abboccato**	Umbria	Perugia
	Prosecco	Veneto	Venice
	Red Wines		
Semidry reds	**Lambrusco**	Emilia Romagna	Bologna
Dry light-bodied reds	**Bardolino Valpolicella**	Veneto Veneto	Lake Garda

TYPE OF WINE	SUGGESTED VARIETIES	REGION OF ORIGIN	MAJOR CITY
Dry medium-bodied reds	**Castel del Monte Rosso**	Apulia	Bari
	Cabernet	Trentino	Bolzano
	Chianti	Tuscany	Florence
	Dolcetto Freisa Grignolino Nebbiolo	Piedmont	Turin
	Montepulciano d'Abruzzo	Abruzzo and Molise	L'Aquila Campobasso
	Merlot	Friuli-Venezia Giulia	Udine
	Sangiovese di Romagna	Emilia Romagna	Bologna
	Sassella	Lombardy	Milan
	Torgiano Rosso	Umbria	Perugia
Robust Reds			
	Barbaresco Barbera d'Asti Barolo Carema Gattinara Ghemme	Piedmont	Turin

TYPE OF WINE	SUGGESTED VARIETIES	REGION OF ORIGIN	MAJOR CITY
	Brunello di Montalcino Chianti Riserva Vino Nobile di Montepulciano	Tuscany	Florence
	Inferno	Lombardy	Milan
Rosé Wines			
	Castel del Monte	Apulia	Bari
	Chiaretto	Lombardy	Milan
Dessert Wines			
	Caluso Passito	Piedmont	Turin
	Marsala Moscato di Pantelleria	Sicily	Palermo
	Vin Santo	Trentino Alto Adige	Bolzano
	Moscato d'Asti	Piedmont	Asti
Sparkling Wines			
	Asti Spumante Nebbiolo Spumante	Piedmont	Turin

MEETING PEOPLE

Italians are hospitable. They are curious and friendly, even desirous to get acquainted with travelers.

SMALL TALK

My name is ____.	**Il mio nome è ____.** *eel mEE-oh nOH-meh EH*
Do you live here?	**Lei abita qui?** *lEH-ee AH-bee-tah koo-EE*
Where are you from?	**Lei di dov'è?** *lEH-ee dee doh-vEH*
I am ____.	**Vengo ____.** *vEHn-goh*
■ from the United States	**dagli Stati Uniti** *dAH-ly-ee stAH-tee oo-nEE-tee*
■ from Canada	**dal Canadà** *dAHl kah-nah-dAH*
■ from England	**dall'Inghilterra** *dahl-lEEn-gheel-tEHr-rah*
■ from Australia	**dall'Australia** *dahl-lah-oos-trAH-lee-ah*
I like Italy (Rome) very much.	**L'Italia (Roma) mi piace moltissimo.** *lee-tAH-lee-ah (rOH-mah) mee pee-AH-cheh mohl-tEEs-see-moh*
I would like to go there.	**Mi piacerebbe andarci.** *mee pee-ah-cheh-rAYb-beh ahn-dAHr-chee*
How long will you be staying?	**Quanto tempo resterà qui?** *koo-AHn-toh tEHm-pon reh-steh-rAH koo-EE*
I'll stay for a few days (a week).	**Resterò alcuni giorni (una settimana).** *reh-steh-rOH ahl-kOO-nee jee-OHr-nee (OO-na seht-tee-mAH-nah)*
What hotel are you staying at?	**In quale hotel (albergo) sta?** *een koo-AH-leh oh-tEHl (ahl-bEHr-goh) stAH*

What do you think of it?	**Che ne pensa?**	*kay nay pEHn-sah*
I (don't) like it very much.	**(Non) mi piace tanto.**	*(nohn) mee pee-AH-cheh tAHn-toh*
I think it's ____.	**Penso che sia ____.**	*pEHn-soh kay sEE-ah*
■ beautiful	**bello**	*bEHl-loh*
■ interesting	**interessante**	*een-teh-rehs-sAHn-teh*
■ magnificent	**splendido (magnifico)**	*splEHn-dee-doh (mah-ny-EE-fee-koh)*
■ wonderful	**stupendo**	*stoo-pEHn-doh*
May I introduce ____?	**Posso presentarle ____?**	*pOHs-soh preh-sehn-tAHr-leh*
■ my brother (sister)	**mio fratello (mia sorella)**	*mEE-oh frah-tEHl-loh (mEE-ah soh-rEHl-lah)*
■ my father (mother)	**mio padre (mia madre)**	*mEE-oh pAH-dreh (mEE-ah mAH-dreh)*
■ my friend	**il mio amico**	*eel mEE-oh ah-mEE-koh*
■ my husband (wife)	**mio marito (mia moglie)**	*mEE-oh mah-rEE-toh (mEE-ah mOH-ly-ee-eh)*
■ my sweetheart	**il mio ragazzo (la mia ragazza)**	*eel mEE-oh rah-gAH-tsoh (lah mEE-ah rah-gAH-tsah)*
■ my son (daughter)	**mio figlio (mia figlia)**	*mEE-oh fEE-ly-ee-oh (mEE-ah fEE-ly-ee-ah)*
Glad to meet you.	**Piacere. Lieto(a) di conoscerla.**	*pee-ah-chAY-reh. lee-EH-toh(ah) dee koh-nOH-shehr-lah*
How do you do?	**Come sta?**	*kOH-meh stah*
I am a ____.	**Sono ____.**	*sOH-noh*
■ teacher	**maestro(a)**	*mah-AYs-troh(ah)*

■ doctor **dottore (dottoressa)** *doht-tOH-reh (doht-toh-rAYs-sah)*

■ lawyer **avvocato (avvocatessa)** *ahv-voh-kAH-toh (ahv-voh-kah-tAYs-sah)*

■ businessperson **una persona d'affari** *oo-nah pehr-sOH-nah dahf-fAH-ree*

■ student **studente (studentessa)** *stoo-dEHn-teh (stoo-dehn-tAYs-sah)*

Would you like a picture (snapshot)? **Vuole che le scatti una foto (un'instantanea)?** *voo-OH-leh kay leh skAHt-tee OO-nah fOH-toh (oon-een-stahn-tAH-neh-ah)*

Stand here (there). **Si metta qui (lì).** *see mAYt-tah koo-EE (lEE)*

Don't move. **Non si muova.** *nohn see moo-OH-vah*

| Smile. That's it. | **Sorrida. Ecco fatto.** *sohr-rEE-dah. EH-koh fAHt-toh* |
| Will you take a picture of me (us)? | **Può farmi (farci) una foto?** *poo-OH fAHr-mee (fAHr-chee) OO-nah fOH-toh* |

DATING AND SOCIALIZING

May I have this dance?	**Le piacerebbe ballare con me?** *leh pee-ah-cheh-rAYb-beh bahl-lAH-reh kohn mAY*
With pleasure.	**Con piacere.** *kohn pee-ah-chAY-reh*
Would you like a drink (a cigarette)?	**Potrei offrirle da bere (una sigaretta)?** *poh-trEH-ee ohf-frEEr-leh dah bAY-reh (OO-na see-gah-rAYt-tah)*
Do you have a light (matches)?	**Ha un accendino (un fiammifero)?** *ah oon ah-chayn-dEE-noh (oon fee-ahm-mEE-feh-roh)*
Do you mind if I smoke?	**Le dispiace se fumo?** *leh dee-spee-AH-cheh say fOO-moh*
May I call you?	**Posso telefonarle?** *pOHs-soh teh-leh-foh-nAHr-leh*
May I take you home?	**L'accompagno a casa?** *lahk-kohm-pAH-ny-oh ah kAH-sah*
Are you doing anything tomorrow?	**Che fa domani?** *kay fAH doh-mAH-nee*
Are you free this evening?	**È libero(a) stasera?** *EH lEE-beh-roh(ah) stah-sAY-rah*
Would you like to go to ___ together?	**Le piacerebbe andare insieme a ___?** *leh pee-ah-cheh-rEHb-beh ahn-dAH-reh een-see-EH-meh ah*
I'll wait for you in front of the hotel.	**L'aspetterò davanti all'hotel (all'albergo).** *lah-speht-teh-rOH dah-vAHn-tee ahl-loh-tEHl (ahl-lahl-bEHr-goh)*

I'll pick you up at your house (hotel).	**La verrò a prendere a casa sua (all'hotel).** *lah vehr-rOH ah prAYn-day-reh ah kAH-sah sOO-ah (ahl-loh-tEHl)*
What is your telephone number?	**Qual è il suo numero di telefono?** *koo-ahl-EH eel sOO-oh nOO-meh-roh dee teh-lEH-foh-noh*
Here's my telephone number (address).	**Ecco il mio numero di telefono (indirizzo).** *EHk-koh eel mEE-oh nOO-meh-roh dee teh-lEH-foh-noh (een-dee-rEE-tsoh)*
Will you write to me?	**Mi scriverà?** *mee skree-veh-rAH*
I'm single (married).	**Sono scapolo (nubile) (sposato[a]).** *sOH-noh scAH-poh-loh nOO-bih-leh (spoh-sAH-toh[ah])*
Is your husband (wife) here?	**Sta qui suo marito (la signora)?** *stAH koo-EE sOO-oh mah-rEE-toh (lah see-ny-OH-rah)*
I'm here with my family.	**Sono qui con la mia famiglia.** *sOH-noh koo-EE kohn lah mEE-ah fah-mEE-ly-ee-ah*
Do you have any children?	**Ha bambini?** *AH bahm-bEE-nee*
How many?	**Quanti?** *koo-AHn-tee*
How old are they?	**Quanti anni hanno?** *koo-AHn-tee AHn-nee AHn-noh*

SAYING GOOD-BYE

Nice to have met you.	**È stato un piacere conoscerla.** *EH stAH-toh oon pee-ah-chAY-reh koh-nOH-shehr-lah*
The pleasure was mine.	**Il piacere è stato mio.** *eel pee-ah-chAY-reh EH stAH-toh mEE-oh*

Regards to ____.	**Saluti a ____.** *sah-lOO-tee ah*
Thanks for the evening.	**Grazie della serata.** *grAH-tsee-eh dAYl-lah say-rAH-tah*
I must go home now.	**Adesso devo andarmene a casa.** *ah-dEHs-soh dAY-voh ahn-dAHr-meh-neh ah kAH-sah*
You must come to visit us.	**Deve venire a farci visita.** *dAY-veh veh-nEE-reh ah fAHr-chee vEE-see-tah*

TRAVEL TIP

When you purchase goods in a foreign country, save the receipts in case you have to prove the value of those purchases to customs agents upon returning home. Before you leave home, find out which goods you are likely to purchase that are not subject to duty and which are items you cannot bring back into the country. Consider also, especially if you plan to purchase a large number of heavy items, whether it is more advantageous to ship your purchases home or to pay airline charges for overweight.

SHOPPING

Italian retail stores close for the mid-afternoon, usually between 1 and 4 p.m., but the closing hours vary slightly from place to place and according to the season.

Pharmacies (chemists) also observe the middle-of-the-day closing, but they are open on a rotation basis on holidays (see page 179), including Sundays, when the name and address of the nearest one open is posted on the front door of each pharmacy that is closed.

During the summer, especially from July 15 to September 1, most smaller stores close for vacation periods of their own choosing. For this reason, tourists will find that not all stores are open at a given time during the summer vacation period.

TYPICAL ARTS AND CRAFTS

Italy offers a wide range of traditional arts and crafts. Each region, city, village, or town has its own variety of products. Bargaining for the item you wish is apt to be a new experience but the shopkeepers and merchants expect it. Here are some tips on what to look for in Italy's different regions.

1. VALLE D'AOSTA (AOSTA)—Laces, embossed copper wares, leather articles, and wood-carved jugs.

2. PIEMONTE (TORINO)—Wood-carved chamois and steenbok, woodworked boxes of Gran San Bernardo and local pottery.

3. LOMBARDIA (MILANO)—Pottery of Laveno, printed silk of Como, rubber toys, shoes of Vigevano, laces of Cantù, accordions, and carpets. Best buys: silk dresses, latest fashions in the boutiques, leather goods.

4. TRENTINO ALTO ADIGE (BOLZANO, TRENTO)—Woodworks of Val Gardena, cuckoo clocks, knick-knacks made of onyx and horn, straw hats of Bessanone, bowls of Martello.

5. VENETO (VENEZIA)—Glass and crystals of Murano, laces of Burano, wrought iron, mosaics, leather articles, woodworks, kettles, and pipes. Best buys: glassware, antiques.

6. FRIULI-VENEZIA GIULIA (TRIESTE)—Knives, mosaics, hempen clothes, linen, and wooden shoes.

7. LIGURIA (GENOVA)—Embroidered silk shawls, laces of Santa Margherita, bottled miniature vessels, pottery of Albisona and Savona.

8. EMILIA-ROMAGNA (BOLOGNA, RAVENNA)—Pottery of Faenza, wrought iron and woodwork of Grazzano Visconti, laces of Forlì and copper engravings of Ravenna.

9. TOSCANA (FIRENZE, PISA)—Alabaster of Volterra, statuettes made with marble sawdust of Lucca, straw hats, prime light-grain florentine leathergoods, pottery, and embroidery. Best buys: shoes, cameos, brushed gold *(satinato)*, jewelry, silk.

10. MARCHE (ANCONA)—Accordions of Castelfidardo, Osimo, Numana, or Recanati; pottery of Urbino, Ascoli, and Pesaro; laces of Offida, in the province of Ascoli Piceno, and articles of straw.

11. UMBRIA (PERUGIA)—Artistic pottery of Orvieto, Gubbio, Deruta, Perugia, Gualdo Tadino, and Città di Castello; textiles and laces of Assisi; inlaid furniture, wood carving, and wrought iron of Perugia, Gubbio, and Todi.

12. LAZIO (ROMA)—Copper wares of Fiuggi, carpets of Veroli, pottery of Civita Castellana, wrought iron of Ciociaria, and pillow laces. Best buys: luggage, leather goods, shoes, antiques, old books and prints.

13. ABRUZZO (PESCARA, L'AQUILA)—Embossed copper wares, wrought iron, wood carving, carpets, textiles, laces, jeweler's wares, and artistic pottery.

14. MOLISE (CAMPOBASSO)—Multicolored pottery, laces, dressed stones, wrought iron, watermarked papers, and jeweler's wares.

15. CAMPANIA (NAPOLI)—Porcelain of Capodimonte, leather gloves of Naples, corals of Torre del Greco, pearls, textiles and silk, straw and wickerworks, wrought iron and inlaid furniture. Best buys: coral items, cameos. Note: do not buy tortoise shell; U.S. forbids you to bring it in.

16. PUGLIA (BARI)—Textiles (particularly woolens), tobacco pipes, embroidery, carpets, and tapestry.

17. BASILICATA (POTENZA)—Pottery of Potenza, woodworks, copper wares and wrought iron, embroidery, and handwoven textiles.

18. CALABRIA (REGGIO CALABRIA, CATANZARO)—
Leather articles, laces, inlaid furniture, painted amphorae, and
hand-woven textiles; string instruments of Bisignano and gold
of Crotone.

19. SICILIA (PALERMO)—Sicilian hand-carts, puppets of Palermo, corals, mandolins and guitars of Catania, marble sculptures, and articles of alabaster.

20. SARDEGNA (CAGLIARI)—Carpets, textiles, blankets of
lively colors, baskets made with reeds and rush, laces, earthenware, pottery, and wrought iron.

GOING SHOPPING

Where can I find ____?	**Dove posso trovare ____?** *dOH-veh pOHs-soh troh-vAH-reh*
■ a bakery	**un fornaio** *oon fohr-nAH-ee-oh*
■ a bookstore	**una libreria** *OO-nah lee-bray-rEE-ah*
■ a butcher	**una macelleria** *OO-nah mah-chehl-leh-rEE-ah*
■ a camera shop	**un negozio di fotocine** *oon neh-gOH-tsee-oh dee foh-toh-chEE-neh*
■ a candy store	**un sale e tabacchi** *oon sAH-leh ay tah-bAH-key*
■ a clothing store	**un negozio di abbigliamento** *oon neh-gOH-tsee-oh dee ahb-bee-ly-ee-ah-mEHn-toh*
■ for children's clothes	**per bambini** *pehr bahm-bEE-nee*
■ men's store	**per uomini** *pehr oo-OH-mee-nee*
■ women's boutique	**per signore** *pehr see-ny-OH-reh*
■ a delicatessen	**una salumeria** *OO-nah sah-loo-meh-rEE-ah*
■ a department store	**i grandi magazzini** *ee grAHn-dee mah-gah-tsEE-nee*

■ a pharmacy (chemist)	**una farmacia** *OO-nah fahr-mah-chEE-ah*
■ a florist	**un fioraio** *oon fee-oh-rAH-ee-oh*
■ a gift (souvenir) shop	**un negozio di regali (souvenir)** *oon neh-gOH-tsee-oh dee reh-gAH-lee (soo-vay-nEEr)*
■ a grocery store	**un negozio di alimentari** *oon neh-gOH-tsee-oh dee ah-lee-mehn-tAH-ree*
■ a hardware store (ironmonger)	**un negozio di ferramenta** *oon neh-gOH-tsee-oh dee fehr-rah-mEHn-tah*
■ a jewelry store	**una gioielleria** *OO-nah jee-oh-ee-ehl-leh-rEE-ah*
■ a liquor store	**una enoteca** *OO-nah eh-noh-tEH-kah*
■ a newsstand	**un'edicola (il giornalaio)** *oo-neh-dEE-koh-lah (eel jee-ohr-nah-lAH-ee-oh)*
■ a record store	**un negozio di dischi** *oon nay-gOH-tsee-oh dee dEE-skey*
■ a supermarket	**un supermercato** *oon soo-pehr-mehr-kAH-toh*
■ a tobacco shop	**una tabaccheria** *OO-nah tah-bahk-keh-rEE-ah*
■ a toy store	**un negozio di giocattoli** *oon neh-gOH-tsee-oh dee jee-oh-kAHt-toh-lee*
■ a wine merchant	**una mescita, una cantina, una enoteca** *OO-nah mAY-shee-tah OO-nah kahn-tEE-nah OO-nah eh-noh-tEH-kah*
Young man, can you wait on me?	**Giovanotto, può occuparsi di me?** *jee-oh-vah-nOHt-toh poo-OH ohk-koo-pAHr-see dee meh*
Miss, can you help me?	**Signorina, può aiutarmi?** *see-ny-oh-rEE-nah poo-OH ah-ee-oo-tAHr-mee*

Do you take credit cards?	**Accettano carte di credito?** *ah-chEHt-tah-noh kAHr-teh dee crEH-dee-toh*
Can I pay with a traveler's check?	**Posso pagare con un traveler's check?** *pOHs-soh pah-gAH-reh kohn oon trAH-veh-lehs chEH-keh*

BOOKS

Is there a store that carries English-language books?	**C'è un negozio dove si vendono libri in lingua inglese?** *chEH oon neh-gOH-tzee-oh dOH-veh see vAYn-doh-noh lEE-bree een lEEn-goo-ah een-glAY-seh*
What is the best (biggest) bookstore here?	**Dov'è la migliore (la più grande) libreria qui?** *doh-vEH lah mee-ly-ee-OH-reh (lah pee-OO grAHn-deh) lee-breh-rEE-ah koo-EE*
I'm looking for a copy of ____.	**M'interessa una copia di ____.** *meen-teh-rEHs-sah OO-nah kOH-pee-ah dee*
The author of the book is ____.	**L'autore del libro è ____.** *lah-oo-tOH-reh dayl lEE-broh EH*
I don't know the title (author).	**Non conosco il titolo (l'autore).** *nohn koh-nOH-skoh eel tEE-toh-loh (lah-oo-tOH-reh)*
I'm just looking.	**Sto solo guardando.** *stoh sOH-loh goo-ahr-dAHn-doh*
Do you have books (novels) in English?	**Ha libri (romanzi) in inglese?** *ah lEE-bree (roh-mAHn-tsee) een een-glAY-seh*
I want ____.	**Desidero ____.** *deh-sEE-deh-roh*
■ a guide book	**una guida** *OO-nah goo-EE-dah*
■ a map of this city	**una pianta di questa città** *OO-nah pee-AHn-tah dee koo-AYs-tah cheet-tAH*

■ a pocket dictionary — **un dizionario tascabile** *oon dee-tsee-oh-nAH-ree-oh tah-skAH-bee-leh*

■ an Italian-English dictionary — **un dizionario Italiano-Inglese** *oon dee-tsee-oh-nAH-ree-oh ee-tah-lee-AH-noh een-glAY-seh*

Where can I find ____? — **Dove posso trovare ____?** *dOH-veh pOHs-soh troh-vAH-reh*

■ detective stories — **romanzi gialli** *roh-mAHn-tsee jee-AHl-lee*

■ comics — **fumetti** *foo-mAYt-tee*

■ history books — **libri di storia** *lEE-bree dee stOH-ree-ah*

■ short stories — **una raccolta di novelle** *OO-nah rahk-kOHl-tah dee noh-vEHl-leh*

■ cookbooks — **libri di cucina** *lEE-bree dee koo-chEE-nah*

I'll take these books. — **Prendo questi libri.** *prAYn-doh koo-AYs-tee lEE-bree*

Will you wrap them, please? — **Me l'incarta, per favore?** *meh leen-kAHr-tah pehr fah-vOH-reh*

CLOTHING

Would you please show me ____? — **Per favore, può mostrarmi ____?** *pehr fah-vOH-reh poo-OH moh-strAHr-mee*

■ a belt for man (lady) — **una cintura per uomo (per signora)** *OO-nah cheen-tOO-rah pehr oo-OH-moh (pehr see-ny-OH-rah)*

■ a blouse — **una blusa (camicetta)** *OO-nah blOO-sah (kah-mee-chAYt-tah)*

■ a bra — **un reggiseno** *oon reh-jee-sAY-noh*

■ a dress — **una veste** *OO-nah vEH-steh*

■ an evening gown **un abito da sera** *oon AH-bee-toh dah sAY-rah*

■ leather (suede) gloves **dei guanti di pelle (scamosciata)** *dAY-ee goo-AHn-tee dee pEHl-leh (skah-moh-shee-AH-tah)*

■ handkerchiefs **dei fazzoletti** *dAY-ee fah-tsoh-lAYt-tee*

■ a hat **un cappello** *oon kahp-pEHl-loh*

■ a jacket **una giacca** *OO-nah jee-AHk-kah*

■ an overcoat **un soprabito** *oon soh-prAH-bee-toh*

■ pants **dei pantaloni** *dAY-ee pahn-tah-lOH-nee*

■ panty hose **un collant** *oon koh-lAHn*

■ a raincoat **un impermeabile** *oon eem-pehr-meh-AH-bee-leh*

■ a robe (for lady) **una vestaglia** *OO-nah veh-stAH-ly-ee-ah*

■ a robe (for man) **una veste da camera** *OO-nah vEH-steh dah kAH-meh-rah*

■ a shirt **una camicia** *OO-nah kah-mEE-chee-ah*

■ (a pair of) shoes **un paio di scarpe** *oon pAH-ee-oh dee skAHr-peh*

■ shorts (briefs) **dei pantaloncini (delle mutande)** *dAY-ee pahn-tah-lohn-chEE-nee (dAYl-leh moo-tAHn-deh)*

■ a skirt **una gonna** *OO-nah gOHn-nah*

■ a slip **una sottoveste** *oo-nah soht-toh-vEH-steh*

■ slippers **delle pantofole** *dAYl-leh pahn-tOH-foh-leh*

■ socks **dei calzini** *dAY-ee kahl-tsEE-nee*

■ (nylon) stockings **delle calze (di nylon)** *dAYl-leh kAHl-tseh (dee nAH-ee-lohn)*

■ a suit **un vestito** *oon veh-stEE-toh*

■ a sweater **una maglia** *OO-nah mAH-ly-ee-ah*

■ a tie **una cravatta** *OO-nah krah-vAHt-tah*

■ an undershirt **una canottiera** *OO-nah kah-noht-tee-EH-rah*

■ a tee-shirt **una maglietta** *OO-nah mah-ly-ee-AYt-tah*

■ underwear **della biancheria intima** *dAYl-lah bee-ahn-keh-rEE-ah EEn-tee-mah*

■ a wallet **un portafoglio** *oon pohr-tah-fOH-ly-ee-oh*

Is there a special sale today? **Oggi c'è una vendita d'occasione?** *OH-jee chEH OO-nah vAYn-dee-tah dohk-kah-see-OH-neh*

I'd like a shirt with short (long) sleeves.	**Vorrei una camicia con le maniche corte (lunghe).** *vohr-rEH-ee OO-nah kah-mEE-chee-ah kOHn leh mAH-nee-keh kOHr-teh (lOOn-gheh)*
Do you have anything ____?	**Ha qualche cosa ____?** *AH koo-AHl-keh kOH-sah*
■ cheaper	**più a buon mercato** *pee-OO ah boo-OHn mehr-kAH-toh*
■ else	**d'altro** *dAHl-troh*
■ larger	**più grande** *pee-OO grAHn-deh*
■ less expensive	**meno costoso** *mAY-noh koh-stOH-soh*
■ longer	**più lungo** *pee-OO lOOn-goh*
■ of better quality	**di migliore qualità** *dee mee-ly-ee-OH-reh koo-ah-lee-tAH*
■ shorter	**più corto** *pee-OO kOHr-toh*
■ smaller	**più piccolo** *pee-OO pEE-koh-loh*
I don't like the color.	**Non mi piace il colore.** *nohn mee pee-AH-cheh eel koh-lOH-reh*
Do you have it in ____?	**Lo ha in ____?** *loh AH een*
■ black	**nero** *nAY-roh*
■ blue	**blu** *blOO*
■ brown	**marrone** *mahr-rOH-neh*
■ gray	**grigio** *grEE-jee-oh*
■ green	**verde** *vAYr-deh*
■ pink	**rosa** *rOH-sah*
■ red	**rosso** *rOHs-soh*
■ white	**bianco** *bee-AHn-koh*
■ yellow	**giallo** *jee-AHl-loh*

SALE SIGNS

SVENDITA	(sale)
SALDI DI FINE STAGIONE	(end of season sale)
LIQUIDAZIONE	(everything must go)
VENDITA TOTALE	
PREZZI FISSI	(fixed prices)

I want something in _____.	**Voglio qualche cosa _____.** *vOH-ly-ee-oh koo-AHl-keh kOH-sah*
■ chiffon	**di chiffon** *dee sheef-fOHn*
■ corduroy	**di velluto a coste** *dee vehl-lOO-toh ah kOH-steh*
■ cotton	**di cotone** *dee koh-tOH-neh*
■ denim	**di denim** *dee dEH-nim*
■ felt	**di feltro** *dee fAYl-troh*
■ flannel	**di flanella** *dee flah-nEHl-lah*
■ gabardine	**di gabardine** *dee gah-bahr-dEE-neh*
■ lace	**in pizzo** *een pEE-tsoh*
■ leather	**in pelle** *een pEHl-leh*
■ linen	**di lino** *dee lEE-noh*
■ nylon	**di nylon** *dee nAH-ee-lohn*
■ permanent press	**con piega permanente** *kOHn pee-EH-gah pehr-mah-nEHn-teh*
■ satin	**di raso** *dee rAH-soh*
■ silk	**di seta** *dee sAY-tah*
■ suede	**di renna** *dee rAYn-nah*

■terrycloth	**in tessuto spugnoso** *een tehs-sOO-toh spoo-ny-OH-soh*
■velvet	**di velluto** *dee vehl-lOO-toh*
■wool	**di lana** *dee lAH-nah*
■synthetic (polyester)	**in poliestere** *een poh-lee-EH-steh-reh*
■wash-and-wear	**che non si stira** *kay nohn see stEE-rah*
Show me something _____.	**Mi faccia vedere qualche cosa _____.** *mee fAH-chee-ah veh-dAY-reh koo-AHl-kay kOH-sah*
■in solid color	**a tinta unita** *ah tEEn-tah oo-nEE-tah*
■with stripes	**a righe** *ah rEE-gheh*
■with polkadots	**a pallini** *ah pahl-lEE-nee*
■in plaid	**a quadri** *ah koo-AH-dree*
Please take my measurements.	**Può prendermi le misure?** *poo-OH prEHn-dayr-mee leh mee-sOO-reh*
I take size (my size is) _____.	**La mia taglia è _____.** *lah mEE-ah tAH-ly-ee-ah EH*
■small	**piccola** *pEEk-koh-lah*
■medium	**media** *mEH-dee-ah*
■large	**grande** *grAHn-deh*
Can I try it on?	**Posso provarmelo(la)?** *pOHs-soh proh-vAHr-meh-loh(lah)*
Can you alter it?	**Può aggiustarmelo(la)?** *poo-OH ah-jee-oo-stAHr-meh-loh(lah)*
Can I return the article (if I change my mind)?	**(Se non mi va), posso portarlo indietro?** *(say nOHn mee vAH) pOHs-soh pohr-tAHr-loh een-dee-EH-troh*
Do you have something hand made?	**Non c'è nulla che sia fatto a mano?** *nOHn chEH nOOl-lah kay sEE-ah fAHt-toh ah mAH-noh*

CLOTHING MEASUREMENTS

WOMEN

Shoes

American	4	5	6	7	8	9
British	3	4	5	6	7	8
Continental	35	36	37	38	39	40

Dresses, suits

American	8	10	12	14	16	18
British	10	12	14	16	18	20
Continental	36	38	40	42	44	46

Blouses, sweaters

American	32	34	36	38	40	42
British	34	36	38	40	42	44
Continental	40	42	44	46	48	50

MEN

Shoes

American	7	8	9	10	11	12
British	6	7	8	9	10	11
Continental	39	41	43	44	45	46

Suits, coats

American	34	36	38	40	42	44	46	48
British	44	46	48	50	54	56	58	60
Continental	44	46	48	50	52	54	56	58

Shirts								
American	14	14½	15	15½	16	16½	17	17½
British	14	14½	15	15½	16	16½	17	17½
Continental	36	37	38	39	40	41	42	43

The zipper doesn't work.	**La cerniera non funziona.** *lah chehr-nee-EH-rah nohn fOOn-tsee-OH-nah*
It doesn't fit me.	**Non mi sta bene.** *nohn mee stAH bEH-neh*
It fits very well.	**Mi sta molto bene.** *mee stAH mOHl-toh bEH-neh*
I'll take it.	**Lo(la) prendo.** *loh(lah) prAYn-doh*
Will you wrap it?	**Me lo(la) impacchetta?** *meh loh(lah) eem-pahk-kEHt-tah*
I'd like to see the pair of shoes (boots) in the window.	**Vorrei vedere il paio di scarpe (stivali) in vetrina.** *vohr-rEH-ee veh-dAY-reh eel pAH-ee-oh dee skAHr-peh (stee-vAH-lee) een vay-trEE-nah*
They're too narrow (wide).	**Sono troppo strette (larghe).** *sOH-noh trOHp-poh strAYt-teh (lAHr-gheh)*
They pinch me.	**Mi stanno strette.** *mee stAHn-noh strAYt-teh*
They fit me.	**Mi stanno bene.** *mee stAHn-noh bEH-neh*
I'll take them.	**Le compro.** *leh kOHm-proh*
I also need shoe-laces.	**Ho bisogno anche dei lacci.** *oh bee-sOH-ny-oh AHn-keh dAY-ee lAH-chee*
That's all I want for now.	**Questo è tutto quello che voglio per ora.** *koo-AYs-toh EH tOOt-toh koo-AYl-loh kay vOH-ly-ee-oh pehr OH-rah*

ELECTRICAL APPLIANCES

When buying any electrical items, check the voltage because it may not correspond with the one you have at home.

I want to buy ____. **Vorrei comprare** ____. *vohr-rEH-ee kohm-prAH-reh*

■ a battery **una pila** *OO-nah pEE-lah*

■ an electric shaver **un rasoio elettrico** *oon rah-sOH-ee-oh eh-lEHt-tree-koh*

■ a hair dryer **un asciugacapelli** *oon ah-shee-oo-gah-kah-pAYl-lee*

■ a (portable) radio **una radio (portatile)** *OO-nah rAH-dee-oh (pohr-tAH-tee-leh)*

■ a tape recorder **un registratore** *oon reh-jee-strah-tOH-reh*

FOODS AND HOUSEHOLD ITEMS

See also pages 71–100 and the dictionary (pages 208–258) for more food words. When you go to a food market or shop, bring your own bag along with you to tote home your groceries. A collapsible net bag is very useful.

I'd like ____. **Vorrei** ____. *vohr-rEH-ee*

■ a bar of soap **una saponetta** *oo-nah sah-poh-nEHt-tah*

■ a bottle of juice **un succo di frutta** *oon sOO-koh dee frOOt-tah*

■ a box of cereal **una scatola di cereali** *oo-nah skAH-toh-lah dee cheh-reh-AH-lee*

■ a can (tin) of tomato sauce **una scatola di conserva di pomodoro** *oo-nah skAH-toh-lah dee kohn-sEHr-vah dee poh-moh-dOH-roh*

■ a dozen eggs   **una dozzina d'uova** *oo-nah doh-tsEE-nah doo-OH-vah*

■ a jar of coffee   **un vasetto di caffè** *oon vah-sAYt-toh dee kahf-fEH*

■ a kilo of potatoes (just over 2 pounds)   **un chilo di patate** *oon kEE-loh dee pah-tAH-teh*

■ a half kilo of cherries (just over one pound)   **mezzo chilo di ciliege** *mEH-tsoh kEE-loh dee chee-lee-EH-jeh*

■ a liter of milk (about 1 quart)   **un litro di latte** *oon LEE-troh dee lAHt-teh*

■ a package of candies   **un pacchetto di caramelle** *oon pah-kAYt-toh dee kah-rah-mEHl-leh*

■ 100 grams of cheese (about ¼ pound)   **cento grammi di formaggio (un etto)** *chEHn-toh grAHm-mee dee fohr-mAH-jee-oh (oon EHt-toh)*

■ a roll of toilet paper   **un rotolo di carta igienica** *oon rOH-toh-loh dee kAHr-tah ee-jee-EH-nee-kah*

I'd like a kilo (about 2 pounds) of oranges.   **Vorrei un chilo di arance.** *vohr-rEY-ee oon kEY-loh dee ah-rAHn-chay*

■ a half kilo of butter   **mezzo chilo di burro.** *mAY-tsoh kEY-loh dee bOOr-roh*

■ 200 grams (about ½ pound) of cookies   **due etti di biscotti** *dOO-eh EHt-tee dee bees-kOHt-tee*

■ 100 grams (about ¼ pound) of bologna   **un etto di mortadella** *oon EHt-toh dee mohr-tah-dAYl-lah*

NOTE: Common measurements for purchasing foods are a kilo (**chilo**), or fractions thereof, and 100 (**cento**), 200 (**duecento**), and 500 (**cinquecento**) grams (**grammi**). See also the pages on numbers, 12–15.

METRIC WEIGHTS AND MEASURES

Solid Measures
(approximate measurements only)

OUNCES	GRAMS (GRAMMI)	GRAMS	OUNCES
$\frac{1}{4}$	7	10	$\frac{1}{3}$
$\frac{1}{2}$	14	100	$3\frac{1}{2}$
$\frac{3}{4}$	21	300	$10\frac{1}{2}$
1	28	500	18

POUNDS	KILOGRAMS (CHILI)	KILOGRAMS	POUNDS
1	$\frac{1}{2}$	1	$2\frac{1}{4}$
5	$2\frac{1}{4}$	3	$6\frac{1}{2}$
10	$4\frac{1}{2}$	5	11
20	9	10	22
50	23	50	110
100	45	100	220

Liquid Measures
(approximate measurements only)

OUNCES	MILLILITERS (MILLILITRI)	MILLILITERS	OUNCES
1	30	10	$\frac{1}{3}$
6	175	50	$1\frac{1}{2}$
12	350	100	$3\frac{1}{2}$
16	475	150	5

GALLONS	LITERS (LITRI)	LITERS	GALLONS
1	$3\frac{3}{4}$	1	$\frac{1}{4}$ (1 quart)
5	19	5	$1\frac{1}{3}$
10	38	10	$2\frac{1}{2}$

What is this (that)?	**Che cosa è questo (quello)?** *kay kOH-sah EH koo-AY-stoh (koo-AYl-loh)*
Is it fresh?	**È fresco?** *EH frAY-skoh*

JEWELRY

I'd like to see ____.	**Vorrei vedere** ____. *vohr-rEH-ee veh-dAY-reh*
■ a bracelet	**un braccialetto** *oon brah-chee-ah-lAYt-toh*
■ a brooch	**un fermaglio (una spilla)** *oon fehr-mAH-ly-ee-oh (OO-nah spEE-lah)*
■ a chain	**una catenina** *OO-nah kah-teh-nEE-nah*
■ a charm	**un ciondolo** *oon chee-OHn-doh-loh*
■ some earrings	**degli orecchini** *dAY-ly-ee oh-rehk-kEE-nee*
■ a necklace	**un monile** *oon moh-nEE-leh*
■ a pin	**una spilla** *OO-nah spEEl-lah*
■ a ring	**un anello** *oon ah-nEHl-loh*
■ a rosary	**una corona del rosario** *OO-nah koh-rOH-nah dayl roh-sAH-ree-oh*
■ a (wrist)watch	**un orologio da polso** *oon oh-roh-lOH-jee-oh dah pOHl-soh*
Is this ____?	**Questo è** ____? *koo-AY-stoh EH*
■ gold	**d'oro** *dOH-roh*
■ platinum	**di platino** *dee plAH-tee-noh*
■ silver	**d'argento** *dahr-jEHn-toh*
■ stainless steel	**d'acciaio inossidabile** *dah-chee-AH-ee-oh ee-nohs-see-dAH-bee-leh*
Is it solid or gold plated?	**È oro massiccio oppure oro placcato?** *EH OH-roh mahs-sEE-chee-oh ohp-pOO-reh OH-roh plahk-kAH-toh*
How many carats is it?	**Di quanti carati è?** *dee koo-AHn-tee kah-rAH-tee EH*

What is that (precious) stone?	**Che pietra (preziosa) è?** *kay pee-Eh-trah (preh-tsee-OH-sah) EH*
I want _____.	**Vorrei (voglio) _____.** *vohr-rEH-ee (vOH-ly-ee-oh)*
■ a coral	**un corallo** *oon koh-rAHl-loh*
■ an amethyst	**un'ametista** *oo-nah-meh-tEE-stah*
■ an aquamarine	**un'acquamarina** *oo-nah-koo-ah-mah-rEE-nah*
■ a diamond	**un diamante** *oon dee-ah-mAHn-teh*
■ an emerald	**uno smeraldo** *OO-noh smeh-rAHl-doh*
■ an enamel	**uno smalto** *OO-noh smAHl-toh*
■ ivory	**una cosa d'avorio** *OO-nah kOH-sah dah-vOH-ree-oh*
■ jade	**una giada** *OO-nah jee-AH-dah*
■ onyx	**un 'onice** *oon-OH-nee-cheh*
■ pearls	**delle perle** *dAYl-leh pEHr-leh*
■ a ruby	**un rubino** *oon roo-bEE-noh*
■ a sapphire	**uno zaffiro** *OO-noh tsahf-fEE-roh*
■ a topaz	**un topazio** *oon toh-pAH-tsee-oh*
■ turquoise	**un turchese** *oon toor-kAY-seh*
How much is it?	**Quanto costa?** *koo-AHn-toh kOH-stah*

RECORDS AND TAPES

Is there a record shop around here?	**C'è un negozio di dischi qui vicino?** *chEH oon neh-GOH-tsee-oh dee dEE-skee koo-EE vee-chEE-noh*

I'd like to buy _____.	**Vorrei comprare _____.**	*vohr-rEH-ee kohm-prAH-reh*
■ cassettes	**delle cassette**	*dAYl-leh kahs-sAYt-teh*
■ records	**dei dischi**	*dAY-ee dEE-skee*
■ tapes	**dei nastri**	*dAY-ee nAH-stree*
Do you have an L.P. (45 r.p.m.) of _____?	**Ha un microsolco (a quarantacinque giri) di _____?**	*Ah oon mee-kroh-sOHl-koh (ah koo-ah-rAHn-tah-chEEn-koo-eh jEE-ree) dee*
Where is the _____ section?	**Dov'è la sezione _____?**	*doh-vEH lah seh-tsee-OH-neh*
■ classical music	**di musica classica**	*dee mOO-see-kah clAHs-see-kah*
■ popular music	**di musica popolare**	*dee mOO-see-kah poh-poh-lAH-reh*
■ latest hits	**degli ultimi successi**	*dAY-ly-ee OOl-tee-mee soo-chEHs-see*
■ Italian music	**della musica italiana**	*dAYl-lah mOO-see-kah ee-tah-lee-AH-nah*
■ opera	**di musica d'opera**	*dee mOO-see-kah dOH-peh-rah*

NEWSPAPERS AND MAGAZINES

Do you carry English newspapers (magazines)?	**Ha giornali (riviste) in inglese?** *a jee-ohr-nAH-lee (ree-vEE-steh) een een-glAY-seh*
I'd like to buy some (picture) postcards.	**Vorrei comprare delle cartoline (illustrate).** *vohr-rEH-ee kohm-prAH-reh dAYl-leh kahr-toh-lEE-neh (eel-loo-strAH-teh)*

Do you have stamps?	**Ha francobolli?** *AH frahn-koh-bOHl-lee*
How much is it?	**Quant'è?** *koo-ahn-tEH*

PHOTOGRAPHIC SUPPLIES

For phrases dealing with camera repairs, see page 140.

Where is there a camera shop?	**Dov'è un negozio di fotocine (macchine fotografiche)?** *doh-vEH oon nay-GOH-tsee-oh dee foh-toh-chEE-neh (mAHk-kee-neh foh-toh-grAH-fee-keh)*
Do they develop films?	**Sviluppano i rullini?** *svee-lOOp-pah-noh ee rool-lEE-nee*
How much does it cost to develop a roll?	**Quanto costa far sviluppare un rullino?** *koo-AHn-toh kOH-stah fahr svee-loop-pAH-reh oon rool-lEE-noh*
I want one print of each.	**Voglio una copia per ogni fotografia.** *vOH-ly-ee-oh OO-nah kOH-pee-ah pehr OH-ny-ee foh-toh-grah-fEE-ah*
I want _____.	**Vorrei (voglio) _____.** *vohr-rEH-ee (vOH-ly-ee-oh)*
■ an enlargement	**un ingrandimento** *oon een-grahn-dee-mEHn-toh*
■ with a glossy (matte) finish	**su carta lucida (opaca, matta)** *soo kAHr-tah lOO-chee-dah (oh-pAH-kah, mAHt-tah)*
I want a roll of color (black and white) film.	**Voglio un rullino a colori (in bianco e nero).** *vOH-ly-ee-oh oon rool-lEE-noh ah koh-lOH-ree (een bee-AHn-koh ay nAY-roh)*
I want a roll of 20 (36) exposures (for slides).	**Vorrei un rullino (per diapositive) di venti, trentasei pose.** *vohr-rEH-ee oon rool-lEE-noh (pehr dee-ah-poh-see-tEE-veh) dee vAYn-tee, trehn-tah-sEH-ee pOH-seh*

I want a filmpack _____.	**Vorrei (voglio) un rullino per istantanee (poloroid).** *vohr-REH-ee (vOH-ly-ee-oh) oon rool-lEE-noh pehr ee-stahn-tAH-neh-eh (poloroid)*
When can I pick up the pictures?	**Quando vengo a ritirarle?** *koo-AHn-doh vEHn-goh ah ree-tee-rAHr-leh*
Do you sell cameras?	**Vende macchine fotografiche?** *vAYn-deh mAH-kee-neh foh-toh-grAH-fee-keh*
I want an expensive (inexpensive) camera.	**Voglio una buona macchina fotografica (a buon mercato).** *vOH-ly-ee-oh OO-nah boo-OH-nah mAHk-kee-nah foh-toh-grAH-fee-kah (ah boo-OHn mayr-kAH-toh)*

SOUVENIRS, HANDICRAFTS

I'd like _____.	**Vorrei _____.** *vohr-rEH-ee*
■ a pretty gift	**un bel regalo** *oon bEHl reh-gAH-loh*
■ a small gift	**un regalino** *oon reh-gah-lEE-noh*
■ a souvenir	**un souvenir** *oon soo-veh-nEEr*
It's for _____.	**È per _____.** *EH pehr*
I don't want to spend more than 20 (30) dollars.	**Non voglio spendere più di venti (trenta) dollari.** *nohn vOH-ly-ee-oh spEHn-deh-reh pee-OO dee vAYn-tee (trEHn-tah) dOHl-lah-ree*
Could you suggest something?	**Potrebbe suggerirmi qualche cosa?** *poh-trAYb-beh soo-jeh-rEEr-mee koo-AHl-keh kOH-sah*
Would you show me your selection of _____?	**Che cosa potrebbe mostrarmi di _____?** *kay kOH-sah poh-trAYb-beh moh-strAHr-mee dee*
■ blown glass	**vetro soffiato** *vAY-troh sohf-fee-AH-toh*

■ carved object	**legno intagliato** *lAY-ny-oh een-tah-ly-ee-AH-toh*
■ crystal	**cristallo** *kree-stAHl-loh*
■ earthenware (pottery)	**ceramiche** *cheh-rAH-mee-keh*
■ fans	**ventagli** *vehn-tAH-ly-ee*
■ jewelry	**oggetti preziosi** *oh-jEHt-tee preh-tsee-OH-see*
■ lace	**pizzi** *pEE-tsee*
■ leathergoods	**articoli in pelle** *ahr-tEE-koh-lee een pEHl-leh*
■ liqueurs	**liquori** *lee-koo-OH-ree*
■ musical instruments	**strumenti musicali** *stroo-mEHn-tee moo-see-kAH-lee*
■ perfumes	**profumi** *proh-fOO-mee*
■ (miniature) pictures	**quadretti (in miniatura)** *koo-ah-drAYt-tee (een mee-nee-ah-tOO-rah)*
■ posters	**affissi, manifesti, poster** *ahf-fEEs-see, mah-nee-fEH-stee, pOH-stehr*
■ religious articles	**articoli religiosi** *ahr-tEE-koh-lee reh-lee-jee-OH-see*
■ local handicrafts	**prodotti dell'artigianato locale?** *proh-dOHt-tee dayl-lahr-tee-jee-ah-nAH-toh loh-kAH-leh*

STATIONERY ITEMS

I want to buy _____.	**Voglio comprare _____.** *vOH-ly-ee-oh kohm-prAH-reh*
■ a ball-point pen	**una penna a sfera** *OO-nah pAYn-nah ah sfEH-rah*
■ a deck of cards	**un mazzo di carte** *oon mAH-tsoh dee kAHr-teh*

◼ envelopes	**delle buste** *dAYl-leh bOO-steh*
◼ an eraser	**una gomma per cancellare** *OO-nah gOHm-mah pehr kahn-chehl-lAH-reh*
◼ glue	**della colla** *dAYl-lah kOHl-lah*
◼ a notebook	**un taccuino** *oon tahk-koo-EE-noh*
◼ pencils	**delle matite** *dAYl-leh mah-tEE-teh*
◼ a pencil sharpener	**un temperamatite** *oon tehm-peh-rah-mah-tEE-teh*
◼ a ruler	**una riga** *OO-nah rEE-gah*
◼ Scotch tape	**un nastro adesivo (uno scotch)** *oon nAH-stroh ah-deh-sEE-voh (OO-noh skO-ch)*
◼ some string	**del filo** *dayl fEE-loh*
◼ typing paper	**della carta per battere a macchina** *dAYl-lah kAHr-tah pehr bAHt-teh-reh ah mAH-kee-nah*
◼ wrapping paper	**della carta da imballaggio** *dAYl-lah kAHr-tah dah eem-bahl-lAH-jee-oh*
◼ a writing pad	**un blocchetto di carta** *oon blohk-kAYt-toh dee kAHr-tah*
◼ writing paper	**della carta da scrivere** *dAYl-lah kAHr-tah dah scrEE-veh-reh*

TOBACCO

You can buy cigarettes and other related items at a **Sale e tabacchi** shop. They also sell post cards and stamps.

A pack (carton) of cigarettes, please.	**Un pacchetto (una stecca) di sigarette, per piacere.** *oon pah-kAYt-toh (OO-nah stAYk-kah) dee see-gah-rAYt-teh, pehr pee-ah-chAY-reh*
◼ filtered	**con filtro** *kOHn fEEl-troh*
◼ unfiltered	**senza filtro** *sEHn-tsah fEEl-troh*

◼menthol	**alla menta** *ahl-lah mEHn-tah*
◼king-size	**lunghe** *lOOn-gheh*

Are these cigarettes (very) strong (mild)?
Sono (molto) forti (leggere) queste sigarette? *sOH-noh (mOHl-toh) fOHr-tee (leh-jEH-reh) koo-AY-steh see-gah-rAYt-teh*

Do you have American cigarettes?
Ha sigarette americane? *AH see-gah-rAYt-teh ah-meh-ree-kAH-neh?*

What brand?
Di che marca? *dee kay mAHr-kah*

Please give me a pack of matches also.
Mi dia anche una scatola di fiammiferi, per piacere. *mee dEE-ah AHn-kay OO-nah skAH-toh-lah dee fee-ahm-mEE-fay-ree pehr pee-ah-chAY-reh*

Do you sell _____?
Vendono _____? *vAYn-doh-noh*

◼chewing tobacco	**tabacco da masticare** *tah-bAHk-koh dah mah-stee-kAH-reh*
◼cigarette holders	**portasigarette** *pohr-tah-see-gah-rAYt-teh*
◼cigars	**sigari** *sEE-gah-ree*
◼flints	**pietrine** *pee-eh-trEE-neh*
◼lighter fluid	**benzina per accendini?** *behn-tsEE-nah pehr ah-chen-dEE-nee*
◼pipes	**pipe** *pEE-peh*
◼pipe tobacco	**tabacco da pipa** *tah-bAHk-koh dah pEE-pah*
◼snuff	**tabacco da fiuto** *tah-bAHk-koh dah fee-OO-toh*

TOILETRIES

In Italy drugstores (chemists) carry mostly actual drugs and medicines. For toiletries and perfumes, you would go to a **profumeria**.

Do you have ___?	**Ha ___?** *ah*
■ bobby pins	**delle forcine** *dAYl-leh fohr-chEE-neh*
■ a brush	**una spazzola** *OO-nah spAH-tsoh-lah*
■ cleansing cream	**della crema detergente** *dAYl-lah crEH-mah day-tehr-jEHn-teh*
■ a comb	**un pettine** *oon pEHt-tee-neh*
■ a deodorant	**un deodorante** *oon deh-oh-doh-rAHn-teh*
■ (disposable) diapers	**dei pannolini usa e getta** *dAY-ee pahn-noh-lEE-nee OO-sah ay jEHt-tah*
■ emery boards	**delle limette per le unghie** *dAYl-leh lee-mEHt-teh pehr leh OOn-ghee-eh*
■ eye liner	**un eye liner** *oon "eye liner"*
■ eye shadow	**l'ombretto** *lohm-brAYt-toh*
■ eyebrow pencil	**una matita per le sopracciglia** *OO-nah mah-tEE-tah pehr leh soh-prah-chEE-ly-ee-ah*
■ hair spray	**della lacca per capelli** *dAYl-la lAHk-kah pehr kah-pAYl-lee*
■ lipstick	**il lipstick (rossetto per le labbra)** *eel "lipstick" (rohs-sEHt-toh pehr leh lAHb-brah)*
■ make-up	**il make-up (trucco)** *eel "make up" (trOOk-koh)*
■ mascara	**del mascara** *dAYl mah-skAH-rah*
■ a mirror	**uno specchio** *OO-noh spEHk-key-oh*
■ mouthwash	**del disinfettante per la bocca** *dayl dee-seen-feht-tAHn-teh pehr lah bOHk-kah*
■ nail clippers	**dei tagliaunghie** *dAY-ee tah-ly-ee-ah-OOn-ghee-eh*

■ a nail file **una limetta per le unghie** *OO-nah lee-mAYt-tah pehr leh OOn-ghee-eh*

■ nail polish **dello smalto per le unghie** *dAYl-loh smAHl-toh pehr leh OOn-ghee-eh*

■ nail polish remover **dell'acetone** *dayl-lah-cheh-tOH-neh*

■ a razor **un rasoio di sicurezza** *oon rah-sOH-ee-oh dee see-koo-rAY-tsah*

■ razor blades **delle lamette** *dAYl-leh lah-mAYt-teh*

■ rouge **il rossetto (belletto)** *eel rohs-sEHt-toh (behl-lEHt-toh)*

■ sanitary napkins **degli assorbenti (igienici)** *dAY-ly-ee ahs-sohr-bEHn-tee (ee-jee-EH-nee-chee)*

■ (cuticle) scissors **delle forbicine** *dAYl-leh fohr-bee-chEE-neh*

■ shampoo **dello shampoo** *dAYl-loh shee-AHm-poh*

■ shaving lotion **un dopobarba** *oon doh-poh-bAHr-bah*

■ soap **del sapone** *dayl sah-pOH-neh*

■ a sponge **una spugna** *OO-nah spOO-ny-ah*

■ tampons **dei tamponi** *dAY-ee tahm-pOH-nee*

■ tissues **dei fazzolettini di carta** *dAY-ee fah-tsoh-leht-tEE-nee dee kAHr-tah*

■ toilet paper **della carta igienica** *dAYl-lah kAHr-tah ee-jee-EH-nee-kah*

■ a toothbrush **uno spazzolino per i denti** *OO-noh spah-tsoh-lEE-noh pehr ee dEHn-tee*

■ toothpaste **un dentifricio** *oon dEHn-tee-frEE-chee-oh*

■ tweezers **delle pinzette** *dAYl-leh peen-tsEHt-teh*

PERSONAL CARE AND SERVICES

If your hotel doesn't offer these services, ask the attendant at the desk to recommend someone nearby.

AT THE BARBER

Where is there a good barbershop?	**Dove potrei trovare (una buona barberia) un buon parrucchiere?** *dOH-veh poh-trEH-ee troh-vAH-reh (OO-nah boo-OH-nah bahr-beh-rEE-ah) oon boo-OHn pahr-rook-key-EH-reh*
Do I have to wait long?	**C'è da aspettare molto?** *chEH dah-speht-tAH-reh mOHl-toh*
Am I next?	**È arrivato il mio turno?** *EH ahr-ree-vAH-toh eel mEE-oh tOOr-noh*
I want a shave.	**Voglio farmi la barba.** *vOH-ly-ee-oh fAHr-mee lah bAHr-bah*
I want a haircut.	**Voglio un taglio di capelli.** *vOH-ly-ee-oh oon tAH-ly-ee-oh dee kah-pAYl-lee*
Short in back, long in front.	**Corti dietro, lunghi davanti.** *kOHr-tee dee-EH-troh, lOOn-ghee dah-vAHn-tee*
Leave it long.	**Me li lasci lunghi.** *meh-lee lAH-shee lOOn-ghee*
I want it (very) short.	**Li voglio (molto) corti.** *lee vOH-ly-ee-oh (mOHl-toh) kOHr-tee*
You can cut a little _____.	**Me li può tagliare un po' _____.** *meh lee poo-OH tah-ly-ee-AH-reh oon pOH*
■ in back	**di dietro** *dee dee-EH-troh*
■ in front	**sul davanti** *sool dah-vAHn-tee*
■ off the top	**sopra** *sOH-prah*

Cut a little bit more here.	**Tagli un po' di più qui (per favore).** *tAH-ly-ee oon pOH dee pee-OO koo-EE (pehr fah-vOH-reh)*
That's enough.	**Basta così.** *bAH-stah koh-sEE*
Use the scissors only.	**Usi solamente le forbici.** *OO-see soh-lah-mEHn-teh leh fOHr-bee-chee*
I'd like a razor cut.	**Vorrei un taglio al rasoio.** *vohr-rEH-ee oon tAH-ly-ee-oh ahl rah-sOH-ee-oh*
Please trim ____.	**Può spuntarmi ____.** *poo-OH spoon-tAHr-mee*
■ my beard	**il pizzo (la barba)** *eel pEE-tsoh (lah bAHr-bah)*
■ my moustache	**i baffi** *ee bAHf-fee*
■ my sideburns	**le basette** *leh bah-sAYt-teh*
Where's the mirror?	**Dov'è lo specchio?** *doh-vEH loh spEHK-key-oh*
How much do I owe you?	**Quanto le devo?** *koo-AHn-toh leh dAY-voh*
Is service included?	**È incluso il servizio?** *EH een-klOO-soh eel sehr-vEE-tzee-oh*

AT THE BEAUTY PARLOR

Is there a beauty parlor (hairdresser) near the hotel?	**C'è una parrucchiera vicino all'albergo?** *chEH OO-nah pahr-rook-key-EH-rah vee-chEE-noh ahl-lahl-bEHr-goh*
I'd like an appointment for this afternoon (tomorrow).	**Vorrei un appuntamento per questo pomeriggio (per domani).** *vohr-rEH-ee oon ahp-poon-tah-mEHn-toh pehr koo-AYs-toh poh-meh-rEE-jee-oh (pehr doh-mAH-nee)*

Can you give me ____?	**Può farmi ____?** *poo-OH fAHr-mee*
■ a color rinse	**un cachet** *oon kah-shEH*
■ a facial massage	**un massaggio facciale** *oon mahs-sAH-jee-oh fah-chee-AH-leh*
■ a haircut	**un taglio di capelli** *oon tAH-ly-ee-oh dee kah-pAYl-lee*
■ a manicure	**la manicure** *lah mah-nee-kOO-reh*
■ a permanent	**una permanente** *OO-nah pehr-mah-nAYn-teh*
■ a shampoo	**lo shampoo** *loh shee-AH-mpoh*
■ a wash and set	**shampoo e messa in piega** *shee-AH-mpoh ay mAYs-sah een pee-AY-gah*
I'd like to see a color chart.	**Vorrei vedere il cartellino dei colori.** *vohr-rEH-ee veh-dAY-reh eel kahr-tehl-lEE-noh dAY-ee koh-lOH-ree*
I want ____.	**Voglio ____.** *vOH-ly-ee-oh*
■ auburn	**un color rame** *oon koh-lOHr rAH-meh*
■ (light) blond	**un biondo (chiaro)** *oon bee-OHn-doh (key-AH-roh)*
■ brunette	**un bruno** *oon brOO-noh*
■ a darker color	**un colore più scuro** *oon koh-lOH-reh pee-OO skOO-roh*
■ a lighter color	**un colore più chiaro** *oon koh-lOH-reh pee-OO key-AH-roh*
■ the same color	**lo stesso colore** *loh stAYs-soh koh-lOH-reh*
Don't apply any hair-spray.	**Non mi metta nessuna lacca.** *nohn mee mEHt-tah nays-sOO-nah lAHk-kah*

Not too much hair-spray.	**Non troppa lacca.** *nohn trOHp-pah lAHk-kah*
I want my hair ____.	**Vorrei (voglio) i capelli ____.** *vohr-rEH-ee (vOH-ly-ee-oh) ee kah-pEHl-lee*
■ with bangs	**con la frangia** *kohn lah frAHn-jee-ah*
■ in a bun	**a nodo (a crocchia)** *ah nOH-doh (ah krOHk-key-ah)*
■ in curls	**a boccoli** *ah bOHk-koh-lee*
■ with waves	**ondulati** *ohn-doo-lAH-tee*
Where's the mirror?	**Dov'è lo specchio?** *doh-vEH loh spEHk-key-oh*
How much do I owe you?	**Quanto le devo?** *koo-AHn-toh leh dAY-voh*
Is service included?	**È incluso il servizio?** *EH een-klOO-soh eel sehr-vEE-tzee-oh*

LAUNDRY AND DRY CLEANING

Where is the nearest laundry (dry cleaner's)?	**Dov'è la lavanderia (la tintoria) più vicina?** *Doh-vEH lah lah-vahn-deh-rEE-ah (lah teen-toh-rEE-ah) pee-OO vee-chEE-nah(oh)*
I have a lot of (dirty) clothes to be _____.	**Ho molta biancheria (sporca) da _____.** *oh mOHl-tah bee-ahn-keh-rEE-ah (spOHr-kah) dah*
■ dry cleaned	**lavare a secco** *lah-vAH-reh ah sAYk-koh*
■ washed	**lavare** *lah-vAH-reh*
■ mended	**rammendare** *rahm-mehn-dAH-reh*
■ ironed	**stirare** *stee-rAH-reh*
Here's the list:	**Ecco l'elenco:** *EHk-koh leh-lEHn-koh*
■ 3 shirts (men's)	**tre camicie (da uomo)** *tray kah-mee-cheh (dah oo-OH-moh)*
■ 12 handkerchiefs	**dodici fazzoletti** *dOH-dee-chee fah-tsoh-lAYt-tee*
■ 6 pairs of socks	**sei paia di calzini** *sAY-ee pAH-ee-ah dee kahl-tsEE-nee*
■ 1 blouse (nylon)	**una blusa (di nylon)** *oo-nah blOO-sah (dee nAH-ee-lohn)*
■ 4 shorts	**quattro mutande** *koo-AHt-tro moo-tAHn-deh*
■ 1 pyjamas	**due pigiama** *dOO-eh pee-jee-AH-mah*
■ 2 suits	**due vestiti** *dOO-eh veh-stEE-tee*
■ 3 ties	**tre cravatte** *tray krah-vAHt-teh*
■ 2 dresses (cotton)	**due vesti (di cotone)** *dOO-eh veh-stee (dee koh-tOH-neh)*

■ 2 skirts **due gonne** *dOO-eh gOHn-neh*

■ 1 sweater (wool) **una maglia (di lana)** *oo-na mAH-ly-ah (dee lAH-nah)*

■ 1 pair of gloves **un paio di guanti** *oon pAH-ee-oh dee goo-AHn-tee*

I need them for _____. **Mi occorrono per _____.** *mee ohk-kOHr-roh-noh pehr*

■ as soon as possible **al più presto possibile** *ahl pee-OO preh-stoh pohs-see-bee-leh*

■ tonight **stasera** *stah-sAY-ra*

■ tomorrow **domani** *doh-mAH-nee*

■ next week **la settimana prossima** *lah seht-tee-mAH-nah prOHs-see-mah*

■ the day after tomorrow **dopodomani** *doh-poh doh-mAH-nee*

When will you bring it (them) back? **Quando lo (li) riporterà?** *koo-AHn-doh loh (lee) ree-pohr-teh-rAH*

When will it be ready? **Quando sarà pronto?** *koo-AHn-doh sah-rAH prOHn-toh*

There's a button missing. **Manca un bottone.** *mAHn-kah oon boht-tOH-neh*

Can you sew it on? **Può riattaccarlo?** *poo-OH ree-aht-tahk-kAHr-loh*

This isn't my laundry. **Questa non è la mia biancheria.** *koo-AYs-tah nohn EH lah mEE-ah bee-ahn-keh-rEE-ah*

SHOE REPAIRS

Can you fix these shoes (boots)? **Può ripararmi queste scarpe (questi stivali)?** *poo-OH ree-pah-rAHr-mee koo-AYs-teh skAHr-peh (koo-AY-stee-vAH-lee)*

Put on (half) soles and rubber heels.	**Ci metta le (mezze) suole e i tacchi di gomma.** *chee mEHt-tah leh (mEH-tseh) soo-OH-leh ay ee tAH-key dee gOHm-mah*
I'd like to have my shoes shined too.	**Vorrei anche che mi lucidasse le scarpe.** *vohr-rEH-ee AHn-keh kay mee loo-chee-dAHs-seh leh skAHr-peh*
When will they be ready?	**Quando saranno pronte?** *koo-AHn-doh sah-rAHn-noh prOHn-teh*
I need them by Saturday (without fail).	**Mi occorrono per sabato (assolutamente).** *mee ohk-kOHr-roh-noh pehr sAH-bah-toh (ahs-soh-loo-tah-mEHn-teh)*

WATCH REPAIRS

Can you fix this watch (alarm clock) (for me)?	**(Mi) può aggiustare quest'orologio (questa sveglia)?** *(mee) poo-OH ah-jee-oo-stAH-reh koo-ay-stoh-roh-lOH-jee-oh (koo-AY-stah svAY-ly-ee-ah)*
Can you clean it?	**Può pulirlo(la)?** *poo-OH poo-lEEr-loh(lah)*
I dropped it.	**L'ho lasciato(a) cadere.** *lOH lah-shee-AH-toh(tah) kah-dAY-reh*
It's running slow (fast).	**Va piano (in anticipo).** *vAH pee-AH-noh (een ahn-tEE-chee-poh)*
It's stopped.	**S'è fermato(a).** *sEH fehr-mAH-toh(tah)*
I wind it everyday.	**Lo (la) carico ogni giorno.** *loh (lah) kAH-ree-koh OH-ny-ee jee-OHr-noh*
I need _____.	**Ho bisogno di _____.** *oh bee-sOH-ny-oh dee*
■ a crystal, glass	**un vetro** *oon vAY-troh*
■ an hour hand	**una lancetta delle ore** *OO-nah lahn-chAYt-tah dAYl-leh OH-reh*

■ a minute hand   **una lancetta dei minuti** *OO-nah lahn-chAYt-tah dAY-ee mee-nOO-tee*

■ a second hand   **una lancetta dei secondi** *OO-nah lahn-chAYt-tah dAY-ee seh-kOHn-dee*

■ a stem   **una vite** *oo-nah vEE-teh*

■ a spring   **una molla** *OO-nah mOHl-lah*

■ a battery   **una pila** *oo-nah pEE-lah*

When will it be ready?   **Quando sarà pronto?** *koo-AHn-doh sah-rAH prOHn-toh*

May I have a receipt?   **Posso avere la ricevuta?** *pOHs-soh ah-vAY-reh lah ree-cheh-vOO-tah*

CAMERA REPAIRS

Can you fix this camera (movie camera)?   **Può aggiustare questa macchina fotografica (questa cinepresa)?** *poo-OH ah-jee-oo-stAH-reh koo-AY-stah mAH-kee-nah foh-toh-grAH-fee-kah (koo-AY-stah chee-neh-prAY-sah)*

The film doesn't advance.   **Si è bloccato il rullino.** *see EH bloh-kAH-toh eel rool-lEE-noh*

I think I need new batteries.   **Penso di aver bisogno delle pile nuove.** *pEHn-soh dee ah-vAYr bee-sOH-ny-ee-oh dAYl-leh pEE-leh noo-OH-veh*

How much will the repair cost?   **Quanto mi costerà farla aggiustare?** *koo-AHn-toh mee-koh-steh-rAH fAHr-lah ah-jee-oo-stAH-reh*

When can I come and get it?   **Quando posso venire a ritirarla?** *koo-AHn-doh pOHs-soh veh-nEE-reh ah ree-tee-rAHr-lah*

I need it as soon as possible.   **Ne ho bisogno al più presto possibile.** *nay oh bee-sOH-ny-ee-oh ahl pee-OO prEH-stoh pohs-sEE-bee-leh*

MEDICAL CARE

THE PHARMACY (CHEMIST)

Where is the nearest (all night) pharmacy (chemist)?	**Dov'è la farmacia (notturna) più vicina?** *doh-vEH lah fahr-mah-chEE-ah (noht-tOOr-nah) pee-OO vee-chEE-nah*
At what time does the pharmacy open (close?)	**A che ora apre (chiude) la farmacia?** *ah kay OH-rah AH-preh (key-OO-deh) lah fahr-mah-chEE-ah*
I need something for ____.	**Ho bisogno di qualche cosa per ____.** *oh bee-sOH-ny-ee-oh dee koo-AHl-keh kOH-sah pehr*
■ a cold	**il raffreddore** *eel rahf-frehd-dOH-reh*
■ constipation	**la stitichezza** *lah stee-tee-kAY-tsah*
■ a cough	**la tosse** *lah tOHs-seh*
■ diarrhea	**la diarrea** *lah dee-ahr-rEH-ah*
■ a fever	**la febbre** *lah fEHb-breh*
■ hay fever	**una rinite da fieno** *OO-nah ree-nEE-teh dah fee-EH-noh*
■ a headache	**il mal di testa** *eel mAHl dee tEH-stah*
■ insomnia	**l'insonnia** *leen-sOHn-nee-ah*
■ sunburn	**la scottatura solare** *lah skoht-tah-tOO-rah soh-lAH-reh*
■ motion sickness	**il mal d'auto (di mare)** *eel mAHl dAH-oo-toh (dee mAH-reh)*
■ a toothache	**il mal di denti** *eel mAHl dee dEHn-tee*
■ an upset stomach	**il mal di stomaco** *eel mAHl dee stOH-mah-koh*
I do not have a prescription.	**Non ho la ricetta medica.** *nohn OH lah ree-chEHt-tah mEH-dee-kah*

May I have it right away?	**Posso averla subito?** *pOHs-soh ah-vAYr-lah sOO-bee-toh*
It's an emergency.	**È un'emergenza.** *eH oo-neh-mehr-jEHn-tsah*
How long will it take?	**Quanto tempo ci vorrà** *koo-AHn-toh tEHm-poh chee vohr-rAH*
When can I come for it?	**Quando potrò venire a prenderla?** *koo-AHn-doh poh-trOH veh-nEE-reh ah prAYn-dehr-lah*
I would like ____.	**Vorrei ____.** *vohr-rEH-ee*
■ adhesive tape	**un nastro adesivo** *oon nAH-stroh ah-deh-sEE-voh*
■ alcohol	**dell'alcool** *dayl-lAHl-koh-ohl*
■ an antacid	**un antiacido** *oon ahn-tee-AH-chee-doh*
■ an antiseptic	**un antisettico** *oon ahn-tee-sEHt-tee-koh*
■ aspirins	**delle aspirine** *dAYl-leh ah-spee-rEE-neh*
■ Band-Aids	**dei cerotti** *dAY-ee cheh-rOHt-tee*
■ contraceptives	**dei contraccettivi** *dAY-ee kohn-trah-chEHt-tee-vee*
■ corn plasters	**dei callifughi** *dAY-ee kahl-lEE-foo-ghee*
■ cotton balls	**del cotone idrofilo** *dayl koh-tOH-neh ee-drOH-fee-loh*
■ cough drops/syrup	**delle pasticche (dello sciroppo) per la tosse** *dAYl-leh pah-stEEk-keh (dAHl-loh shee-rOHp-poh) pehr lah tOHs-seh*
■ ear drops	**delle gocce per gli orecchi** *dAYl-leh gOH-cheh pehr ly-ee oh-rAYk-key*
■ eye drops	**del collirio** *dayl kohl-lEE-ree-oh*

■ iodine   **della tintura di iodio** *dAYl-lah teen-tOO-rah dee ee-OH-dee-oh*

■ a (mild) laxative   **un lassativo (leggero)** *oon lahs-sah-tEE-voh (lay-jEH-roh)*

■ milk of magnesia   **della magnesia** *dAYl-lah mah-ny-ee-EH-see-ah*

■ prophylactics   **dei profilattici** *dAY-ee proh-fee-lAHt-tee-chee*

■ sanitary napkins   **degli assorbenti (igienici)** *dAY-ly-ee ahs-sohr-bEHn-tee (ee-jee-EH-nee-chee)*

■ suppositories   **delle supposte** *dAYl-leh soop-pOH-steh*

■ talcum powder   **del borotalco** *dayl boh-roh-tAHl-koh*

■ tampons   **dei tamponi** *dAY-ee tahm-pOH-nee*

■ a thermometer   **un termometro** *oon tehr-mOH-meh-troh*

■ vitamins   **delle vitamine** *dAYl-leh vee-tah-mEE-neh*

WITH THE DOCTOR

I don't feel well.	**Non mi sento bene.** *nohn mee sEHn-toh bEH-neh*
I need a doctor right away.	**Ho bisogno urgente del medico.** *oh bee-sOH-ny-ee-oh oor-jEHn-teh dayl mEH-dee-koh*
Do you know a doctor who speaks English?	**Conosce un dottore che parla inglese?** *koh-nOH-sheh oon doht-tOH-reh kay pAHr-lah een-glAY-seh*
Where is his office (surgery)?	**Dov'è il suo ambulatorio?** *doh-vEH eel sOO-oh ahm-boo-lah-tOH-ree-oh*

Will the doctor come to the hotel?	**Il dottore potrà venire all'hotel?** *eel doht-tOH-reh poh-trAH veh-NEE-reh ahl-loh-tEHl*	
I feel dizzy.	**Mi gira la testa (ho le vertigini).** *mee jEE-rah lah tEH-stah (oh leh vehr-tEE-jee-nee)*	
I feel weak.	**Mi sento debole.** *mee sEHn-toh dAY-boh-leh*	

PARTS OF THE BODY

head	**la testa**	*lah tEH-stah*
face	**il viso**	*eel vEE-soh*
ear	**l'orecchio**	*loh-rAY-key-oh*
eye	**l'occhio**	*lOH-key-oh*
nose	**il naso**	*eel nAH-soh*
mouth	**la bocca**	*lah bOH-kah*
tooth	**il dente**	*eel dEHn-teh*
throat	**la gola**	*lah gOH-lah*
neck	**il collo**	*eel kOHl-loh*
shoulder	**la spalla**	*lah spAHl-lah*
breast	**il petto**	*eel pEHt-toh*
heart	**il cuore**	*eel koo-OH-reh*
arm	**il braccio**	*eel brAH-chee-oh*
elbow	**il gomito**	*eel gOH-mee-toh*
wrist	**il polso**	*eel pOHl-soh*
hand	**la mano**	*lah mAH-noh*
appendix	**l'appendicite**	*lahp-pehn-dee-chEE-teh*
liver	**il fegato**	*ell fEH-gah-toh*
hip	**l'anca**	*l'AHn-kah*

leg	**la gamba**	*lah gAHm-bah*
knee	**il ginocchio**	*eel jee-nOH-key-oh*
ankle	**la caviglia**	*lah kah-vEE-ly-ah*
foot	**il piede**	*eel pee-EH-deh*
skin	**la pelle**	*lah pEHl-leh*
I (think I) have _____.	**(Credo che) ho _____.**	*(kreh-doh kay) oh*
■ an abscess	**un ascesso**	*oon ah-shEHs-soh*
■ a broken bone	**una frattura**	*OO-nah frat-tOO-rah*
■ a bruise	**una contusione**	*OO-nah kohn-too-see-OH-neh*
■ a burn	**un'ustione**	*oo-noo-stee-oH-neh*
■ something in my eye	**qualche cosa nell'occhio**	*koo-AHl-keh kOH-sah nayl-lOHk-key-oh*
■ the chills	**i brividi**	*ee brEE-vee-dee*
■ a cold	**un raffreddore**	*oon rahf-frehd-dOH-reh*
■ constipation	**stitichezza**	*stee-tee-kAY-tsah*
■ stomach cramps	**crampi allo stomaco**	*krAHm-pee AHl-loh stOH-mah-koh*
■ a cut	**una ferita (un taglio)**	*OO-nah feh-rEE-tah (oon tAH-ly-ee-oh)*
■ diarrhea	**la diarrea**	*lah dee-ahr-rEH-ah*
■ a fever	**la febbre**	*la fEHb-breh*
■ a headache	**un mal di testa**	*oon mAHl dee tEH-stah*
■ an infection	**un'infezione**	*oo-neen-feh-tsee-OH-neh*
■ a lump	**un gonfiore**	*oon gohn-fee-OH-reh*
■ a sore throat	**un mal di gola**	*oon mAHl dee gOH-lah*

■ a stomachache | **un mal di stomaco** *oon mAHl dee stOH-mah-koh*

■ rheumatism | **i reumatismi** *ee reh-oo-mah-tEE-smee*

TELLING THE DOCTOR

It hurts me here. | **Mi fa male qui.** *mee fah mAH-leh koo-EE*

I've had this pain since yesterday. | **Ho questo dolore da ieri.** *oh koo-AY-stoh doh-lOH-reh dah ee-EH-ree*

There's a (no) history of asthma (diabetes) in my family. | **(Non) c'è anamnesi di asma (diabete) nella mia famiglia.** *(nohn) chEH ah-nahm-nEH-see dee AH-smah (dee-ah-bEH-teh) nAYl-lah mEE-ah fah-mEE-ly-ee-ah*

I'm (not) allergic to antibiotics (penicillin). | **(Non) sono allergico agli antibiotici (alla penicillina).** *(nohn) sOH-noh ahl-lEHr-jee-koh AH-ly-ee ahn-tee-bee-OH-tee-chee (AHl-lah peh-nee-cheel-lEE-nah)*

I have a pain in my chest. | **Ho un dolore al petto.** *oh oon doh-lOH-reh ahl pEHt-toh*

I had a heart attack ____. | **Ho avuto un attacco cardiaco ____.** *oh ah-vOO-toh oon aht-tAHk-koh kahr-dEE-ah-koh*

■ last year | **l'anno scorso** *lAHn-noh skOHr-soh*

■ (three) years ago | **(tre) anni fa** *trEH AHn-nee fah*

I'm taking this medicine (insulin). | **Sto prendendo questa medicina (insulina).** *stOH prehn-dEHn-doh koo-AY-stah meh-dee-chEE-nah (een-soo-lEE-nah)*

I'm pregnant. | **Sono incinta.** *sOH-noh een-chEEn-tah*

I feel better (worse). | **Mi sento meglio (peggio).** *mee sEHn-toh mEH-ly-ee-oh (pEH-jee-oh)*

Is it serious (contagious)?	**È serio (contagioso)?** *EH sEH-ree-oh (kohn-tah-jee-OH-soh)*
Do I have to go to the hospital?	**Devo andare in ospedale?** *dAY-voh ahn-dAH-reh een oh-speh-dAH-leh*
When can I continue my trip?	**Quando potrò continuare la mia gita?** *koo-AHn-doh poh-trOH kohn-tee-noo-AH-reh lah mEE-ah jEE-tah*

DOCTOR'S INSTRUCTIONS

Apra la boca.	Open your mouth.
Tiri fuori la lingua.	Stick out your tongue.
Tossisca.	Cough.
Respiri profondamente.	Breathe deeply.
Si spogli.	Take off your clothing.
Si sdrai.	Lie down.
Si alzi.	Stand up.
Si vesta.	Get dressed.

FOLLOWING UP

Are you giving me a prescription?	**Mi darà una ricetta?** *mee dah-rAH oo-nah ree-chEHt-tah*
How often must I take this medicine (these pills)?	**Quante volte devo prendere questa medicina (queste pillole)?** *koo-AHn-teh vOHl-teh dAY-voh prAYn-deh-reh koo-AYs-tah meh-dee-chEE-nah (koo-AYs-teh pEEl-loh-leh)*
(How long) do I have to stay in bed?	**(Quanto) devo rimanere a letto?** *(koo-AHn-toh) dAY-voh ree-mah-nAY-reh ah lEHt-toh*
Thank you (for everything) doctor.	**Grazie (di tutto), dottore.** *grAH-tsee-eh (dee tOOt-toh) doht-tOH-reh*

How much do I owe you for your services? — **Quanto le devo per la visita?** *koo-AHn-toh leh dAY-voh pehr lah vEE-see-tah*

I have medical insurance. — **Ho l'assicurazione (l'assistenza) medica.** *oh lahs-see-koo-rah-tsee-OH-neh (lahs-sees-stEHn-tsah) mEH-dee-kah*

IN THE HOSPITAL (ACCIDENTS)

Help! — **Aiuto!** *ah-ee-OO-toh*

Get a doctor, quick! — **Chiamate un medico, subito!** *key-ah-mAH-teh oon mEH-dee-koh sOO-bee-toh*

Call an ambulance! — **Chiamate un'ambulanza!** *key-ah-mAH-teh oo-nahm-boo-lAHn-tsah*

Take him to the hospital. — **Portatelo in ospedale.** *pohr-tAH-teh-loh een oh-speh-dAH-leh*

I've fallen. — **Sono caduto(a).** *sOH-noh kah-dOO-toh(ah)*

I was knocked down. — **Mi hanno buttato(a) a terra.** *mee AHn-noh boot-tAH-toh(ah) ah tEHr-rah*

She was run over.	**È stata investita.** *EH stAH-tah een-veh-stEE-tah*
I think I've had a heart attack.	**Credo che ho avuto un collasso cardiaco.** *krEH-do kay oh ah-vOO-toh oon kohl-lAHs-soh kahr-dEE-ah-koh*
I burned myself.	**Mi sono ustionato(a).** *mee sOH-noh oo-stee-oh-nAH-toh(ah)*
I cut myself.	**Mi sono tagliato.** *mee sOH-noh tah-ly-ee-AH-toh*
I'm bleeding.	**Sto sanguinando.** *stOH sahn-goo-ee-nAHn-doh*
He's lost a lot of blood.	**Ha perduto molto sangue.** *ah pehr-dOO-toh mOHl-toh sAHn-goo-eh*
I think the bone is broken (dislocated).	**Penso che mi si sia fratturato (lussato) l'osso.** *pEHn-soh kay mee see sEE-ah fraht-too-rAH-toh (loos-sAH-toh) lOHs-soh*
The leg is swollen.	**La gamba è gonfia.** *lah gAHm-bah EH gOHn-fee-ah*
The wrist is sprained (twisted).	**Mi si è slogato (storto) il polso.** *mee see-EH sloh-gAH-toh (stOHr-toh) eel pOHl-soh*
The ankle is sprained (twisted).	**Mi si è slogata (storta) la caviglia.** *mee see-EH sloh-gAH-tah (stOHr-tah) lah kah-vEE-ly-ee-ah*
I can't move my elbow (knee).	**Non posso muovere il gomito (il ginocchio).** *nohn pOHs-soh moo-OH-veh-reh eel gOH-mee-toh (eel jee-nOHk-key-oh)*

AT THE DENTIST

Can you recommend a dentist?	**Può raccomandarmi un dentista?** *poo-OH rahk-koh-mahn-dAHr-mee oon dehn-tEE-stah*

I have a toothache that's driving me crazy.	**Ho un mal di denti che mi fa impazzire.** *oh oon mAHl dee dEHn-tee kay mee fah eem-pah-tsEE-reh*
I've lost a filling.	**Ho perduto l'otturazione.** *oh payr-dOO-toh loht-too-rah-tsee-OH-neh*
I've a broken tooth.	**Mi son rotto un dente.** *mee sOHn rOHt-toh oon dEHn-teh*
My gums hurt me.	**Mi fanno male le gengive.** *mee fAHn-noh mAH-leh leh jehn-jEE-veh*
Is there an infection?	**C'è un'infezione?** *chEH oo-neen-feh-tsee-OH-neh*
Will you have to extract the tooth?	**Deve estrarre il dente?** *dAY-veh ehs-trAHr-reh eel dEHn-teh*
I'd prefer you filled it ____.	**Preferisco farlo otturare ____.** *preh-feh-rIH-skoh fAHr-loh oht-too-rAH-reh*
▪ with amalgam	**con l'algama** *kOHn lAHl-gah-mah*
▪ with gold	**con oro** *kOHn OH-roh*
▪ with silver	**con argento** *kOHn ahr-jEHn-toh*
▪ for now temporarily	**provvisoriamente** *prohv-vee-soh-ree-ah-mEHn-teh*
Can you fix ____?	**Può riparare ____?** *poo-OH ree-pah-rAH-reh*
▪ this bridge	**questo ponte** *koo-AY-stoh pOHn- teh*
▪ this crown	**questa corona** *koo-AY-stah koh-rOH-nah*
▪ these dentures	**questi denti finti** *koo-AY-stee dEHn-tee fEEn-tee*
When should I come back?	**Quando dovrei ritornare?** *koo-AHn-doh doh-vrEH-ee ree-tohr-nAH-reh*
How much do I owe you for your services?	**Quanto le devo per la visita?** *koo-AHn-toh leh dAY-voh pehr lah vEE-see-tah*

WITH THE OPTICIAN

Can you repair these glasses (for me)?	**Può aggiustar(mi) questi occhiali?** *poo-OH ah-jee-oo-stAHr-(mee) koo-AY-stee oh-key-AH-lee*
I've broken a lens (the frame).	**Mi si è rotta una lente (la montatura).** *mee see-EH rOHt-tah OO-nah lEHn-teh (lah mohn-tah-tOO-rah)*
Can you put in a new lens?	**Può metterci una lente nuova?** *poo-OH mAYt-tehr-chee OO-nah lEHn-teh noo-OH-vah*
I do not have a prescription.	**Non ho la ricetta medica.** *nohn OH lah ree-chEHt-tah mEH-dee-kah*
Can you tighten the screw?	**Può stringere la vite?** *poo-OH strEEn-jeh-rEH lah vEE-teh*
I need the glasses as soon as possible.	**Ho bisogno degli occhiali al più presto possibile.** *oh bee-sOH-ny-ee-oh dAY-ly-ee oh-key-AH-lee ahl pee-OO prEH-stoh pohs-sEE-bee-leh*
I don't have any others.	**Non ne ho altri.** *nohn nay-OH AHl-tree*
I have lost a contact lens.	**Ho perduto una lente a contatto.** *oh pehr-dOO-toh OO-nah lEHn-teh ah kohn-tAHt-toh*
Can you replace it quickly?	**Può darmene un'altra subito?** *poo-OH dAHr-meh-neh oo-nAHl-trah sOO-bee-toh*

TRAVEL TIP

Simple toiletries such as toothpaste and shaving cream can be purchased easily when you arrive at your destination, but prescription medicines should be brought from home.

COMMUNICATIONS

POST OFFICE

Post offices in Italy can be identified by a sign **Poste e Telecomunicazioni** or the initials **PT**. All post offices are open weekdays 8:15 a.m. to 2 p.m. and Saturdays from 8:15 a.m. to 12 noon. In the largest cities (Rome, Milan, Turin, Naples, etc.) the central post office **(posta centrale)** is open until 9 p.m.

Stamps are sold at windows usually marked **Raccomandate/Francobolli** (Registered Letters/Stamps). Always have the clerk weigh air-mail letters since overweight letters will be sent surface mail rather than returned to the sender. Urgent letters may be sent **espresso** (special delivery) with additional postage.

Italian post offices are often very crowded because **conti correnti** (current bills for taxes, electricity and gas, and telephone) are paid at the post office.

Stamps for letters of normal weight and postcards can be purchased more conveniently at a tobacco shop **(tabaccheria)**. The tobacconist has a schedule of postal rates. There are no stamp-dispensing machines in Italy.

Letter boxes, which are red and attached to the wall rather than freestanding, are found in front of post offices and in the vicinity of tobacco shops. If there are two letter boxes side by side, be sure *not* to put letters and postcards for other destinations, including overseas, in the box marked **Città** (City).

General delivery letters should be addressed as follows:

Name of addressee
c/o Ufficio Postale Centrale
Fermo Posta
City

I want to mail a letter.	**Voglio spedire una lettera.** *vOH-ly-ee-oh speh-dEE-reh OO-nah lAYt-teh-rah*

Where's the post office?	**Dov'è l'ufficio postale?** *doh-vEH loof-fEE-chee-oh poh-stAH-leh*
Where's a letter box?	**Dov'è una cassetta postale?** *doh-vEH OO-nah kas-sAYt-tah poh-stAH-leh*
What is the postage on _____ to the United States (Canada, England, Australia)?	**Qual è l'affrancatura per _____ per gli Stati Uniti (Canada, Inghilterra, Australia)?** *koo-ah-lEH lahf-frahn-kah-tOO-rah pehr pehr ly-ee stAH-tee oo-nEE-tee (kah-nah-dAH, een-gheel-tEHr-rah, ahoo-strAH lee-ah)*
■ a letter	**una lettera** *OO-nah lAYt-teh-rah*
■ an air-mail letter	**una lettera via aerea** *oo-nah layt-teh-rah vEE-ah ah-EH-reh-ah*
■ an insured letter	**una lettera assicurata** *OO-nah lAYt-teh-rah ahs-see-koo-rAH-tah*
■ a registered letter	**una lettera raccomandata** *OO-nah lAYt-teh-rah rahk-koh-mahn-dAH-tah*
■ a special delivery letter	**una lettera espresso** *OO-nah lAYt-teh-rah ehs-prEHs-soh*
■ a package	**un pacco** *oon pAHk-koh*
■ a postcard	**una cartolina postale** *OO-nah kahr-toh-lEE-nah poh-stAH-leh*
When will it arrive?	**Quando arriverà?** *koo-AHn-doh ahr-ree-veh-rAH*
Which is the _____ window?	**Qual è lo sportello per _____?** *koo-ah-lEH loh spohr-tEHl-loh pehr*
■ general delivery	**il fermo posta** *eel fAYr-moh pOH-stah*
■ money order	**i vaglia postali** *ee vAH-ly-ee-ah poh-stAH-lee*
■ stamp	**i francobolli** *ee frahn-koh-bOHl-lee*

Are there any letters for me? My name is ____.	**Ci sono lettere per me? Il mio nome è ____.** *chee sOH-noh lAYt-teh-reh pehr mAY? eel mEE-oh nOH-meh EH*
I'd like ____.	**Vorrei ____.** *vohr-rEH-ee*
■ 10 post cards	**dieci cartoline postali** *dee-EH-chee kahr-toh-lEE-neh poh-stAH-lee*
■ 5 (air mail) stamps	**cinque francobolli (via aerea)** *chEEn-koo-eh frahn-koh-bOHl-lee (vEE-ah ah-EH-reh-ah)*
Do I fill out a customs receipt?	**Devo compilare una ricevuta?** *dAY-voh kohm-pee-lAH-reh oo-nah ree-cheh-vOO-tah*

TELEGRAMS

How late is the telegraph window open (till what time?)	**L'ufficio Poste e Telegrafi sta aperto fino a tardi (fino a che ora)?** *loof-fEE-chee-oh pOHs-teh ay teh-lEH-grah-fee stah ah-pEHr-toh fEE-noh ah tAHr-dee (fEE-noh ah kay OH-rah)*
I'd like to send a telegram to ____.	**Vorrei spedire un telegramma a ____.** *vohr-rEH-ee speh-dEE-reh oon teh-leh-grAHm-mah ah*
How much is it per word?	**Quanto costa per parola?** *koo-AHn-toh kOH-stah pehr pah-rOH-lah*
I want to send it collect.	**Voglio spedirlo(la) a carico del destinatario.** *vOH-ly-ee-oh speh-dEEr-loh(lah) ah kAH-ree-koh dayl deh-stee-nah-tAH-ree-oh*
When will it arrive?	**Quando sarà recapitato(a)?** *koo-AHn-doh sah-rAH reh-kah-pee-tAH-toh(ah)*

TELEPHONES

You'll find public telephones in cafés, bars, and station terminals. Buy the tokens (**gettoni,** *jeht-tOH-nee*) before making phone calls or have some change ready. At several telephone centers there are "clicking" timers. You will pay after having completed the phone call and will be charged by the number of **scatti** (*skAHt-tee*) or "clicks" marked by the timer.

While the telephone is ringing, you'll be able to hear two different signals. The long *too, too* sounds signify that the line is free and the bell is ringing; the short and repeated *too, too, too* sounds signify that the line is busy.

If you have difficulty operating the telephone or feel you will not be able to understand the person who answers the call, ask the clerk at your hotel to make the call for you.

Where is _____?	**Dov'è** _____? *doh-vEH*
■ a public telephone	**un telefono pubblico?** *oon teh-lEH-foh-noh pOOb-blee-koh*
■ a telephone booth	**una cabina telefonica?** *OO-nah kah-bEE-nah teh-leh-fOH-nee-kah*
■ a telephone directory	**un elenco telefonico?** *oon eh-lEHn-koh teh-leh-fOH-nee-koh*
May I use your phone?	**Posso usare il suo telefono?** *pOHs-soh oo-sAH-reh eel sOO-oh teh-lEH-foh-noh*
Can I call direct?	**Posso telefonare direttamente?** *pOHs-soh teh-leh-foh-nAH-reh dee-reht-tah-mEHn-teh*
I want to reverse the charges.	**Desidero fare una riversibile.** *deh-sEE-deh-roh fAH-reh oo-nah ree-vehr-sEE-bee-leh*
Do I need tokens for the phone?	**Occorrono i gettoni per il telefono?** *ohk-kOHr-roh-noh ee jeht-tOH-nee pehr eel teh-lEH-foh-noh*

I want to make a _____ to _____.	**Vorrei fare una _____ a _____.** *vohr-rEH-ee fAH-reh OO-nah _____ ah _____.*
■ local call	**telefonata urbana** *teh-leh-foh-nAH-tah oor-bAH-nah*
■ long-distance call	**una telefonata in teleselezione (interurbana, internazionale)** *OO-nah teh-leh-foh-nAH-tah een teh-leh-seh-leh-tsee-OH-neh (een-tehr-oor-bAH-nah, een-tehr-nah-tsee-oh-nAH-leh)*
■ person-to-person call	**una telefonata diretta con preavviso** *OO-nah teh-leh-foh-nAH-tah dee-rEHt-tah kohn preh-ahv-vEE-soh*
How do I get the operator?	**Come si ottiene il centralino?** *kOH-meh see oht-tee-EH-neh eel chehn-trah-lEE-noh*
Operator, can you give me _____?	**Signorina (signore, centralino), può darmi _____?** *see-ny-oh-rEE-nah (see-ny-OH-reh, chehn-trah-lEE-noh), poo-OH dAhr-mee*
■ number 23 345	**il ventitrè trecentoquarantacinque** *eel vayn-tee-trEH treh-chEHn-toh-koo-ah-rahn-tah-chEEn-koo-eh*
■ extension 19	**interno diciannove** *een-tEHr-noh dee-chee-ahn-nOH-veh*
■ area code	**prefisso numero** *preh-fEEs-soh nOO-meh-roh*
■ country code	**prefisso internazionale** *preh-fEEs-soh een-tehr-nah-tzee-oh-nAH-leh*
■ city code	**prefisso interurbano** *preh-fEEs-soh een-tehr-oor-bAH-noh*
My number is _____.	**Il mio numero è _____.** *eel mEE-oh nOO-meh-roh EH*
May I speak to _____?	**Potrei parlare con _____?** *poh-trEH-ee pahr-lAH-reh kohn*

Speaking.	**Sono io.** *sOH-noh EE-oh*
Hello.	**Pronto.** *prOHn-toh*
Who is it?	**Chi è?** *key EH*

PROBLEMS ON THE LINE

I can't hear.	**Non si sente bene.** *nOHn see sEHn-teh bEH-neh*
Speak louder (please).	**Parli più forte (per favore).** *pAHr-lee pee-OO fOHr-teh (pehr fah-vOH-reh)*
Don't hang up.	**Non appenda il ricevitore.** *nohn ahp-pEHn-dah eel ree-cheh-vee-tOH-reh*
This is ____.	**Parla ____.** *pAHr-lah*
Operator, there is no answer (they don't answer).	**Centralino, non risponde nessuno.** *chehn-trah-lEE-noh nohn ree-spOHn-deh nehs-sOO-noh*
The line is busy.	**La linea è occupata.** *lah lEE-neh-ah EH ohk-koo-pAH-tah*

You gave me (that was) a wrong number.	**Mi ha dato (era) un numero sbagliato.** *mee ah dAH-toh (EH-rah) oon nOO-meh-roh sbah-ly-ee-AH-toh*
I was cut off.	**È caduta la linea.** *EH kah-dOO-tah lah lEE-neh-ah*
Please dial it again.	**Per favore, rifaccia il numero.** *pehr fah-vOH-reh ree-fAH-chee-ah eel nOO-meh-roh*
I want to leave a message.	**Voglio lasciare un (messaggio) appunto.** *vOH-ly-ee-oh lah-shee-AH-reh oon (mehs-sAH-jee-oh) ahp-pOOn-toh*

PAYING UP

| How much do I have to pay? | **Quanto devo pagare?** *koo-AHn-toh dEH-voh pah-gAH-reh* |
| How many clicks did I have? | **Quanti scatti sono?** *koo-AHn-tee skAHt-tee sOH-noh* |

TRAVEL TIP

If you have had to change your plans and cannot use your airline ticket, you can apply for a complete refund. Treat your ticket as if it were cash, and return it to your travel agent or to the airline for your money back. Note, however, that some charter tickets are nonrefundable. If you do not use the ticket, you have lost the money, but if you take out special flight insurance, you can collect your refund for that charter ticket from the insuring company.

DRIVING A CAR

To drive in Italy you will be best off with an International Driving Permit (equivalent to a regular driver's license), best obtained before you leave home. You will need the car's registration documents with the **bollo** (*bOHl-loh*), the annual circulation charge, and a hazard triangle. Insurance is compulsory.

The Italian police (**Polizia Stradale, Carabinieri,** and **Vigili**) (*Poh-lee-tsEE-ah Strah-dAH-leh, kah-rah-bee-nee-EH-ree* and *vEE-jee-lee*) can stop at will any car on the road for spot checks and for traffic offenses. Tickets are paid on the spot. The traffic moves on the right, and passing is on the left. The speed limit—90–140 kilometers per hour or 56–87 miles per hour—depends upon engine capacity.

The roads in Italy are classified as **Autostrade** (*ah-oo-toh-strAH-deh*) with "pay tolls" (motor ways or expressways); **S.S., Strade Statali** (*strAH-deh stah-tAH-lee*), state roads; **S.P., Strade Provinciali** (*strAH-deh proh-veen-chee-AH-lee*), provincial roads; **S.C., Strade Comunali** (*strAH-deh koh-moo-nAH-lee*), village roads.

For road emergency, dial 116.

For police and ambulance, dial 113.

CAR RENTALS

Rentals can be arranged before departure for Italy through a travel agent or upon arrival in Italy at a rental office in the major airports or in or near the railroad station in a larger city or town. Some automobile rental companies are nationwide or worldwide organizations (like Avis and Hertz), enabling you to pick up and drop off a rented car at local offices throughout Italy.

To rent an automobile, you must be at least 21 years old and have an International Driving Permit, obtainable before departure or in Italy at the nearest office of the Automobile Club of Italy.

Where can I rent _____?	**Dove posso noleggiare _____?**
	dOH-veh pOHs-soh noh-leh-jee-AH-reh
■ a car	**una macchina** *OO-nah mAHk-keę-nah*

■ a motorcycle	**una motocicletta** *OO-nah moh-toh-chEE-klAYt-tah*
■ a motorscooter	**una vespa (una lambretta)** *OO-nah vEH-spah (OO-nah lahm-brAYt-tah)*
■ a moped	**un motorino** *oon moh-toh-rEE-noh*
■ a bicycle	**una bicicletta** *OO-na bee-chee-klAYt-tah*
I want (I'd like) _____.	**Voglio (Vorrei) _____.** *vOH-ly-ee-oh (vohr-rEH-ee)*
■ a small car	**una macchina piccola** *OO-nah mAHk-kee-nah pEE-koh-lah*
■ a large car	**una macchina grande** *OO-nah mAHk-kee-nah grAHn-deh*
■ a sport car	**una macchina sportiva** *OO-nah mAHk-kee-nah spohr-tEE-vah*
I prefer automatic transmission.	**Preferisco il cambio automatico.** *preh-feh-rEE-skoh eel kAHm-bee-oh ah-oo-toh-mAH-tee-koh*
How much does it cost _____?	**Quanto costa _____?** *koo-AHn-toh kOH-stah*
■ per day	**al giorno** *ahl jee-OHr-noh*
■ per week	**alla settimana** *AHl-lah seht-tee-mAH-nah*
■ per kilometer	**per chilometro** *pehr key-lOH-meh-troh*
■ for unlimited mileage	**a chilometraggio illimitato** *ah key-loh-meh-trAH-jee-oh eel-lee-mee-tAH-toh*
How much is the (complete) insurance?	**Quant'è l'assicurazione (completa)?** *koo-ahn-tEH lahs-see-koo-rah-tsee-OH-neh (kohm-plEH-tah)*
Is gas included?	**È inclusa la benzina?** *EH een-klOO-sah lah behn-tsEE-nah*

Do you accept credit cards?	**Accetta (no) carte di credito?** *ah-chEHt-tah(noh) kAHr-teh dee krEH-dee-toh*
Here's my (international) driver's license.	**Ecco la mia patente (internazionale) di guida.** *EHk-koh lah mEE-ah pah-tEHn-teh (een-tehr-nah-tsee-oh-nAH-leh) dee goo-EE-dah*
Do I have to leave a deposit?	**Devo lasciare un acconto (un deposito)?** *dAY-voh lah-shee-AH-reh oon ahk-kOHn-toh (oon day-pOH-see-toh)*
Is there a drop-off charge?	**C'è un supplemento per la consegna dell'auto?** *chEH oon soop-pleh-mEHn-toh pehr lah kohn-seh-ny-ee-ah dayl-lAH-oo-toh*
I want to rent the car here and leave it in Turin.	**Desidero noleggiare l'auto qui e consegnarla a Torino.** *day-sEE-deh-roh noh-lay-jee-AH-reh lAH-oo-toh koo-EE ay kohn-say-ny-ee-AHr-lah ah toh-rEE-noh*
What kind of gasoline does it take?	**Che tipo di carburante usa?** *kay tEE-poh dee kahr-boo-rAHn-teh OO-sah*

PARKING

Parallel parking is prohibited in the centers of many Italian cities and towns, especially where the street is so narrow that parked cars would obstruct traffic. Moreover, the historical center (**centro storico**) of a city or town may sometimes be entirely or partly closed to automobile traffic (as, for example, in Rome and Verona).

In larger cities and towns, automobiles should be left in an attended parking place (**posteggio**) or in a garage (**auto-rimessa**). When an automobile is left in an attended outdoor parking place—often a square (**piazza**) or widening of the street (**largo**)—the driver must pay the attendant (**posteggia-tore**) on leaving the vehicle (sometimes also leaving the keys) and tip him on reclaiming it.

Guarded railroad crossing

Yield

Stop

Right of way

Dangerous intersection
ahead

Gasoline (petrol) ahead

Parking

No vehicles allowed

Dangerous curve

Pedestrian crossing

Oncoming traffic
has right of way

No bicycles allowed

No parking allowed

No entry

No left turn

No U-turn

No passing

Border crossing

Traffic signal ahead

Speed limit

Traffic circle (roundabout) ahead

Minimum speed limit

All traffic turns left

End of no passing zone

One-way street

Detour

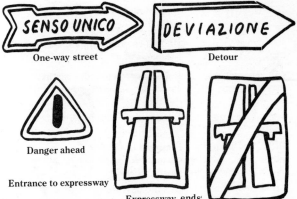

Danger ahead

Entrance to expressway

Expressway ends

ON THE ROAD

Excuse me. Can you tell me _____?	**Mi scusi. Può dirmi _____?** *mee skOO-see poo-OH dEEr-mee*
■ which way is it to _____?	**qual'è la via per _____?** *koo-ah-lEH lah vEE-ah pehr*
■ how I get to _____?	**come potrei raggiungere _____?** *kOH-meh poh-trEH-ee rah-jee-OOn-jeh-reh*
I think we're lost.	**Penso che ci siamo perduti(e).** *pEHn-soh kay chee see-AH-moh pehr-dOO-tee(eh)*
Is this the road (way) to _____?	**È questa la strada (via) per _____?** *EH koo-AYs-tah lah strAH-dah (vEE-ah) pehr*
Where does this road go?	**Dove porta questa strada?** *dOH-veh pOHr-tah koo-AYs-tah strAH-dah*
How far is it from here to the next town?	**Quanto dista da qui la prossima città?** *koo-AHn-toh dEE-stah dah koo-EE lah prOHs-see-mah cheet-tAH*
How far away is _____?	**Quanto dista _____?** *koo-AHn-toh dEE-stah*
Do you have a road map?	**Ha una cartina stradale?** *AH OO-nah kahr-tEE-nah strah-dAH-leh*
Can you show it to me on the map?	**Può indicarmelo sulla cartina?** *poo-OH een-dee-kAHr-meh-loh sOOl-lah kahr-tEE-nah*
Is it a good road?	**È buona la strada?** *EH boo-OH-nah lah strAH-dah*
Is this the shortest way?	**È questa la via più corta?** *EH koo-AY-stah lah vEE-ah pee-OO kOHr-tah*
Are there any detours?	**Ci sono deviazioni?** *chee sOH-noh day-vee-ah-tsee-OH-nee*

Do I go straight?	**Posso proseguire diritto?** *pOHs-soh proh-seh-goo-EE-reh dee-rEEt-toh*
Turn to the right (to the left).	**Giri a destra (a sinistra).** *jEE-ree ah dEH-strah (ah see-nEE-strah)*

AT THE SERVICE STATION

Gasoline is sold by the liter in Europe, and for the traveler accustomed to gallons, it may seem confusing, especially if you want to calculate your mileage per gallon (kilometer per liter). Here are some tips on making those conversions.

LIQUID MEASURES (APPROXIMATE)		
LITERS	U.S. GALLONS	IMPERIAL GALLONS
30	8	$6\frac{1}{2}$
40	$10\frac{1}{2}$	$8\frac{3}{4}$
50	$13\frac{1}{2}$	11
60	$15\frac{3}{4}$	13
70	$18\frac{1}{2}$	$15\frac{1}{2}$
80	21	$17\frac{1}{2}$

DISTANCE MEASURES (APPROXIMATE)	
KILOMETERS	MILES
1	.62
5	3
10	6
20	12
50	31
100	62

Where is there a gas (petrol) station?	**Dov'è una stazione di servizio?** *doh-vEH OO-nah stah-tsee-OH-neh dee sayr-vEE-tsee-oh*
Give me 15 (25) liters.	**Mi dia quindici (venticinque) litri.** *mee dEE-ah koo-EEn-dee-chee (vayn-tee-chEEn-koo-eh) lEE-tree*

Fill'er up with _____.	**Faccia il pieno di _____.** *fAH-chee-ah eel pee-AY-noh dee*
■ diesel	**diesel** *dEE-eh-sehl*
■ regular (standard)	**normale** *nohr-mAH-leh*
■ super (premium)	**super** *sOO-pehr*
Please check _____.	**Per favore mi controlli _____.** *pehr fah-vOH-reh mee kohn-trOHl-lee*
■ the battery	**la batteria** *lah baht-teh-rEE-ah*
■ the carburetor	**il carburatore** *eel kahr-boo-rah-tOH-reh*
■ the oil	**l'olio** *lOH-lee-oh*
■ the spark plugs	**le candele** *leh kahn-dAY-leh*
■ the tires	**i pneumatici (le gomme)** *ee pnay-oo-mAH-tee-chee (leh gOHm-meh)*
■ the tire pressure	**la pressione delle gomme** *lah prehs-see-OH-neh dAYl-leh gOHm-meh*
■ the antifreeze	**l'acqua** *lAH-koo-ah*
Change the oil (please).	**Mi cambi l'olio (per favore).** *mee kAHm-bee lOH-lee-oh (pehr fah-vOH-reh)*
Lubricate the car (please).	**Mi lubrifichi la macchina (per favore).** *mee loo-brEE-fee-key lah mAHk-kee-nah (pehr fah-vOH-reh)*
Charge the battery.	**Mi carichi la batteria.** *mee kAH-ree-key lah baht-teh-rEE-ah*
Change this tire.	**Mi cambi questa ruota.** *mee kAHm-bee koo-AY-stah roo-OH-tah*
Wash the car.	**Mi faccia il lavaggio alla macchina.** *mee fAH-chee-ah eel lah-vAH-jee-oh AHl-lah mAHk-kee-nah*
Where are the rest rooms?	**Dove sono i gabinetti?** *dOH-veh sOH-noh ee gah-bee-nAYt-tee*

ACCIDENTS AND REPAIRS

My car has broken down.	**Mi si è guastata la macchina.** *mee see-EH goo-ah-stAH-tah lah mAHk-kee-nah*
It overl.eats.	**Si surriscalda.** *see soor-ree-skAHl-dah*
It doesn't start.	**Non si avvia.** *nohn see ahv-vEE-ah*

TIRE PRESSURES			
LBS. PER SQ. IN.	KG. PER CM.	LBS. PER SQ. IN.	KG. PER CM.
17	1.2	30	2.1
18	1.3	31	2.2
20	1.4	33	2.3
21	1.5	34	2.4
23	1.6	36	2.5
24	1.7	37	2.6
26	1.8	38	2.7
27	1.9	40	2.8
28	2.0		

I have a flat tire.	**Ho una gomma bucata.** *oh OO-nah gOHm-mah boo-kAH-tah*
The radiator is leaking.	**Il radiatore perde acqua.** *eel rah-dee-ah-tOH-reh pEHr-deh AH-koo-ah*
The battery is dead.	**La batteria è scarica.** *lah baht-teh-rEE-ah EH skAH-ree-kah*
The keys are locked inside the car.	**Le chiavi sono rimaste chiuse in macchina.** *leh key-AH-vee sOH-noh ree-mAH-steh key-OO-seh een mAHk-kee-nah*
Is there a garage near here?	**C'è un'autorimessa qui vicino?** *chEH oon-ah-oo-toh-ree-mEHs-sah koo-EE vee-chEE-noh*
I need a mechanic (tow truck).	**Ho bisogno di un meccanico (carroattrezzi).** *oh bee-sOH-ny-ee-oh dee oon mehk-kAH-nee-koh (kAHr-roh-aht-trAY-tsee)*

Can you give me a push?	**Può darmi una spinta?** *poo-OH dAHr-mee OO-nah spEEn-tah*
I don't have any tools.	**Non ho gli attrezzi.** *nohn-OH ly-ee aht-trAY-tsee*
Can you lend me ____?	**Può prestarmi ____?** *poo-OH preh-stAHr-mee*
■ a flashlight	**una lampadina tascabile** *OO-nah lahm-pah-dEE-nah tah-skAH-bee-leh*
■ a hammer	**un martello** *oon mahr-tEHl-loh*
■ a jack	**un cricco** *oon krEEk-koh*
■ a monkey wrench	**una chiave inglese** *OO-nah key-AH-veh een-glAY-seh*
■ pliers	**delle pinze** *dAYl-leh pEEn-tseh*
■ a screwdriver	**un cacciavite** *oon kah-chee-ah-vEE-teh*
I need ____.	**Ho bisogno di ____.** *oh bee-sOH-ny-ee-oh dee*
■ a bulb	**una lampadina** *OO-nah lahm-pah-dEE-nah*
■ a filter	**un filtro** *oon fEEl-troh*
■ a fuse	**un fusibile** *oon foo-sEE-bee-leh*
Can you fix the car?	**Può ripararmi la macchina?** *poo-OH ree-pah-rAHr-mee lah mAHk-kee-nah*
Can you repair it temporarily?	**Può farmi una riparazione provvisoria?** *poo-OH fAHr-mee OO-nah ree-pah-rah-tsee-OH-neh prohv-vee-sOH-ree-ah*
Do you have the part?	**Ha il pezzo di recambio?** *ah eel pEH-tsoh dee ree-kAHm-bee-oh*
I think there's something wrong with ____.	**Penso che ci sia un guasto ____.** *pEHn-soh kay chee sEE-ah oon goo-AH-stoh*
■ the directional signal	**alla freccia** *AHl-lah frAY-chee-ah*

- the door handle

alla maniglia della porta *AHl-lah mah-nEE-ly-ee-ah dAYl-la pOHr-tah*

- the electrical system

all'impianto elettrico *ahl-leem-pee-AHn-toh eh-lEHt-tree-koh*

- the fan

alla ventola *AHl-lah vEHn-toh-lah*

- the fan belt

alla cinghia del ventilatore *AHl-lah chEEn-ghee-ah dayl vehn-tee-lah-tOH-reh*

- the fuel pump

alla pompa della benzina *AHl-lah pOHm-pah dAHl-lah behn-tsEE-nah*

- the gear shift

al cambio *ahl kAHm-bee-oh*

- the headlights

agli abbaglianti *AH-ly-ee ahb-bah-ly-ee-AHn-tee*

- the horn

al clacson *ahl klAH-ksohn*

- the ignition

all'accensione *ahl-lah-chehn-see-OH-neh*

- the radio

alla radio *AHl-lah rAH-dee-oh*

- the starter

al motorino d'avviamento *ahl moh-toh-rEE-noh dahv-vee-ah-mEHn-toh*

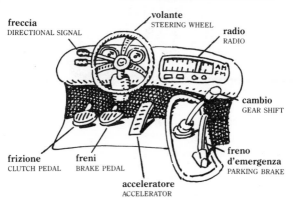

freccia DIRECTIONAL SIGNAL

volante STEERING WHEEL

radio RADIO

cambio GEAR SHIFT

freno d'emergenza PARKING BRAKE

frizione CLUTCH PEDAL

freni BRAKE PEDAL

acceleratore ACCELERATOR

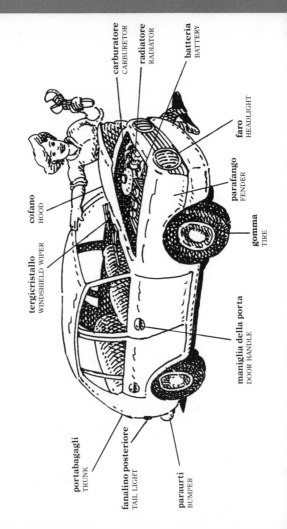

carburatore
CARBURETOR

radiatore
RADIATOR

batteria
BATTERY

faro
HEADLIGHT

parafango
FENDER

gomma
TIRE

cofano
HOOD

tergicristallo
WINDSHIELD WIPER

maniglia della porta
DOOR HANDLE

portabagagli
TRUNK

fanalino posteriore
TAIL LIGHT

paraurti
BUMPER

■ the steering wheel	**al volante** *ahl voh-lAHn-teh*
■ the tail light	**al fanalino posteriore** *ahl fah-nah-lEE-noh poh-steh-ree-OH-reh*
■ the transmission	**alla trasmissione** *AHl-lah trah-smees-see-OH-neh*
■ the water pump	**alla pompa dell'acqua** *AHl-lah pOHm-pah dayl-AH-koo-ah*
■ the windshield (windscreen) wiper	**al tergicristallo** *ahl tehr-jee-kree-stAHl-loh*
Can you take a look at (check out) _____?	**Può dare un'occhiata (una controllata) _____?** *poo-OH dAH-reh oo-noh-key-AH-tah (OO-nah kohn-trohl-lAH-tah)*
■ the brakes	**ai freni** *ah-ee frAY-nee*
■ the bumper	**al paraurti** *ahl pah-rah-OOr-tee*
■ the exhaust system	**al tubo di scappamento** *ahl tOO-boh dee skahp-pah-mEHn-toh*
■ the fender	**al parafango** *ahl pah-rah-fAHn-goh*
■ the gas tank	**al serbatoio (della benzina)** *ahl sehr-bah-tOH-ee-oh dAYl-lah behn-tsEE-nah*
■ the hood	**al cofano** *ahl kOH-fah-noh*
■ the trunk (boot)	**al portabagagli** *ahl pohr-tah-bah-gAH-ly-ee*
What's the matter?	**Che cosa c'è che non va?** *kay kOH-sah chEH kay nohn vAH*
Is it possible to (can you) fix it today?	**È possibile (può) aggiustarlo oggi?** *EH pohs-sEE-bee-leh (poo-OH) ah-jee-oo-stAHr-loh OH-jee*
How long will it take?	**Quanto tempo ci vorrà?** *koo-AHn-toh tEHm-poh chee vohr-rAH*
How much do I owe you?	**Quanto le devo?** *koo-AHn-toh leh dAY-voh*

GENERAL INFORMATION

TELLING TIME

What time is it?	**Che ora è?** *kay OH-rah EH*

When telling time in Italian, *it is* is expressed by è for 1:00, noon, and midnight; **sono** is used for all other numbers.

It's 1:00.	**È l'una.** *eh lOO-nah*
It's 12 o'clock (noon).	**È mezzogiorno.** *eh meh-tsoh-jee-OHr-noh*
It's midnight.	**È mezzanotte.** *eh meh-tsah-nOHt-teh*
It's early (late).	**È presto (tardi).** *eh prEH-stoh (tAHr-dee)*
It's 2:00.	**Sono le due.** *sOH-noh leh dOO-eh*
It's 3:00, etc.	**Sono le tre.** *sOH-noh leh trAY*

The number of minutes after the hour is expressed by adding **e** ("and"), followed by the number of minutes.

It's 4:10.	**Sono le quattro e dieci.** *sOH-noh leh koo-AHt-roh ay dee-EH-chee*
It's 5:20.	**Sono le cinque e venti.** *sOH-noh leh chEEn-koo-eh ay vAYn-tee*

Fifteen minutes after the hour and half past the hour are expressed by placing **e un quarto** and **e mezzo** after the hour.

It's 6:15.	**Sono le sei e un quarto.** *sOH-noh leh sEH-ee ay oon koo-AHr-toh*
It's 7:30.	**Sono le sette e mezzo.** *sOH-noh leh sEHt-teh ay mEH-tsoh*

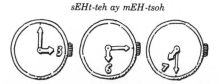

After passing the half-hour point on the clock, time is expressed in Italian by *subtracting* the number of minutes to the *next* hour.

It's 7:40.	**Sono le otto meno venti.** *sOH-noh leh OHt-toh mEH-noh vayn-tee*
It's 8:50.	**Sono le nove meno dieci.** *sOH-noh leh nOH-veh mAY-noh dee-EH-chee*
At what time?	**A che ora?** *ah kay OH-rah*
At 1:00.	**All'una.** *ahl-lOO-nah*
At 2:00 (3:00, etc.).	**Alle due (tre, . . .).** *AHl-leh dOO-eh (trAY)*
A.M. (in the morning)	**del mattino** *dAYl maht-tEE-noh*
P.M. (in the afternoon)	**del pomeriggio** *dAYl poh-meh-rEE-jee-oh*
At night.	**Della notte.** *dAYl-lah nOHt-teh*

Official time is based on the 24-hour clock. You will find train schedules and other such times expressed in terms of a point within a 24-hour sequence.

The train leaves at 15.30.	**Il treno parte alle quindici a tenta.** *eel trEH-noh pAHr-teh ahl-leh koo-EEn-dee-chee ay treHn-tah*

The time is now 21.15.	**Ora sono le ventuno e quindici.** *OH-rah sOH-noh leh vayn-too-noh ay koo-EEn-dee-chee.*	

DAYS OF THE WEEK

What day is it today?	**Che giorno è oggi?**	*kAY jee-OHr-noh EH OH-jee*

The days of the week are *not* capitalized in Italian.

Today is ___.	**Oggi è ___.**	*OH-jee EH*
■ Monday	**lunedí**	*loo-neh-dEE*
■ Tuesday	**martedí**	*mahr-teh-dEE*
■ Wednesday	**mercoledí**	*mehr-koh-leh-dEE*
■ Thursday	**giovedí**	*jee-oh-veh-dEE*
■ Friday	**venerdí**	*veh-nehr-dEE*
■ Saturday	**sabato**	*sAH-bah-toh*
■ Sunday	**domenica**	*doh-mAY-nee-kah*
■ yesterday	**ieri**	*ee-EH-ree*
■ tomorrow	**domani**	*doh-mAH-nee*
■ the day after tomorrow	**dopodomani**	*doh-poh-doh-mAH-nee*
■ last week	**la settimana passata**	*lah seht-tee-mAH-nah pahs-sAH-tah*

■ next week	**la settimana prossima**	*lah seht-tee-mAH-nah prOHs-see-mah*
■ tonight	**questa notte (stanotte)**	*koo-AY-stah nOHt-teh (stah-nOHt-teh)*
■ last night	**la notte passata**	*lah nOHt-teh pahs-sAH-tah*

MONTHS OF THE YEAR

The months of the year are *not* capitalized in Italian.

January	**gennaio**	*jehn-nAH-ee-oh*
February	**febbraio**	*fehb-brAH-ee-oh*
March	**marzo**	*mAHr-tsoh*
April	**aprile**	*ah-prEE-leh*
May	**maggio**	*mAH-jee-oh*
June	**giugno**	*jee-OO-ny-ee-oh*
July	**luglio**	*lOO-ly-ee-oh*
August	**agosto**	*ah-gOH-stoh*
September	**settembre**	*seht-tEHm-breh*
October	**ottobre**	*oht-tOH-breh*
November	**novembre**	*noh-vEHm-breh*
December	**dicembre**	*dee-chEHm-breh*
What's today's date?	**Che data è oggi?**	*kay dAH-ta EH OH-jee*

The first of the month is *il primo* (an ordinal number). All other dates are expressed with *cardinal* numbers.

Today is August *first*.	**Oggi è il primo di agosto.**	*OH-jee EH eel prEE-moh dee ah-gOH-stoh*
■ second	**il due**	*eel dOO-eh*

■ fourth	**il quattro**	*eel koo-AHt-troh*
■ 25th	**il venticinque**	*eel vayn-tee-chEEn-koo-eh*
This month	**Questo mese**	*koo-AY-stoh mAY-seh*
Last month	**Il mese scorso**	*eel mAY-seh skOHr-soh*
Next month	**Il mese prossimo**	*eel mAY-seh prOHs-see-moh*
Last year	**L'anno scorso**	*lAHn-noh skOHr-soh*
Next year	**L'anno prossimo**	*lAHn-noh prOHs-see-moh*
May 1, 1876	**Il primo maggio, mille ottocento settanta sei**	*EEl prEE-moh mAH-jee-oh mEEl-leh oht-toh-chEHn-toh seht-tAHn-tah sEH-ee*
July 4, 1984	**Il quattro luglio, mille novecento ottanta quattro**	*eel koo-AHt-troh lOO-ly-ee-oh mEEl-leh noh-veh-chEHn-toh oht-tAHn-tah koo-AHt-troh*

THE FOUR SEASONS

Spring	**la primavera**	*lah pree-mah-vEH-rah*
Summer	**l'estate**	*leh-stAH-teh*
Fall	**l'autunno**	*lah-oo-tOOn-noh*
Winter	**l'inverno**	*leen-vEHr-noh*

THE WEATHER

How is the weather today?	**Che tempo fa oggi?**	*kay tEHm-poh fAH OH-jee*
It's good (bad) weather.	**Fa bel (cattivo) tempo.**	*fah behl (kaht-tEE-voh) tEHm-poh*

It's hot.	**Fa caldo.** *fah kAHl-doh*
■ cold	**freddo** *frAYd-doh*
■ cool	**fresco** *frAY-skoh*
It's windy.	**Tira vento.** *tEE-rah vEHn-toh*
It's sunny.	**C'è il sole.** *chEH eel sOH-leh*
It's raining.	**Piove.** *pee-OH-veh*
It's snowing.	**Nevica.** *nAY-vee-kah*
It's drizzling.	**Pioviggina.** *pee-oh-vEE-jee-nah*

TEMPERATURE CONVERSIONS

To change Fahrenheit to Centigrade, subtract 32 and multiply by $\frac{5}{9}$.

To change Centigrade to Fahrenheit, multiply by $\frac{9}{5}$ and add 32.

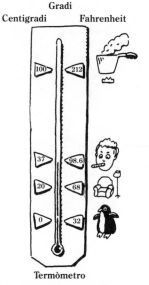

Gradi
Centigradi   Fahrenheit

Termòmetro

CLIMATE

CITIES FROM N TO S IN ORDER OF LATITUDE	COLD MONTHS (JAN.–FEB.)		HOT MONTHS (JULY–AUG.)		AVERAGE ANNUAL TEMPERATURE	
	°C	°F	°C	°F	°C	°F
Bolzano	−1	30	23	72	12	54
Trento	−3	23.5	23	72	11.5	53
Trieste	4	39	23.5	74	13.5	57
Milano	−2	29	24	75	12.5	55
Venezia	2.5	37	24.5	76	13.5	57
Torino	−6	21	23	72	12	55
Bologna	1.5	35	24.5	76	13	56
Genova	7.5	45	24	75	15.5	60
Firenze	5	41	24.5	76	14.5	58
Pisa	6	43	23.5	74	14.5	58
Ancona	5.5	52	25.5	78	15.5	60
Iesi	6	43	26	79	16	61
Siena	4.5	40	23.5	74	13.6	57
Perugia	4	39	23	72	13	56
L'Aquila	1	34	21.5	71	11	52
R O M A	6.5	43	25	77	15.5	60
Sassari	8.5	47	24	75	15	59
Napoli	8	46	25	77	16	61
Foggia	6.5	43	26	79	16	61
Bari	8	46	24	75	16	61
Potenza	3	38	20.5	69	11	52
Lecce	9	48	25	77	16.5	62
Cagliari	9.5	49	25	77	16.5	62
Reggio C.	11.5	53	25	77	18	65
Palermo	10.5	51	25	77	17.5	64
Catania	11	52	26.5	80	18.5	66

NATIONAL HOLIDAYS

Banks, post offices, retail stores, and public offices are closed on national holidays.

January 1	New Year's Day	**Capodanno**
Varies	Easter Monday	**Lunedí dopo Pasqua**
April 25	Liberation Day (1945)	**Festa della Resistenza**
May 1	Labor Day	**Festa del Lavoro**
June 2	Proclamation of Republic	**Festa della Repubblica**
August 15	Assumption Day (known as Ferragosto)	**Assunzione**
November 1	All Saints Day	**Ognissanti**
December 8	Immaculate Conception	**Immacolata Concezione**
December 25	Christmas	**Natale**

LOCAL HOLIDAYS

Stores and offices in some cities are closed on feast days honoring their patron saints.

Bari	December 6	San Nicola
Bologna	October 4	San Petronio
Florence and Genoa	June 24	San Giovanni Battista (John the Baptist)
Milan	December 7	Sant'Ambrogio
Naples	September 19	San Gennaro
Palermo	July 15	Santa Rosalia
Rome	June 29	Santi Pietro e Paolo
Turin	June 24	San Giovanni Battista
Venice	April 25	San Marco

COUNTRIES AND NATIONALITIES

Where are you from?	**Di dov'è lei?**	*dee doh-vEH leh-ee*
I'm from ___.	**Vengo** ___.	*vEHn-goh*
I'm ___.	**Sono** ___.	*sOH-noh*

	COUNTRY	NATIONALITY
Argentina	**dall'Argentina** *dahl-lahr-jehn-tEE-nah*	**argentino(a)** *ahr-jehn-tEE-noh (ah)*
Bolivia	**dalla Bolivia** *dAHl-lah boh-lEE-vee-ah*	**boliviano(a)** *boh-lee-vee-AH-noh(ah)*
Brazil	**dal Brasile** *dahl brah-sEE-leh*	**brasiliano(a)** *brah-see-lee-AH-noh(ah)*
Canada	**dal Canada** *dahl kah-nah-dAH*	**canadese** *kah-nah-dAY-seh*
Chile	**dal Cile** *dahl chEE-leh*	**cileno(a)** *chee-lAY-noh(ah)*
China	**dalla Cina** *dAHl-lah chEE-nah*	**cinese** *chee-nAY-seh*
Colombia	**dalla Colombia** *dAHl-lah koh-lOHm-bee-ah*	**colombiano(a)** *koh-lohm-bee-AH-noh(ah)*
Costa Rica	**da Costa Rica** *dah koh-stah-rEE-kah*	**costaricense** *koh-stah-ree-chEHn-seh*
Cuba	**da Cuba** *dah kOO-bah*	**cubano(a)** *koo-bAH-noh(ah)*
Denmark	**dalla Danimarca** *dAHl-lah dah-nee-mAHr-kah*	**danese** *dah-nAY-seh*
Ecuador	**dall'Ecuador** *dahl-leh-koo-ah-dOHr*	**ecuadoriano(a)** *eh-koo-ah-doh-ree-AH-noh(ah)*

	COUNTRY	NATIONALITY
Egypt	**dall'Egitto** *dahl-lay-jEEt-toh*	**egiziano(a)** *ay-jee-tsee-AH-noh(ah)*
El Salvador	**dal Salvador** *dahl sahl-vah-dOHr*	**salvadoregno(a)** *sahl-vah-doh-rAY-ny-ee-oh(ah)*
England	**dall'Inghilterra** *dahl-lEEn-gheel-tEHr-ah*	**inglese** *een-glAY-seh*
Europe	**dall'Europa** *dahl-leh-oo-rOH-pah*	**europeo(a)** *eh-oo-roh-pEH-oh(ah)*
Finland	**dalla Finlandia** *dahl-lah feen-lAHn-dee-ah*	**finlandese** *feen-lahn-dAY-seh*
France	**dalla Francia** *dahl-lah frAHn-chee-ah*	**francese** *frahn-chAY-seh*
Germany	**dalla Germania** *dahl-la jehr-mAH-nee-ah*	**tedesco(a)** *tay-dAYs-koh(ah)*
Greece	dalla Grecia *dahl-lah grEH-chee-ah*	**greco(a)** *grEH-koh(ah)*
Guatemala	**dalla Guatemala** *dahl-lah goo-ah-teh-mAH-lah*	**guatemalteco(a)** *goo-ah-teh-mahl-tAY-koh(ah)*
Holland	**dall'Olanda** *dahl-loh-lAHn-dah*	**olandese** *oh-lahn-dAY-seh*
Iceland	**dall'Islanda** *dahl-lees-lAHn-dah*	**islandese** *ees-lahn-dAY-seh*
Ireland	**dall'Irlanda** *dahl-leer-lAHn-dah*	**irlandese** *eer-lahn-dAY-seh*
Israel	**da Israel** *dah EE-srah-EHl*	**israeliano(a)** *ee-srah-eh-lee-AH-noh(ah)*

	COUNTRY	NATIONALITY
Italy	**dall'Italia** *dahl-lee-tAH-lee-ah*	**italiano(a)** *ee-tah-lee-AH-noh(ah)*
Japan	**dal Giappone** *dahl jee-ahp-pOH-neh*	**giapponese** *jee-ahp-poh-nAY-seh*
Mexico	**dal Messico** *dahl mEHs-see-koh*	**messicano(a)** *mehs-see-kAH-noh(ah)*
Nicaragua	**dal Nicaragua** *dahl nee-kah-rAH-goo-ah*	**nicaraguese** *nee-kah-rah-goo-AY-seh*
Norway	**dalla Norvegia** *dahl-lah nohr-vEH-jee-ah*	**norvegese** *nohr-veh-jAY-seh*
Panama	**da Panama** *dah pAH-nah-mah*	**panamegno(a)** *pah-nah-mAY-ny-ee-oh(ah)*
Paraguay	**dal Paraguay** *dahl pah-rah-goo-AH-ee*	**paraguaiano(a)** *pah-rah-goo-ah-ee-AH-noh(ah)*
Peru	**dal Perù** *dahl peh-rOO*	**peruviano(a)** *peh-roo-vee-AH-noh(ah)*
Poland	**dalla Polonia** *dahl-lah poh-lOH-nee-ah*	**polacco(a)** *poh-lAH-koh(ah)*
Portugal	**dal Portogallo** *dahl pohr-toh-gAHl-loh*	**portoghese** *pohr-toh-ghAY-seh*
Puerto Rico	**dal Porto Rico** *dahl pOHr-toh rEE-koh*	**portoricano(a)** *pohr-toh-ree-kAH-noh(ah)*
Russia	**dalla Russia** *dahl-lah rOOs-see-ah*	**russo(a)** *rOOs-soh(ah)*

	COUNTRY	NATIONALITY
Spain	**dalla Spagna** *dahl-lah spAH-ny-ee-ah*	**spagnolo(a)** *spah-ny-ee-OH-loh(ah)*
Sweden	**dalla Svezia** *dahl-lah svEH-tsee-ah*	**svedese** *svay-dAY-seh*
Switzer-land	**dalla Svizzera** *dahl-lah svEE-tseh-rah*	**svizzero(a)** *svEE-tseh-roh(ah)*
Turkey	**dalla Turchia** *dahl-lah toor-kEE-ah*	**turco(a)** *tOOr-koh(ah)*
United States	**dagli Stati Uniti** *dAH-ly-ee stAH-tee oo-nEE-tee*	**americano(a)** *ah-meh-ree-kAH-noh(ah)*
Uruguay	**dall'Uruguay** *dahl-loo-roo-goo-AH-ee*	**uruguaiano(a)** *oo-roo-goo-ah-ee-AH-noh(ah)*
Venezuela	**dalla Venezuela** *dahl-lah veh-neh-tsoo-EH-lah*	**venezuelano(a)** *veh-neh-tsoo-EH-lAH-noh(ah)*

IMPORTANT SIGNS

Acqua (non)potabile	(Not) potable water
Alt	Stop
Aperto	Open
Ascensore	Elevator (Lift)
Attenzione	Caution, watch out
Avanti	Enter (come in, go, walk [at the lights])

Caldo or "C"	Hot
Cassa	Cashier
Chiuso	Closed
Divieto di sosta	No parking
Divieto di transito	No entrance, keep out
Freddo or "F"	Cold
Gabinetti (WC)	Toilets
Ingresso	Entrance
Libero	Vacant
Non calpestare le aiuole	Keep off the grass
Non ostruire l'ingresso	Don't block entrance
Non toccare	Hands off, don't touch
Occupato	Occupied
Pericolo	Danger
Riservato	Reserved
Si affitta (si loca)	For rent
Si vende	For sale
Signora	Women's room
Signore	Men's room
Spingere	Push
Strada privata	Private road
Tirare	Pull
Uscita	Exit
Vietato fumare	No smoking
Vietato nuotare	No bathing
Vietato sputare	No spitting

COMMON ABBREVIATIONS

AA	Azienda Autonoma di Soggiorno e Turismo	Local Tourist Information Center
ACI	Automobile Club d'Italia	Automobile Club of Italy
Cap.	Capoluogo	Province
C.P.	Casella Postale	Post Office Box
CAP	Codice Postale	Zip Code
ENIT	Ente Nazionale per il Turismo	Italian State Tourist Office
EPT	Ente Provinciale per il Turismo	Provincial Tourist Information Center
F.lli	Brothers	Inc.
FS	Ferrovie dello Stato	Italian State Railways
IVA	Imposte sul Valore Aggiunto	Italian State Tax
L.	Lire	Italian currency
N., n°	Numero	Number
Pro Loco	Ente Locale per il Turismo	Local Tourist Information Office
Prov.	Provincia	Province
P.za	Piazza	(City) Square
S.	San, Santo(a)	Saint
S.A.	Società Anonima	Inc.
Sig.	Signor	Mr.
Sig.na	Signorina	Miss
Sig.ra	Signora	Mrs.
TCI	Touring Club Italiano	Italian Touring Club
v.	Via	Street
v.le	Viale	Boulevard

CENTIMETERS/INCHES

It is usually unnecessary to make exact conversions from your customary inches to the metric system used in Italy, but to give you an approximate idea of how they compare, we give you the following guide.

To convert **centimetri** into inches, multiply by .39.

To convert inches into **centimetri,** multiply by 2.54.

Centimetri

Pollici

METERS/FEET

How tall are you in meters? See for yourself.

FEET/INCHES	METERS/CENTIMETERS
5	1.52
5 1	1.545
5 2	1.57
5 3	1.595
5 4	1.62
5 5	1.645
5 6	1.68
5 7	1.705
5 8	1.73
5 9	1.755
5 10	1.78
5 11	1.805
6	1.83
6 1	1.855

1 meter (metro) = 39.37 inches
= 3.28 feet
= 1.09 yards

1 foot = 0.3 meters
1 yard = 0.9 meters

WHEN YOU WEIGH YOURSELF

1 kilogram **(chilo)** = 2.2 pounds
1 pound   = 0.45 kilogram

KILOGRAMS	POUNDS
40	88
45	99
50	110
55	121
60	132
65	143
70	154
75	165
80	176
85	187
90	198
95	209
100	220

LIQUID MEASUREMENTS

1 liter = 1.06 quarts
4 liters = 1.06 gallons

For quick approximate conversion, multiply the number of gallons by 4 to get liters **(litri).** Divide the number of liters by 4 to get gallons.

NOTE: You will find other conversion charts on pages 117, 118, 122, 165, 167, 177, 178 .

A MINI-DICTIONARY FOR BUSINESS TRAVELERS

For other commercial terms, see Money and Banking, pages 21–25 and Abbreviations, p. 185.

amount	**ammontare, somma, totale** *ahm-mohn-tAH-reh, sOHm-mah, toh-tAH-leh*

appraise (to)	**stimare, valutare** *stee-mAH-reh, vah-loo-tAH-reh*
authorize (to)	**autorizzare** *ah-oo-toh-ree-tsAH-reh*
■ authorized edition	**edizione autorizzata** *ay-dee-tsee-OH-neh ah-oo-toh-ree-tsAH-tah*
bill	**fattura** *faht-tOO-rah*
■ bill of exchange	**cambiale** *kahm-bee-AH-leh*
■ bill of lading	**polizza di carico** *poh-lEE-tsah dee kAH-ree-koh*
■ bill of sale	**atto di vendita** *AHt-toh dee vAYn-dee-tah*
business operations	**attività commerciali** *aht-tee-vee-tAH kohm-mehr-chee-AH-lee*
cash	**denaro, contanti** *deh-nAH-roh, kohn-tAHn-tee*
■ to buy, sell, for cash	**comprare, vendere in contanti** *kohm-prAH-reh, vAYn-deh-reh een kohn-tAHn-tee*
cash a check (to)	**riscuotere un assegno** *ree-skoo-OH-teh-reh oon ahs-sAY-ny-oh*
certified check	**assegno vistato, autenticato** *ahs-sAY-ny-oh vees-tAH-toh, ah-oo-tehn-tee-kAH-toh*
Chamber of Commerce	**Camera di Commercio** *kAH-meh-rah dee kohm-mEHr-chee-oh*
compensation for damage	**compenso (risarcimento) dei danni** *kohm-pEHn-soh (ree-sahr-chee-mEHn-toh) dAY-ee dAHn-nee*
competition	**concorrenza** *kohn-kohr-rEHn-tsah*
competitive price	**prezzo di concorrenza** *prEH-tsoh dee kohn-kohr-rEHn-tsah*
contract	**contratto** *kohn-trAHt-toh*

contractual obligation	**obbligazione (obbligo) contrattuale** *ohb-blee-gah-tsee-OH-neh (OHb-blee-goh)*
controlling interest	**controllo delle azioni** *kohn-trOHl-loh dAYl-leh ah-tsee-OH-nee*
co-owner	**comproprietario(a)** *kohm-proh-pree-eh-tAH-ree-oh(ah)*
co-partner	**consocio(a)** *kohn-sOH-chee-oh(ah)*
down payment	**acconto, anticipo, caparra** *ahk-kOHn-toh, ahn-tEE-chee-poh, kah-pAHr-rah*
due	**dovuto** *doh-vOO-toh*
enterprise	**impresa, iniziativa** *eem-prAY-sah, ee-nee-tsee-ah-tEE-vah*
expedite delivery (to)	**sollecitare la consegna** *sohl-lay-chee-tAH-reh lah kohn-sAY-ny-ah*
expenses	**spese, indennità** *spAY-seh, een-dehn-nee-tAH*
goods	**merci** *mEHr-chee*
infringement of patent	**contraffazione di brevetto** *kohn-trahf-fah-tsee-OH-neh dee breh-vAYt-toh*
■ rights	**usurpazione di diritti** *oo-soor-pah-tsee-OH-neh dee dee-rEEt-tee*
insurance against all risks	**assicurazione comprendente tutti i rischi** *ahs-see-koo-rah-tsee-OH-neh kohm-prehn-dEHn-teh tOOt-tee ee rEEs-key*
international law	**legge internazionale** *lAY-jeh een-tehr-nah-tsee-oh-nAH-leh*
lawful possessor	**legittimo proprietario** *leh-jEEt-tee-moh proh-pree-eh-tAH-ree-oh*
lawsuit	**causa, processo** *kAH-sah, proh-chEHs-soh*

lawyer | **avvocato (avvocatessa)** *ahv-voh-kAH-toh (ahv-voh-kah-tAYs-sah)*

mail-order business | **ordinazione (di merci) per corrispondenza** *ohr-dee-nah-tsee-OH-neh dee mEHr-chee pehr kohr-rees-pohn-dEHn-tsah*

market value | **valore di mercato** *vah-lOH-reh dee mehr-kAH-toh*

manager | **direttore (direttrice)** *dee-reht-tOH-reh (dee-reht-trEE-cheh)*

payment | **pagamento** *pah-gah-mEHn-toh*

■ part payment | **pagamento parziale** *pah-gah-mEHn-toh pahr-tsee-AH-leh*

past due | **arretrato** *ahr-reh-trAH-toh*

post office box | **casella postale** *kah-sEHl-lah pohs-tAH-leh*

property | **proprietà** *proh-pree-eh-tAH*

purchasing agent | **agente compratore** *ah-jEHn-teh kohm-prah-tOH-reh*

put (to) on the American market | **mettere in vendita sul mercato americano** *mAYt-teh-reh een vAYn-dee-tah sool mehr-kAH-toh ah-meh-ree-kAH-noh*

sale | **vendita, liquidazione, saldi** *vAYn-dee-tah, lee-koo-ee-dah-tsee-OH-neh, sAHl-dee*

sell (to) | **vendere** *vAYn-deh-reh*

send (to) | **mandare, inviare, spedire** *mahn-dAH-reh, een-vee-AH-reh, speh-dEE-reh*

■ send back | **rinviare, mandare indietro** *reen-vee-AH-reh, mahn-dAH-reh een-dee-AY-troh*

■ send C.O.D.	**spedire contro assegno** *speh-dEE-reh kOHn-troh ahs-sEH-ny-oh*
shipment	**spedizione (di merci), carico** *speh-dee-tsee-OH-neh (dee mEHr-chee), kAH-ree-koh*
tax	**tassa, imposta** *tAHs-sah, eem-pOHs-tah*
■ tax-exempt	**esente da tasse** *ay-sEHn-teh dah tAHs-seh*
■ sales tax	**imposta sulle vendite** *eem-pOHs-tah sOOl-leh vAYn-dee-teh*
■ value added tax	**imposta sui valori aggiunti** *eem-pOHs-tah sOO-ee vah-lOH-ree ah-jee-OOn-tee*
trade (n.)	**commercio** *kohm-mEHr-chee-oh*
■ trade (to)	**commerciare** *kohm-mehr-chee-AH-reh*
transact business (to)	**trattare un affare** *traht-tAH-reh oon ahf-fAH-reh*
transfer (to)	**trasferire** *trahs-feh-rEE-reh*
transportation charges	**spese di trasporto** *spAY-seh dee trahs-pOHr-toh*
via	**per, via** *pEHr, vEE-ah*
yield a profit (to)	**rendere interesse, fruttare un guadagno** *rEHn-deh-reh een-teh-rEHs-seh, froot-tAH-reh oon goo-ah-dAH-ny-oh*

QUICK GRAMMAR GUIDE

Your facility with Italian will be greatly enhanced if you know a little of its grammar. Here are a few simple rules governing the use of the various parts of speech.

NOUNS

In contrast with English, in which inanimate objects are considered neuter, Italian nouns are designated either masculine or feminine. In the singular, you'll find that feminine nouns often end in *a* while masculine nouns often end in *o*. Other nouns, which can be either masculine or feminine, often end in *e*. There are still others, however, which you simply have to learn as either masculine or feminine because their endings give you no clue as to their gender. With this in mind, you can follow these simple rules to make a singular noun plural.

1. When a feminine noun ends in *a*, make it plural by changing the *a* to *e*.
2. When a masculine noun ends in *o*, make it plural by changing the *o* to *i*.
3. For masculine or feminine nouns ending in *e*, make them plural by changing the *e* to *i*.
4. For masculine or feminine nouns with endings different from those above, keep the same ending for both singular and plural forms.

GENDER	SINGULAR	PLURAL
feminine	cas*a* (house)	cas*e* (houses)
masculine	libr*o* (book)	libr*i* (books)
masculine or feminine	pied*e* (foot) vest*e* (dress)	pied*i* (feet) vest*i* (dresses)
masculine or feminine	bar (bar) metropoli (city)	bar (bars) metropoli (cities)

Some nouns end in *co* or *go;* these change to *chi* and *ghi* in the plural. Other nouns ending in *ca* or *ga* change to *che* and *ghe* in the plural.

banco (desk)   **banchi** (desks)
fungo (mushroom)   **funghi** (mushrooms)
barca (boat)   **barche** (boats)
alga (alga)   **alghe** (algae)

ARTICLES

Articles (*the, a, an*) agree in gender (masculine or feminine) and number (singular or plural) with the nouns they modify. Separate rules apply to the definite and indefinite articles.

The **definite article** (*the*) is different in both the singular and plural forms, depending on the noun it is being paired with. Select the proper word for *the*, depending on the sounds that are part of the noun.

il (plural, **i**)	Use before consonants (except *s* followed by another consonant, *a, gn, ps,* and *x*): **il libro** (the book), **i libri** (the books); **il soldato** (the soldier), **i soldati** (the soldiers).
lo (**gli**)	Use before *z, gn, ps, x,* and *s* followed by another consonant: **lo zio** (the uncle), **gli zii** (the uncles); **lo stadio** (the stadium), **gli stadi** (the stadiums).
lo (**gli**)	Drops the *o* and becomes *l'* before vowels in the singular: **l'amico** (the friend), **gli amici** (the friends); **l'elefante** (the elephant), **gli elefanti** (the elephants).
la (**le**)	Use before consonants: **la casa** (the house), **le case** (the houses); **la ragazza** (the girl), **le ragazze** (the girls).
la (**le**)	Drops the *a* and becomes *l'* before vowels in the singular: **l'ora** (the hour), **le ore** (the hours); **l'edizione** (the edition), **le edizioni** (the editions).

The **indefinite articles** (*a, an*) also follow certain rules. Use *un* or *uno* for masculine forms and *una* and *un'* for feminine ones. Use *qualche* to indicate the plural forms (*some, any*).

un	Use before vowels and consonants (except *s* followed by another consonant, *z*, *gn*, *ps*, and *x*): **un amico** (a friend), **qualche amico** (some friends); **un dollaro** (a dollar), **qualche dollaro** (some dollars).
uno	Use before *s* followed by another consonant, *z*, *gn*, *ps*, and *x*: **uno specchio** (a mirror), **qualche specchio** (some mirrors); **uno zaino** (a knapsack), **qualche zaino** (some knapsacks).
una	Use before consonants: **una casa** (a house), **qualche casa** (some houses); **una chiesa** (a church), **qualche chiesa** (some churches).
un'	Use before vowel(s): **un'idea** (an idea), **qualche idea** (some ideas); **un'amica** (a girlfriend), **qualche amica** (some girlfriends).

Some and *any* are often also expressed by *alcuni(e)* + the plural of the noun.

un piatto (a dish)	**alcuni piatti** (some dishes)
una ragazza (a girl)	**alcune ragazze** (some girls)

Some and *any* can also be indicated by using *di* + the definite article in a contracted form.

una macchina (a car)	**delle macchine** (some cars)

To determine which contracted form is appropriate, use the following guide:

	MASCULINE			FEMININE	
singular	di+il	di+lo	di+l'	di+la	di+l'
	del	dello	dell'	della	dell'
plural	di+i	di+gli		di+le	
	dei	degli		delle	

del (dei)	Use before consonants (except *x* followed by another consonant, *z*, *gn*, *ps*, and *x*): **del vino** (some wine), **dei vini** (some wines).
dello (degli)	Use before *s*, followed by another consonant, *z*, *gn*, *ps*, and *x*: **dello zucchero** (some sugar), **degli zuccheri** (some sugars).
dello (degli)	Drops the *o* and becomes *dell'* before vowels in the singular: **dell'olio** (some oil), **degli olii** (some oils).
della (delle)	Use before consonants: **della birra** (some beer), **delle birre** (some beers).
della (delle)	Use before vowels: **dell'aranciata** (some orangeade), **delle aranciate** (some orangeades).

ADJECTIVES

Adjectives agree in gender and in number with the nouns they modify. Descriptive adjectives are generally placed after the noun.

la casa bianca(the white house)
il ragazzo alto(the tall boy)
le signore belle(the pretty women)
i libri costosi(the expensive books)

The plurals of adjectives are formed following the same rules as for nouns.

1. For adjectives ending in *a*, change *a* to *e*.
2. For adjectives ending in *o*, change *o* to *i*.
3. For adjectives ending in *e*, change *e* to *i*.

The following show the adjectives in their singular and plural forms.

la carta azzurra (the blue paper)	**le carte azzurre** (the blue papers)

il vestito rosso (the red dress)

i vestiti rossi (the red dresses)

l'abito verde (the green suit)

gli abiti verdi (the green suits)

Articles, possessives, and limiting adjectives agree in number and gender with the nouns they modify. Usually they are placed before the noun.

molte cose (many things)

pochi americani (few Americans)

In English, the possessive adjective agrees with the person who possesses the object, but in Italian, the possessive adjective agrees in gender and number with the object possessed. The possessive adjective is usually placed alongside the article.

il mio libro (my book)

i miei libri (my books)

la mia amica (my girlfriend)

le mie amiche (my girlfriends)

Use the following table to determine the correct form of the possessive, both for masculine and feminine forms and also for singular and plural forms.

POSSESSIVE	MASCULINE	FEMININE
my	il mio (i miei)	la mia (le mie)
your	il tuo (i tuoi)	la tua (le tue)
his/her/your (formal)	il suo (i suoi)	la sua (le sue)
our	il nostro (i nostri)	la nostra (le nostre)
your	il vostro (i vostri)	la vostra (le vostre)
their/your (formal)	il loro (i loro)	la loro (le loro)

There are a few exceptions to the above rules.

mio padre (my father)

mio zio (my uncle)

mia madre (my mother)

mia zia (my aunt)

mio fratello (my brother)   **mio nonno** (my grandfather)
mia sorella (my sister)   **mia nonna** (my grandmother)

Demonstrative adjectives (*this, these*) are placed in front of the nouns they modify. They agree in number and gender with the nouns that they modify. The adjective *this* has the following forms: **questo** (masculine singular), **questa** (feminine singular), **questi** (masculine plural), **queste** (feminine plural).

questo libro (this book)   **questi libri** (these books)

questa casa (this house)   **queste case** (these houses)

The demonstrative adjectives *that* and *those* are handled differently. **Quello** (that) has the following forms, depending on the article of the nouns being modified.

	MASCULINE			FEMININE	
singular	que+il	que+lo	que+l'	que+la	que+l'
	quel	quello	quell'	quella	quell'
plural	que+i	que+gli		que+le	
	quei	quegli		quelle	

For example, the singular forms.

il ragazzo (the boy)   **quel ragazzo** (that boy)
lo zio (the uncle)   **quello zio** (that uncle)
l'albero (the tree)   **quell'albero** (that tree)
l'oca (the goose)   **quell'oca** (that goose)
la casa (the house)   **quella casa** (that house)

Now the plural forms.

i ragazzi (the boys)   **quei ragazzi** (those boys)
gli zii (the uncles)   **quegli zii** (those uncles)
gli alberi (the trees)   **quegli alberi** (those trees)
le oche (the geese)   **quelle oche** (those geese)
le case (the houses)   **quelle case** (those houses)

PRONOUNS

Subject pronouns (*I, you, he, she,* etc.) have both singular and plural forms.

io (I)   **noi** (we)

tu (you, familiar)   **voi** (you, familiar)

Lei (you, polite)   **Loro** (you, polite)

egli, lui (he)   **loro, essi** (they, masculine)

ella, lei (she)   **loro, esse** (they, feminine)

Direct object pronouns (*me, you, him, it, us, them*) are used as direct objects of verbs. They have both singular and plural forms, and their placement before or after the verb varies. Italians usually place the direct object pronouns before the verb except for emphasis.

SINGULAR		PLURAL	
(me)	(You love me)	(us)	(You love us)
after verb	Tu ami *me*	after verb	Tu ami *noi*
before verb	Tu *mi* ami	before verb	Tu *ci* ami
(you)	(I love you)	(you)	(I love you)
after verb	Io amo *te*	after verb	Io amo *voi*
before verb	Io *ti* amo	before verb	Io *vi* amo
(him/it)	(I love him)	(them, masc./ you, polite)	(I love them)
after verb	Io amo *lui*	after verb	Io amo *loro*
before verb	Io *lo* amo	before verb	Io *li* amo

SINGULAR		PLURAL	
(her/it/you, polite)	(I love her/it/ you)	(them, fem./ you, polite)	(I love them)
after verb	Io amo lei/essa	after verb	Io amo *loro*
before verb	Io *la* amo	before verb	Io *le* amo

Indirect object pronouns are pronouns serving as indirect objects. They take the following forms, depending upon whether they are placed before or after the verb.

SINGULAR		PLURAL	
(to me)	(You give me a kiss)	(to us)	(You give us a kiss)
after verb	Tu dai un bacio *a me*	after verb	Tu dai un bacio *a noi*
before verb	Tu *mi* dai un bacio	before verb	Tu *ci* dai un bacio
(to you)	(I give you a kiss)	(to you)	(I give you a kiss)
after verb	Io do un baci *a te*	after verb	Io do un bacio *a voi.*
before verb	Io *ti* do un bacio	before verb	Io *vi* do un bacio
(to him)	(I give him a kiss)	(to them/ you, polite)	(I give them/ you a kiss)
after verb	Io do un bacio *a lui*	after verb	Io do un bacio *a loro*
before verb	Io *gli* do un bacio	after verb	Io do *loro* un bacio
(to her/you, polite)	(I give her/ it a kiss)	(to them/ you, polite)	(I give them/ you a kiss)
after verb	Io do un bacio *a lei*	after verb	Io do un bacio *a loro*
before verb	Io *le* do un bacio	before verb	Io do *loro* un bacio

VERBS

In this phrase book, we limit the use of verbs to the present tense, since this is the most likely one for you to use as a tourist. Most Italian verbs in the infinitive end in either *are, ere,* or *ire.*

parlare (to speak)
vedere (to see)
partire (to leave)

In order to conjugate a verb, this infinitive ending must be removed and replaced by the appropriate ending found in the following table.

PARLARE (TO SPEAK)	
io parlo (I speak)	noi parliamo (we speak)
tu parli (you speak, familiar)	voi parlate (you speak, familiar)
Lei parla (you speak, polite)	Loro parlano (you speak, polite)
egli parla (he speaks) lui	loro parlano (they speak, essi masculine)
ella parla (she speaks) lei	loro parlano (they speak, esse masculine)

Two other examples of verbs with regular conjugations are:

VEDERE (TO SEE)	
vedo (I see)	vediamo (we see)
vedi (you see)	vedete (you see)
vede (he, she, you see(s))	vedono (they, you see)

PARTIRE (TO LEAVE)	
parto (I leave)	partiamo (we leave)
parti (you leave)	partite (you leave)
parte (he, she, you leave(s)	partono (they, you leave)

Some *ire* verbs add *sc* to the stem before the endings in the *io, tu, egli, essi* forms. For example, with the verb **finire** (to finish):

io finisco	**egli finisce**
tu finisci	**essi finiscono**

Not all verbs are regular. Here are some of the common irregular ones, with their conjugations.

ANDARE (TO GO)	
vado (I go)	andiamo (we go)
vai (you go)	andate (you go)
va (he, she, you go)	vanno (they you go)

DARE (TO GIVE)	
do (I give)	diamo (we give)
dai (you give)	date (you give)
da (he, she, you give)	danno (they, you give)

FARE (TO DO/TO MAKE)	
faccio (I do/make)	facciamo (we do/make)
fai (you do/make)	fate (you do/make)
fa (he, she, you do/make)	fanno (they, you do/make)

BERE (TO DRINK)	
bevo (I drink)	beviamo (we drink)
bevi (you drink)	bevete (you drink)
beve (he, she, you drink(s))	bevono (they, you drink)

DOVERE (TO HAVE TO)	
devo (I have to)	dobbiamo (we have to)
devi (you have to)	dovete (you have to)
deve (he, she, you has (ve) to)	devono (they, you have to)

POTERE (TO BE ABLE TO/CAN)

posso (I am able to) — possiamo (we are able to)
puoi (you are able to) — potete (you are able to)
può (he, she — possono (they, you are able to)

RIMANERE (TO STAY)

rimango (I stay) — rimaniamo (we stay)
rimani (you stay) — rimanete (you stay)
rimane (he, she, you — rimangano (they, you stay)
stay(s))

SAPERE (TO KNOW)

so (I know) — sappiamo (we know)
sai (you know) — sapete (you know)
sa (he, she, you know(s)) — sanno (they, you know)

VOLERE (TO WANT)

voglio (I want) — vogliamo (we want)
vuoi (you want) — volete (you want)
vuole (he, she, you want(s)) — vogliono (they, you want)

USCIRE (TO GO OUT)

esco (I go out) — usciamo (we go out)
esci (you go out) — uscite (you go out)
esce (he, she, you go(es) — escono (they, you go out)
out)

VENIRE (TO COME)

vengo (I come) — veniamo (we come)
vieni (you come) — venite (you come)
viene (he, she, you come(s)) — vengono (they, you come)

CONOSCERE (TO KNOW A PERSON)

conosco (I know) — conosciamo (we know)
conosci (you know) — conoscete (you know)
conosce (he, she, you — conoscono (they, you know)
know(s))

The verb **piacere** means to like something, but how it is conjugated depends on whether you like one thing or several. This is best shown as follows.

mi piace (I like—one thing) **mi piacciono** (I like—several things)

Thus, the forms of **piacere** are as follows:

	ONE THING	SEVERAL THINGS
I	mi piace	mi piacciono
you (familiar)	ti piace	ti piacciono
he she you (formal)	gli le piace	gli le piacciono
we	ci piace	ci piacciono
you (familiar)	vi piace	vi piace
they you (formal)	piace a loro	piacciono a loro

Used in sentences, they would be as follows:

Le piace Venezia? (Do you like Venice?)

Le piace ballare? (Do you like dancing?)

Le piace Roma? (Do you like Rome?)

Le piacciono i monumenti? (Do you like the monuments?)

Note the following constructions, which vary depending on the meaning intended.

Ti piaccio? (Am I pleasing to you?—familiar form of singular you)

Le piaccio? (Am I pleasing to you?—polite form of singular you)

Vi piaccio? (Am I pleasing to you?—familiar form of plural you)

Piaccio a loro? (Am I pleasing to them?—plural form of third person, polite form of plural you)

Or, in the form of a statement.

Mi piaci. (You are pleasing to me, I like you. —familiar form of singular you)

Mi piace. (You are pleasing to me, I like her/him. —singular form of third person, polite form of singular you)

Mi piacete. (You are pleasing to me, I like you. —familar form of plural you)

Mi piacciono. (They are pleasing to me. I like them. —plural form of third person, polite form of plural you)

As in English, many verbs are used in conjunction with auxiliary verbs. Three of the most common are given below, with their conjugations.

AVERE (TO HAVE)	
ho (I have)	abbiamo (we have)
hai (you have)	avete (you have)
ha (he, she, you has(ve)	hanno (they, you have)
ESSERE (TO BE)	
sono (I am)	siamo (we are)
sei (you are)	siete (you are)
è (he, she, you is(are)	sono (they, you are)
STARE (TO BE)	
sto (I am)	stiamo (we are)
stai (you are)	state (you are)
sta (he, she, you is(are)	stanno (they, you are)

Stare is used when expressing an action in progress.

Che cosa sta facendo? (What are you doing?)

Io sto camminando (I am walking.)

Essere is used mostly with intransitive verbs denoting motion such as to go. (The past participle with which it is linked agrees with its subject in gender and number.)

Sono andato a fare la spesa. (I have gone shopping.)

Maria è appena arrivata. (Mary has just arrived.)

Avere is used with verbs that may take an object, such as to buy.

> **Che cosa ha comprato?** (What have you bought?)
>
> **Ho comprato un regalo.** (I have bought a gift.)

To form the past participle of a verb, use the following patterns for all regular verbs.

> **parlare: parl + ato**   **ho parlato** (I have spo-
> (spoken)   ken)
>
> **vedere: ved + uto**   **ha veduto** (he, she, you
> (seen)   have seen)
>
> **partire: part + ito**   **sono partiti** (they, you
> (left)   have left)

There are several idiomatic uses of the verb avere (to have), in which the verb is being used to express the English *to be:*

> **aver freddo** (to be cold)
>
> **aver sete** (to be thirsty)
>
> **aver fame** (to be hungry)
>
> **aver sonno** (to be sleepy)
>
> **aver caldo** (to be hot)
>
> **aver fretta** (to be in a hurry)
>
> **aver paura** (to be afraid)
>
> **aver ragione** (to be right)
>
> **aver torto** (to be wrong)

Used in context, we have some examples of **avere.**

> **Non ho caldo, ho freddo.** (I'm not hot, I'm cold.)
>
> **Ha fame?** (Are you hungry?)
>
> **No, ho sete.** (No, I am thirsty.)
>
> **Abbiamo fretta.** (We're in a hurry.)
>
> **Egli ha venti anni.** (He's 20 years old.)*
>
> **Ho ragione.** (I'm right.)

*NOTE: In Italian, to express one's age, you use the verb **avere:** to have _____ years.

PREPOSITIONS

The following most common Italian prepositions are listed in the alphabetical order of their English equivalents.

after	**dopo** *(dOH-poh)*
before (in time)	**prima** *(prEE-mah)*
before, in front of	**davanti** *(dah-vAHn-tee)*
behind, in back of	**dietro** *(dee-AY-troh)*
down	**giù** *(jee-oo)*
during	**durante** *(doo-rAHn-tay)*
for, through	**per** *(pehr)*
from	**da** *(dah)*
in	**in** *(een)*
in, into	**a** *(ah)*
inside	**dentro** *(dEHn-troh)*
outside	**fuori** *(foo-OH-ree)*
toward	**verso** *(vEHr-soh)*
through, across	**attraverso** *(aht-trah-vEHr-soh)*
until	**fino a** *(fEE-noh ah)*
up	**su** *(soo)*
without	**senza** *(sEHn-tsah)*

TO FORM NEGATIVE EXPRESSIONS

The most common negative word in Italian is *non*. It always precedes the verb.

Io non ho soldi. (I have no money; I don't have any money.)

Other negative words are:

nessuno (no one)   **Nessuno viene.** (No one is coming.)

niente (nothing)   **Non vedo niente.** (I don't see anything; I see nothing.)

mai (never)   **Mai mangiamo in casa.** (We never eat at home.)

neppure (neither)   **Lei non ha soldi e neppure io.** (She has no money and neither do I.)

Any one of the negative words except *non* may be used either before or after the verb. If one is used after the verb, *non* is also used before the verb (forming double negative).

Nessuno parla.
Non parla nessuno.   (Nobody is speaking.)

Mai vado da solo(a).
Non vado mai da solo(a).   (I never go alone.)

TO FORM QUESTIONS

Some common interrogative words in Italian are the following:

Dove? (Where?)   **Per che cosa?** (What for?)

Come? (How?)   **Perché?** (Why?)

Quale? (Which?)   **Che (cosa)?** (What?)

Quanto? (How much?)   **Chi?** (Who?)

Quanti? (How many?)

To form a question in Italian, place the subject *after* the verb or raise your intonation at the end of the sentence.

Lei parla italiano. (You speak Italian.)
Parla lei italiano? (Do you speak Italian?)
Maria ha il biglietto. (Mary has the ticket.)
Ha Maria il biglietto? (Does Mary have the ticket?)
Voi andate al cinema. (You are going to the movies.)
Andate voi al cinema? (Are you going to the movies?)

ENGLISH-ITALIAN DICTIONARY

A

a, an un, uno, una *oon, OO-noh, OO-nah*

about circa *chEEr-kah*

above sopra *sOH-prah*

abscess ascesso *ash-EHs-soh*

to accept accettare *ah-cheht-tAH-reh*

ace asso *AHs-soh*

across attraverso *aht-trah-vEHr-soh*

address indirizzo *een-dee-rEE-tsoh*

adhesive tape nastro adesivo *nAHs-troh ah-day-sEE-voh*

advance anticipo *ahn-tEE-chee-poh*

adventure avventura *ahv-vehn-tOO-rah*

to adore adorare *ah-doh-rAH-reh*

after dietro *dee-AY-troh*; dopo *dOH-poh*

afternoon pomeriggio *poh-may-rEE-jee-oh*

again ancora *ahn-kOH-rah*

agency agenzia *ah-jehn-tsEE-ah*

air aria *AH-ree-ah*;
 air-conditioned aria condizionata *AH-ree-ah kohn-dee-tsee-oh-nAH-tah*; **air mail** posta aerea *pOHs-tah ah-EH-reh-ah*

airplane aereo *ah-EH-reh-oh*

airport aeroporto *ah-eh-roh-pOHr-toh*

aisle corridoio *kohr-ree dOH-ee-oh*

album album *AHl-boom*

alcohol alcool *AHl-koh-ohl*

all tutto *tOOt-toh*

allergic allergico *ahl-lEHr-jee-koh*

to allow permettere *pehr-mAYt-teh-reh*

almond mandorla *mAHn-dohr-lah*

almost quasi *kwAH-zee*

alone solo *sOH-loh*

also anche *AHn-keh*

always sempre *sEHm-preh*

amalgam amalgama *ah-mAHl-gah-mah*

ambulance autoambulanza *ah-oo-toh-ahm-boo-lAHn-tsah*

American americano *ah-may-ree-kAH-noh*

amethyst ametista *ah-may-tEEs-tah*

among fra *frAH*; tra *trAH*

amount ammontare *ahm-mohn-tAH-reh*; somma *sOHm-mah*

anchovy acciuga *ah-chee-OO-gah*

and e *ay*

ankle caviglia *kah-vEE-ly-ee-ah*

another un altro *oon-AHl-troh*

to answer rispondere *rees-pOHn-day-reh*

antacid antiacido *ahn-tee-AH-chee-doh*

antibiotic antibiotico *ahn-tee-bee-OH-tee-koh*

antiseptic antisettico *ahn-tee-sEHt-tee-koh*

apartment appartamento *ahp-pahr-tah-mEHn-toh*

apéritif aperitivo *ah-peh-ree-tEE-voh*

appendicitis appendicite *ahp-payn-dee-chEE-teh*

appetizer antipasto *ahn-tee-pAHs-toh*

apple mela *mAY-lah*

appointment appuntamento *ahp-poon-tah-mEHn-toh*

apricot albicocca *ahl-bee-kOH-kah*

April aprile *ah-prEE-leh*

aquamarine acquamarina *ah-koo-ah-mah-rEE-nah*

Arab arabo *AH-rah-boh*

area code prefisso *pray-fEEs-soh*

Argentinian argentino *ahr-jehn-tEE-noh*

arm braccio *brAH-chee-oh*

around attorno *aht-tOHr-noh*

to arrive arrivare *ahr-ree-vAH-reh*

arrival arrivo *ahr-rEE-voh*

article articolo *ahr-tEE-koh-loh*

ashtray portacenere *pohr-tah-chAY-nay-reh*

to ask chiedere *key-AY-day-reh*

asparagus asparagi *ahs-pAH-ra-jee*

aspirin aspirina *ahs-pee-rEE-nah*

to assist assistere *ahs-sEEs-teh-reh*

asthma asma *AHs-mah*

at a *ah*; **at least** almeno *ahl-mAY-noh*; **at once** subito *sOO-bee-toh*

attention attenzione *aht-tehn-tsee-OH-neh*

attentive attento *aht-tEHn-toh*

attraction attrazione *aht-trah-tsee-OH-neh*

auburn castano *kahs-tAH-noh*

August agosto *ah-gOHs-toh*

aunt zia *tsEE-ah*

Austrian austriaco *ah-oos-trEE-ah-koh*

author autore *ah-oo-tOH-reh*

automatic automatico *ah-oo-toh-mAH-tee-koh*

autumn autunno *ah-oo-tOOn-noh*

awful terribile *tehr-rEE-bee-leh*

away via *vEE-ah*

B

baby bambino *bahm-bEE-noh*

bachelor scapolo *skAH-poh-loh*

back schiena *skee-AY-nah*

backwards dietro *dee-AY-troh*

bacon pancetta *pahn-chAYt-tah*

bad cattivo *kaht-tEE-voh*

bag (handbag) borsa *bOHr-sah*; borsetta *bohr-sAYt-tah*; **bag (suitcase)** valigia *vah-lEE-jee-ah*; **bag snatching** scippo *shEEp-poh*

baggage bagaglio *bah-gAH-ly-ee-oh*

baked al forno *ahl-fOHr-noh*

bakery fornaio *fohr-nAH-ee-oh*

balcony: (house) balcone *bahl-kOH-neh*; **(theater)** galleria *gahl-leh-rEE-ah*

ball (play ball) palla *pAHl-lah*

banana banana *bah-nAH-nah*

bandage fascia *fAH-shee-ah*

Band-Aid cerotto *chay-rOHt-toh*

bang(s) (hair) frangia *frAHn-jee-ah*

bangle bracciale *brah-chee-AH-leh*

bank banca *bAHn-kah*

bank note banconota *bahn-koh-nOH-tah*

barber barbiere *bahr-bee-AY-reh*; parrucchiere *pahr-roo-key-AY-reh*

baritone baritono *bah-rEE-toh-noh*

barley orzo *OHr-tsoh*

barn stalla *stAHl-lah*

bass: (singer) basso *bAHs-soh*; **(fish)** branzino *brahn-tsEE-noh*

bath bagno *bAH-ny-oh*

bathing suit costume da bagno *kohs-tOO-may dah bAH-ny-oh*

bathrobe accappatoio *ah-kahp-pah-tOH-ee-oh*

bathroom bagno *bAH-ny-oh*

bathtub vasca *vAHs-kah*

battery batteria *baht-teh-rEE-ah;* pila *pEE-lah* (for radio, camera, etc.)

to be essere *EHs-seh-reh;* stare *stAH-reh*

beach spiaggia *spee-AH-jee-ah*

bean (shell) fagiolo *fah-jee-OH-loh*

beard barba *bAHr-bah*

beautiful bello *bEHl-loh*

because perché *pehr-kAY*

bed letto *lEHt-toh;* **bedroom** camera da letto *kAH-meh-rah dah lEHt-toh*

beef manzo *mAHn-tsoh;* **(beef) steak** bistecca *bees-tAY-kah;* **(grilled)** ai ferri *ah-ee fEHr-ree;* **(medium)** a puntino *ah poon-tEE-noh;* **(rare)** al sangue *ahl sAHn-goo-eh;* **(well-done)** ben cotta *behn kOHt-tah*

beer birra *bEEr-rah;* **beer on tap** birra alla spina *bEEr-rah ahl-lah spEE-nah*

before prima *prEE-mah*

to begin cominciare *koh-meen-chee-AH-reh*

behind dietro *dee-AY-troh*

Belgian belga *bEHl-gah*

to believe credere *krAY-deh-reh*

below sotto *sOHt-toh*

belt cintura *cheen-tOO-rah*

berth cuccetta *koo-chAYt-tah*

beside accanto *ahk-kAHn-toh*

best il migliore *eel-mee-ly-ee-OH-reh*

better meglio *mEh-ly-ee-oh;* migliore *mee-ly-ee-OH-reh*

between fra *frAH;* tra *trAH*

bicycle bicicletta *bee-chee-klAYt-tah*

big grande *grAHn-deh;* grosso *grOHs-soh*

bill conto *kOHn-toh*

bird uccello *oo-chEHl-loh*

birth nascita *nAH-shee-tah*

bite boccone *boh-kOH-neh;* **to**

have a bite mangiare un boccone *mahn-jee-AH-reh oon boh-kOH-neh*

bitter amaro *ah-mAH-roh*

black nero *nAY-roh*

blade lama *lAH-mah;* **razor blades** lamette *lah-mAYt-teh*

blank modulo *mOH-doo-loh*

blanket coperta *koh-pEHr-tah*

blender frullatore *frool-lah-tOH-reh*

blond biondo *bee-OHn-doh*

blood sangue *sAHn-goo-eh;* **I'm bleeding** sto sanguinando *stOH sahn-goo-ee-nAHn-doh*

blouse blusa *blOO-sah;* camicetta *kah-mee-chAYt-tah*

blue blu *blOO;* azzurro *ah-tsOOr-roh*

body corpo *kOHr-poh*

boiled bollito *bohl-lEE-toh*

bolt bullone *bool-lOH-neh*

book libro *lEE-broh;* **bookstore** libreria *lee-breh-rEE-ah*

boot stivale *stee-vAH-leh*

booth cabina telefonica *kah-bEE-nah teh-leh-fOH-nee-kah*

botanic botanico *boh-tAH-nee-koh*

both tutti e due *toot-tee ay dOO-eh*

to bother seccare *say-kAH-reh;* dare fastidio *dAH-reh fas-tEE-dee-oh;* **don't bother me!** non darmi fastidio! *nohn dAHr-mee fahs-tEE-dee-oh!*

bottle bottiglia *boht-tEE-ly-ee-ah*

box scatola *skAH-toh-lah*

bowling bowling

boy ragazzo *rah-gAH-tsoh*

bra, brassiere reggiseno *reh-jee-sAY-noh*

bracelet bracciale *brah-chee-AH-leh*

brain cervello *chehr-vEHl-loh*

brakes freni *frAY-nee*

Brazilian brasiliano *brah-see-lee-AH-noh*

bread pane *pAH-neh*; **soft part of bread** mollica *mohl-lEE-kah*; **toasted bread** pan tostato *pAHn tohs-tAH-toh*

to break rompere *rOHm-pay-reh*

breakdown (car) guasto *goo-AHs-toh*

breakfast colazione *koh-lah-tsee-OH-neh*

to breathe respirare *rays-pee-rAH-reh*

bridge ponte *pOHn-teh*

to bring portare *pohr-tAH-reh*; **bring me . . .** mi porti . . . *mee pOHr-tee*

broken rotto *rOHt-toh*

brooch fermaglio *fehr-mAH-ly-ee-oh*; spilla *spEEl-lah*

brook ruscello *roo-shEHl-loh*

broth brodo *brOH-doh*

brother fratello *frah-tEHl-loh*

brown marrone *mahr-rOH-neh*

bruise contusione *kohn-too-see-OH-neh*

brunette bruna *brOO-nah*; brunetta *broo-nAYt-tah*

brush spazzola *spAH-tsoh-lah*

bulb (light) lampadina *lahm-pah-dEE-nah*

bumper paraurti *pah-rah-OOr-tee*

bun: (bread) rosetta *roh-sAYt-tah*; **(hair)** crocchia *krOH-key-ah*

to burn bruciare *broo-chee-AH-reh*

burn ustione *oos-tee-OH-neh*

burnt ustionato *oos-tee-oh-nAH-toh*

bus autobus *ah-oo-toh-bOOs*

business affare *ahf-fAH-reh*

busy occupato *oh-koo-pAH-toh*

but ma, però *mah; peh-rOH*

butcher shop macelleria *mah-chehl-leh-rEE-ah*

butter burro *bOOr-roh*

button bottone *boht-tOH-neh*

to buy comprare *kohm-prAH-reh*

C

cabbage cavolo *kAH-voh-loh*

cabin cabina *kah-bEE-nah*

cake torta *tOHr-tah*

calf vitello *vee-tEHl-loh*

to call chiamare *key-ah-mAH-reh*; telefonare *teh-leh-foh-nAH-reh*

camera macchina fotografica *mAH-kee-nah foh-toh-grAH-fee-kah*; **camera store** negozio fotocine *neh-gOH-tsee-oh fOH-toh-chEE-neh*; negozio di articoli fotografici *neh-gOH-tsee-oh dee ahr-tEE-koh-lee foh-toh-grAH-fee-chee*

camping campeggio *kahm-pAY-jee-oh*

Canadian canadese *kah-nah-dAY-seh*

cancel cancellare *kahn-chehl-lAH-reh*

candle candela *kahn-dAY-lah*

candy dolci *dOHl-chee*; caramelle *kah-rah-mEHl-leh*

capon cappone *kahp-pOH-neh*

car (auto) auto *AH-oo-toh*; **(train)** carrozza *kahr-rOH-tsah*; vagone *vah-gOH-neh*; **dining car** vagone ristorante *vah-gOH-neh rees-toh-rAHn-teh*

carburetor carburatore *kahr-boo-rah-tOH-reh*

card: identification card carta d'identità *kAHr-tah dee-dEHn-tee-tAH*; **(playing) cards** carte da gioco *kAHr-teh dah jee-OH-koh*; **(deck of)** mazzo di carte *mAH-tsoh dee kAHr-toh*

careful attento *aht-tEHn-toh*; **be careful!** stia attento! *stEE-ah aht-tEHn-toh!*

carrot carota *kah-rOH-tah*

to carry portare *pohr-tAH-reh*

carton of cigarettes stecca di sigarette *stAY-kah dee see-gah-rAYt-teh*

carved intagliato *een-tah-ly-ee-AH-toh*

cashier cassa *kAHs-sah*; cassiere *kahs-see-AY-reh*

to catch prendere *prAYn-day-reh*

cathedral cattedrale *kaht-tay-drAH-leh*

Catholic cattolico *kaht-tOH-lee-koh*

centimeter centimetro *chayn-tEE-meh-troh*

center centrale *chayn-trAH-leh*

ceramics ceramiche *chay-rAH-mee-keh*

cereals cereali *cheh-reh-AH-lee*

chain (gold) catenina *kah-tay-nEE-nah*

chair sedia *sEH-dee-ah*; **chaise longue** sedia a sdraio *sEH-dee-ah ah sdrAH-ee-oh*

chambermaid cameriera *kah-meh-ree-AY-rah*

to change cambiare *kahm-bee-AH-reh*

change (money) resto *rEHs-toh*; **small change** spiccioli *spEE-chee-oh-lee*

character personaggio *pehr-soh-nAH-jee-oh*

charm ciondolo *chee-OHn-doh-loh*

chart cartellino *kahr-tehl-lEE-noh*

cheap a buon mercato *ah boo-OHn mehr-kAH-toh*; **cheaper** più a buon mercato *pee-OO ah boo-OHn mehr-kAH-toh*

check (chess game) scacco *skAH-koh*; **(money)** assegno *ahs-sAY-ny-oh*; **checkmate** scaccomatto *skAH-koh-mAHt-toh*

checkers dama *dAH-mah*

checkroom guardaroba *goo-AHr-dah-rOH-bah*

cheek guancia *goo-AHn-chee-ah*

cheers! salute! *sah-lOO-teh!*

cheese formaggio *fohr-mAH-jee-oh*

chess scacchi *skAH-key*; **chessboard** scacchiera *skah-key-AY-rah*

chest petto *pEHt-toh*; **a chest cold** un colpo d'aria al petto *oon kOHl-poh dAH-ree-ah ahl pEHt-toh*

chestnuts castagne *kahs-tAH-ny-eh*

to chew masticare *mahs-tee-kAH-reh*; **chewing gum** gomma masticante *gOHm-mah mahs-tee-kAHn-teh*

chicken pollo *pOHl-loh*

chiffon chiffon

child bambino *bahm-bEE-noh*

Chilean cileno *chee-lAY-noh*

chill brivido *brEE-vee-doh*

chin mento *mEHn-toh*

Chinese cinese *chee-nAY-seh*

chocolate cioccolato *chee-oh-kOH-lah-toh*

chop (meat) cotoletta *koh-toh-lAYt-tah*

Christmas Natale *nah-tAH-leh*

church chiesa *key-AY-sah*

cider sidro *sEE-droh*

cigar sigaro *sEE-gah-roh*; **cigar store** tabaccaio *tah-bah-kAH-ee-oh*; tabaccheria *tah-bah-kEH-ree-ah*

cigarette sigaretta *see-gah-rAYt-tah*; **cigarette lighter** accendino *ah-chayn-dEE-noh*

cinema cinema *chEE-neh-mah*

city città *cheet-tAH*

class classe *klAHs-seh*

to clean pulire *poo-lEE-reh*

clear chiaro *key-AH-roh*

clerk impiegato *eem-pee-ay-gAH-toh*

to close chiudere *key-OO-deh-reh*; **may I close?** posso chiudere? *pOHs-soh key-OO-deh-reh?*; **closed** chiuso *key-OO-soh*

cloth panno *pAHn-noh*

clothing vestiti *vays-tEE-tee*; **evening clothes** abiti da sera *AH-bee-tee dah sAY-rah*

club club; **night club** night club; **golf clubs** mazze da golf *mAH-tseh dah gOHlf*

clutch frizione *free-tsee-OH-neh*

coat cappotto *kahp-pOHt-toh*

cocktail cocktail *kOH-ktayl*

coconut noce di cocco *nOH-cheh dee kOH-koh*

codfish merluzzo *mehr-lOO-tsoh*

coffee caffè *kahf-fEH*

cold freddo *frAYd-doh*; **I have a cold** ho il raffreddore *OH eel rahf-frayd-dOH-reh*

cold cuts affettati *ahf-fayt-tAH-tee*; salumi *sah-lOO-mee*

color colore *koh-lOH-reh*; **light color** color chiaro *koh-lOHr key-AH-roh*

comb pettine *pEHt-tee-neh*

to come venire *vay-nEE-reh*; **come in!** entri! avanti! *AYn-tree! ah-vAHn-tee!*

comedy commedia *kohm-mEH-dee-ah*

commercial commerciale *kohm-mehr-chee-AH-leh*

compartment compartimento *kohm-pahr-tee-mEHn-toh*

concert concerto *kohn-chEHr-toh*; **concert hall** sala da concerti *sAH-lah dah kohn-chEHr-tee*

to confirm confermare *kohn-fayr-mAH-reh*

consomme consommé *kohn-sohm-mAY*

constipation stitichezza *stee-tee-kAY-tsah*

consulate consolato *kohn-soh-lAH-toh*

contagious contagioso *kohn-tah-jee-OH-soh*

to continue continuare *kohn-tee-noo-AH-reh*

contraceptive contraccettivo *kohn-trah-cheht-tEE-voh*

cooked cotto *kOHt-toh*

cookies dolci *dOHl-chee*

cool fresco *frAYs-koh*

copy copia *kOH-pee-ah*

coral corallo *koh-rAHl-loh*

corn plaster callifugo *kahl-lEE-foo-goh*

corner angolo *AHn-goh-loh*; **at the corner** all'angolo *ahl-lAHn-goh-loh*

correct corretto *kohr-rEHt-toh*

cosmetic cosmetico *kohs-mEH-tee-koh*

to cost costare *kohs-tAH-reh*

cottage villino *veel-lEE-noh*

cotton cotone *koh-tOH-neh*; **sanitary cotton** cotone idrofilo *koh-tOH-neh ee-drOH-fee-loh*

cough tosse *tOHs-seh*; **cough drops** pasticche per la tosse *pahs-tEE-keh pehr lah tOHs-seh*

countryside campagna *kahm-pAH-ny-ah*

course: golf course campo di golf *kAHm-poh dee gOHlf*, **of course** naturalmente *nah-too-rahl-mEHn-teh*; (of • **meals**) portata *pohr-tAH-tah*

courtyard cortile *kohr-tEE-leh*

crabs granchi *grAHn-key*

cramps crampi *krAHm-pee*; **stomach cramps** crampi allo stomaco *krAHm-pee AHl-loh stOH-mah-koh*

cream crema *krEH-mah*

credit credito *krEH-dee-toh*; **credit card** carta di credito *kAHr-tah dee krEH-dee-toh*

croissant cornetto *kohr-nAYt-toh*

crossroad incrocio *een-krOH-chee-oh*

crossing traversata *trah-vehr-sAH-tah*; passaggio a livello *pahs-sAH-jee-oh ah lee-vEHl-loh*

crown corona *koh-rOH-nah*

to crush calpestare *kahl-pehs-tAH-reh*

crust crosta *krOHs-tah*

crystal cristallo *krees-tAHl-loh*

Cuban cubano *koo-bAH-noh*

cucumber cetriolo *chay-tree-OH-loh*

cup tazza *tAH-tsah*

curls riccioli *rEE-chee-oh-lee*

currency valuta *vah-lOO-tah*

current corrente *kohr-rEHn-teh*

curse maledizione *mah-lay-dee-tsee-OH-neh*

curve (road) curva *kOOr-vah*

customs dogana *doh-gAH-nah*

to cut tagliare *tah-ly-ee-AH-reh*; **to cut cards** tagliare il mazzo *tah-ly-ee-AH-reh eel mAH-tsoh*

cut taglio *tAH-ly-ee-oh*; **a haircut** un taglio di capelli *oon tAH-ly-ee-oh dee kah-pAYl-lee*; **a shortcut** un'accorciatoia *oo-nah-kOHr-chee-ah-tOH-ee-ah*

cutlet cotoletta *koh-toh-lAYt-tah*; **veal cutlet** cotoletta di vitello *koh-toh-lAYt-tah dee vee-tEHl-loh*

Czech cecoslovacco *chay-kohs-loh-vAH-koh*

D

daily quotidiano *koo-oh-tee-dee-AH-noh*

to dance ballare *bahl-lAH-reh*

dancing floor pista di ballo *pEEs-tah dee bAHl-loh*

danger pericolo *peh-rEE-koh-loh*; **dangerous** pericoloso *peh-ree-koh-lOH-soh*

Danish danese *dah-nAY-seh*

dark scuro *skOO-roh*

darn it! maledizione! *mah-leh-dee-tsee-OH-neh!*

date data *dAH-tah*; **what's today's date?** che data è oggi? *kay dAH-tah EH OH-jee?*

dates (fruit) datteri *dAHt-teh-ree*

daughter figlia *fEE-ly-ee-ah*

day giorno *jee-OHr-noh*; **good morning** buon giorno *boo-OHn jee-OHr-noh*

to deal the cards dare le carte *dAH-reh leh kAHr-teh*

decayed (tooth) cariato *kah-ree-AH-toh*

December dicembre *dee-chEHm-breh*

to declare dichiarare *dee-key-ah-rAH-reh*

deer cervo *chEHr-voh*

delay ritardo *ree-tAHr-doh*

to deliver consegnare *kohn-say-ny-AH-reh*

dental dentale *dayn-tAH-leh*; **dental prosthesis** protesi dentale *prOH-teh-see dayn-tAH-leh*

dentist dentista *dehn-tEEs-tah*

deodorant deodorante *day-oh-doh-rAHn-teh*

to depart partire *pahr-tEE-reh*

department store magazzino *mah-gah-tsEE-noh*

to desire desiderare *day-see-day-rAH-reh*

detective stories gialli *jee-AHl-lee*

detergent detersivo *day-tayr-sEE-voh*

detour (road) deviazione *day-vee-ah-tsee-OH-neh*

to develop sviluppare *svee-loop-pAH-reh*

devil diavolo *dee-AH-voh-loh;* **what the devil do you want?** ma che diavolo vuole? *mah kay dee-AH-voh-loh voo-OH-leh?*

diabetes diabete *dee-ah-bEH-teh*

diamond diamante *dee-ah-mAHn-teh*

diarrhea diarrea *dee-ahr-rEH-ah*

dictionary dizionario *dee-tsee-oh-nAH-ree-oh*

to dine pranzare *prahn-tsAH-reh*

dining room sala da pranzo *sAH-lah dah prAHn-tsoh*

dinner pranzo *prAHn-tsoh*

to direct indicare *een-dee-kAH-reh*

direction direzione *dee-ray-tsee-OH-neh;* **direction indicator (car)** freccia *frAY-chee-ah*

director direttore *dee-reht-tOH-reh*

dirty sporco *spOHr-koh*

discotheque discoteca *dees-koh-tEH-kah*

dish piatto *pee-AHt-toh*

disk disco *dEEs-koh*

to dislike detestare *day-teh-stAH-reh*

to disturb disturbare *dees-toor-bAH-reh*

dizzy: I feel dizzy mi gira la testa *mee-jEE-lah tEHs-tah*

to do fare *fAH-reh*

doctor dottore *doht-tOH-reh;* **doctor's office** ambulatorio *ahm-boo-lah-tOH-ree-oh*

document documento *doh-koo-mEHn-toh*

doll bambola *bAHm-boh-lah*

dollar dollaro *dOHl-lah-roh*

dominoes (game) domino *dOH-mee-noh*

door porta *pOHr-tah;* **doorknob** maniglia *mah-nEE-ly-ee-ah*

dot puntino *poon-tEE-noh;* **dots** pallini *pahl-lEE-nee*

doubt dubbio *dOOb-bee-oh*

down giù *jee-OO*

dozen dozzina *doh-tsEE-nah*

drama dramma *drAHm-mah*

to dress vestire *vays-tEE-reh;* **get dressed!** si vesta! *see vEHs-tah!*

dress (garment) abito *AH-bee-toh*

to drink bere *bAY-reh*

drink (beverage) bibita *bEE-bee-tah;* **drinking glass** bicchiere *bee-key-AY-reh*

drinkable potabile *poh-tAH-bee-leh*

to drive guidare *goo-ee-dAH-reh;* **driver's license** patente di guida *pah-tEHn-teh dee goo-EE-dah*

dry secco *sAY-koh*

to dry-clean lavare a secco *lah-vAH-reh ah sAY-koh;* **dry cleaner** tintoria *teen-toh-rEE-ah*

duck (bird) anatra *AH-nah-trah*

during durante *door-AHn-teh*

dust polvere *pOHl-vay-reh*

duty (customs) dogana *doh-gAH-nah*

dye tintura *teen-tOO-rah*

dysentery dissenteria *dEEs-sehn-teh-rEE-ah*

E

each ogni *OH-ny-ee*

ear orecchio *oh-rAY-key-oh*

early presto *prEHs-toh*

earrings orecchini *oh-ray-kEY-nee*

earth terra *tEHr-rah*

east est *ehst*

easy facile *FAH-chee-leh*

to eat mangiare *mahn-jee-AH-reh*

eel anguilla *ahn-goo-EEl-lah*

egg uovo *oo-OH-voh*; **hard-cooked eggs** uova sode *oo-OH-vah sOH-deh*; **scrambled eggs** uova strapazzate *oo-OH-vah strah-pah-tsAH-teh*; **soft-boiled eggs** uova alla coque *oo-OH-vah AHl-lah kOHk*

eggplant melanzana *may-lahn-tsAH-nah*

eight otto *OHt-toh*; **eight hundred** ottocento *OHt-toh-chEHn-toh*

eighteen diciotto *dee-chee-OHt-toh*

eighth ottavo *oht-tAH-voh*

eighty ottanta *oht-tAHn-tah*

elbow gomito *gOH-mee-toh*

electric elettrico *ay-lEHt-tree-koh*; **electricity** elettricità *ay-leht-tree-chee-tAH*

elevator ascensore *ah-shayn-sOH-reh*

eleven undici *OOn-dee-chee*

emerald smeraldo *smeh-rAHl-doh*

emergency emergenza *eh-mehr-jEHn-tsah*

enamel smalto *smAHl-toh*

to end finire *fee-nEE-reh*

to endorse firmare *feer-mAH-reh*

English inglese *een-glAY-seh*

enlargement ingrandimento *een-grahn-dee-mEHn-toh*

enough abbastanza *ahb-bah-stAHn-tsah*; **that's enough!** basta! *bAHs-tah!*

to enter entrare *ayn-trAH-reh*

entrance ingresso *een-grEHs-soh*

envelope busta *bOOs-tah*

equipment equipaggiamento *ay-koo-ee-pah-jee-ah-mEHn-toh*

eraser gomma *gOHm-mah*

even pari *pAH-reh*

evening sera *sAY-rah*; **evening gown** abito da sera *AH-bee-toh dah sAY-rah*

every ogni *OH-ny-ee*; **everyone** ognuno *oh-ny-oo-noh*; **everything** tutto *tOOt-toh*

to examine esaminare *ay-sah-mee-nAH-reh*

except eccetto *ay-chEH-toh*

to exchange cambiare *kahm-be-AH-reh*; **the exchange rate** il cambio *eel kAHm-bee-oh*; **exchange office** ufficio di cambio *off-fEE-chee-oh dee kAHm-bee-oh*

excursion escursione *ays-koor-see-OH-neh*; gita *jEE-tah*

to excuse scusare *skoo-sAH-reh*; **excuse me!** mi scusi! *mee skOO-see!*

exhaust pipe tubo di scappamento *tOO-boh dee skahp-pah-mEHn-toh*

exit uscita *oo-shEE-tah*

expensive caro *kAH-roh*; costoso *kohs-tOH-soh*

express espresso *ays-prEHs-soh*

to extract estrarre *ays-trAHr-reh*

eye occhio *OH-key-oh*; **eye doctor** oculista *oh-koo-lEEs-tah*; **eye drops** collirio *kohl-lEE-ree-oh*

eye shadow ombretto *ohm-brAYt-toh*

eyebrows sopracciglia *soh-prah-chEE-ly-ee-ah*

eyeglasses occhiali *oh-key-AH-lee*; **sunglasses** occhiali da sole *Oh-key-AH-lee dah sOH-leh*

eyelashes ciglia *chEE-ly-ee-ah*

eyeliner eye liner

F

to face dare su *dAH-reh soo*

face faccia *fAH-chee-ah*

facial facciale *fah-chee-AH-leh*

to faint svenire *svay-nEE-reh*

fall (autumn) autunno *ah-oo-tOOn-noh*

to fall cadere *kah-dAY-reh*

family famiglia *fah-mEE-ly-ee-ah*

fan ventaglio *vehn-tAH-ly-ee-oh*; ventola *vEHn-toh-lah*; **fan belt** cinghia del ventilatore *chEEn-ghee-ah dayl vehn-tee-lah-tOH-reh*

far lontano *lohn-tAH-noh*

fare corsa *kOHr-sah*; biglietto *bee-ly-ee-AYt-toh*

farm fattoria *faht-toh-rEE-ah*

fast veloce *vay-lOH-cheh*; **faster** più veloce *pee-OO vay-lOH-cheh*

father padre *pAH-dreh*

faucet rubinetto *roo-bee-nAYt-toh*

favor favore *fah-vOH-reh*

February febbraio *fayb-brAH-ee-oh*

to feel sentire *sayn-tEE-reh*; **I don't feel well** non mi sento bene *nOHn mee sEHn-toh bEH-neh*

felt (cloth) feltro *fAYl-troh*

fender parafango *pah-rah-fAHn-goh*

fever febbre *fEHb-breh*

few, a few alcuni *ahl-kOO-nee*; qualche *koo-AHl-keh*

field campo *kAHm-poh*

fifteen quindici *koo-EEn-dee-chee*

fifth quinto *koo-EEn-toh*

fifty cinquanta *cheen-koo-AHn-tah*

fig fico *fEE-koh*

(nail) file limetta *lee-mAYt-tah*

to fill, to fill out riempire *ree-ehm-pEE-reh*

filling (tooth) otturazione *oht-too-rah-tsee-OH-neh*

film film; pellicola *pehl-lEE-koh-lah*

filter filtro *fEEl-troh*

to find trovare *troh-vAH-reh*

finger dito *dEE-toh*; **fingers** dita *dEE-tah*

to finish finire *fee-nEE-reh*

fire fuoco *foo-OH-koh*; **fire!** al fuoco! *ahl foo-OH-koh!*

first primo *prEE-moh*; **first class** prima classe *prEE-mah clAHs-seh*; **first aid** pronto soccorso *prOHn-toh soh-kOHr-soh*

fish pesce *pAY-sheh*

five cinque *chEEn-koo-eh*; **five hundred** cinquecento *chEEn-koo-eh-chEHn-toh*

to fix aggiustare *ah-jee-oos-tAH-reh*; riparare *ree-pah-rAH-reh*

flannel flanella *flah-nEHl-lah*

flashlight lampadina tascabile *lahm-pah-dEE-nah tahs-kAH-bee-leh*

flat tire gomma bucata *gOHm-mah boo-kAH-tah*

flight volo *vOH-loh*

flint pietrina *pee-ay-trEE-nah*

florist fioraio *fee-oh-rAH-ee-oh*

flour semola *sAY-moh-lah*; farina *fah-rEE-nah*

flu influenza *een-floo-EHn-tsah*

fluid (for cigarette lighters) benzina *bayn-tsEE-nah*

folklore, folkloric folklore folcloristico *fohl-klOH-ray fohl-kloh-rEEs-tee-koh*

to follow seguire *say-goo-EE-reh*

foot piede *pee-EH-deh*; **to go on foot, walk** andare a piedi *ahn-dAH-reh ah pee-EH-dee*

for per *pehr*

forbidden vietato *vee-ay-tAH-toh*

forehead fronte *frOHn-teh*

forest bosco *bOHs-koh*; foresta *foh-rEHs-tah*

to forget dimenticare *dee-mehn-tee-kAH-reh*

fork forchetta *fohr-kAYt-tah*

form modulo *mOH-doo-loh*

fortune fortuna *fohr-tOO-nah*

forty quaranta *koo-ah-rAHn-tah*

to forward spedire *spay-dEE-reh*; **forward (direction)** avanti *ah-vAHn-tee*

fountain fontana *fohn-tAH-nah*

four quattro *koo-AHt-troh*; **four hundred** quattrocento *koo-AHt-troh chEHn-toh*

fourteen quattordici *koo-aht-tOHr-dee-chee*

fourth quarto *koo-AHr-toh*

fracture frattura *fraht-tOO-rah*

frame montatura *mohn-tah-tOO-rah*

free libero *lEE-beh-roh*

French francese *frahn-chAY-seh*

fresh fresco *frAYs-koh*

Friday venerdì *veh-nehr-dEE*

fried fritto *frEEt-toh*

friend amico *ah-mEE-koh*

from da *dah*

front davanti *dah-vAHn-tee*

fruit frutta *frOOt-tah*; **fresh-fruit salad** macedonia *mah-chay-dOH-nee-ah*

fuel pump pompa della benzina *pOHm-pah dAYl-lah bayn-tsEE-nah*

fuel tank serbatoio *sehr-bah-tOH-ee-oh*

full pieno *pee-AY-noh*

fullback (sport) terzino *tehr-tsEE-noh*

furnished ammobiliato *ahm-moh-bee-lee-AH-toh*

G

game (sports) partita *pahr-tEE-tah*; **(birds)** selvaggina *sayl-vah-jEE-nah*

garage autorimessa *AH-oo-toh-ree-mAYs-sah*

garden aiuola *ah-ee-oo-OH-lah*; giardino *jee-ahr-dEE-noh*

garlic aglio *AH-ly-ee-oh*

garnish contorno *kohn-tOHr-noh*

gasoline benzina *bayn-tsEE-nah*

gate porta *pOHr-tah*; cancello *kahn-chAYl-loh*; uscita *oo-shEE-tah*

gears ingranaggi *een-grah-nAH-jee*

general delivery fermo posta *fAYr-moh pOHs-tah*

gentleman signore *see-ny-OH-reh*

German tedesco *tay-dAYs-koh*

to get ottenere *oht-teh-nAY-reh*; **to get back (to return)** ritornare *ree-tohr-nAH-reh*; **to get dressed** vestirsi *vays-tEEr-see*; **to get off** scendere *shAYn-day-reh*; **to get on** montare *mohn-tAH-ray*; **to get up** alzarsi *ahl-tzAH-ray*

gift regalo *ray-gAH-loh*

girl ragazza *rah-gAH-tsah*

to give dare *dAH-reh*; **to give back** ridare *ree-dAH-reh*

glands ghiandole *ghee-AHn-doh-leh*

glass vetro *vAY-troh*; **blown glass** vetro soffiato *vAY-troh sohf-fEE-ah-toh*

glue colla *kOHl-lah*

goat (kid) capra, capretto *kAH-prah kah-prAYt-toh*

to go andare *ahn-dAH-reh*; **let's go!** andiamo! *ahn-dee-AH-moh!*; **go!** forza! *fOHr-tsah!*; **to go back** ritornare *ree-tohr-nAH-reh*; **to go down** scendere *shAYn-day-reh*; **to go home** andare a casa *ahn-dAH-reh ah kAH-sah*; **to go in** entrare *ayn-trAH-reh*; **to go out** uscire *oo-shEE-reh*; **to go shopping** andare a fare la spesa *ahn-dAH-reh ah fAH-reh lah spAY-sah*; **to go up** salire *sah-lEE-rah*

gold oro *OH-roh*; **solid gold** oro massiccio *OH-roh mahs-sEE-chee-oh*; **gold plated** oro placcato *OH-roh plah-kAH-toh*

good buono *boo-OH-noh*

good-bye arrivederci *ahr-rEE-veh-dAYr-chee*; **(friendly)** ciao *chee-AH-oh*

goose oca *OH-kah*

gram grammo *grAHm-moh*

grapefruit pompelmo *pohm-pAYl-moh*

grass erba *EHr-bah*

gray grigio *grEE-jee-oh*

to grease lubrificare *loo-bree-fee-kAH-reh*

great! magnifico! *mah-ny-EE-fee-koh!*

Greek greco *grEH-koh*

green verde *vAYr-deh*

greetings saluti *sah-lOO-tee*

guide, guidebook guida *goo-EE-dah*

gums (teeth) gengive *jayn-jEE-veh*

H

hair capelli *kah-pAYl-lee*; **hair bleach** tintura per capelli *teen-tOO-rah pehr kah-pAYl-lee*; **hair dryer** asciugacapelli *ah-shee-OO-gah-kah-pAYl-lee*; fono *fOH-noh*; **hair lotion** frizione *free-tsee-OH-neh*; brillantina *breel-lahn-tEE-nah*; **hair rinse** cachet *kah-shEH*; **hair spray** lacca *lAH-kah*

haircut taglio di capelli *tAH-ly-ee-oh dee kah-pAYl-lee*

hairdresser parrucchiere per signore *pahr-roo-key-EH-reh pehr see-ny-OH-reh*

hairpin forcina *fohr-chEE-nah*

hake (fish) nasello *nah-sehl-loh*

half mezzo *mEH-tsoh*

ham (cured) prosciutto *proh-shee-OOt-toh*

hamburger hamburger

hammer martello *mahr-tEHl-loh*

hand mano *mAH-noh*; **give me a hand** mi dia una mano *mee dEE-ah oo-nah mAH-noh*

handbag borsetta *bohr-sAYt-tah*

handkerchief fazzoletto *fah-tsoh-lAYt-toh*

handmade fatto a mano *fAHt-toh ah mAH-noh*

hanger grucce *grOO-cheh*; attaccapanni *aht-tAH-kah-pAHn-nee*

to happen succedere *soo-chEH-deh-reh*; **what's happening?** ma che cosa succede? *mah kay kOH-sah soo-chEH-deh?*

happy lieto *lee-AY-toh*

harbor porto *pOHr-toh*

hard duro *dOO-roh*

hardware store ferramenta *fehr-rah-mEHn-tah*

hare lepre *lEH-preh*

hat cappello *kahp-pEHl-loh*

to have avere *ah-vAY-reh*; **to have to** dovere *doh-vAY-reh*

hay fever febbre del fieno *fEHb-breh dayl fee-AY-noh*

hazelnuts noccioline *noh-chee-oh-lEE-neh*

he egli *AY-ly-ee*; lui *lOO-ee*

head capo *kAH-poh*; **headache** mal di testa *mAHl dee tEHs-tah*

headlights fari abbaglianti *fAH-ree ahb-bah-ly-ee-AHn-tee*

health salute *sah-lOO-teh*

to hear sentire *sayn-tEE-reh*

heart cuore *koo-OH-reh*; **heart attack** attacco cardiaco *aht-tAH-koh kahr-dEE-ah-koh*

heat calore *kah-lOH-reh*

heaven cielo *chee-EH-loh*

heavy pesante *pay-sAHn-teh*

hectogram ettogrammo *eht-toh-grAHm-moh*

heel (foot) tallone *tahl-lOH-neh*; **(shoe)** tacco *tAH-koh*

hello! (telephone) pronto! *prOHn-toh!*

to help aiutare *ah-ee-oo-tAH-reh*; assistere *ahs-sEEs-tay-reh*; **help!** aiuto! *ah-ee-OO-toh!*

her lei *lEH-ee*; la *lah*; le *lay*

here qui *koo-EE*; qua *koo-AH*; **here is** ecco *EHk-koh*

herring aringa *ah-rEEn-gah*

high alto *AHl-toh*

highway autostrada *ah-oo-toh-strAH-dah*

hill collina *kohl-lEE-nah*

him lui *lOO-ee*; lo *loh*

hip anca *AHn-kah*

to hold tenere *tay-nAY-reh*

home casa *kAH-sah*

hood (car) cofano *kOH-fah-noh*

horn (car) clacson *clAH-ksohn*

hors d'oeuvre antipasto *ahn-tee-pAHs-toh*

horse cavallo *kah-vAHl-loh*

hostel (youth) ostello della gioventù *ohs-tEHl-loh dAYl-lah jee-oh-vehn-tOO*

hot caldo *kAHl-doh*

hotel hotel; albergo *ahl-bEHr-goh*

hour ora *OH-rah*; **at what time?** a che ora? *ah kay OH-rah?*

house casa *kAH-sah*

how come *kOH-meh*; **how are you?** come sta? *kOH-meh stAH?*; **how far is it?** quanto dista? *koo-AHn-toh dEEs-tah?*; **how long does it take to get there?** quanto tempo ci vuole per andarci? *koo-AHn-toh*

tEHm-poh chee voo-OH-leh pehr ahn-dAHr-chee?; **how much is it?** quanto costa? *koo-AHn-toh kOHs-tah?*

however però *peh-rOH*

hundred cento *chEHn-toh*

hunger fame *fAH-meh*; **I'm hungry** ho fame *OH fAH-meh*

to hurry sbrigarsi *sbree-gAHr-see*; **hurry up!** si sbrighi! *see sbrEE-ghee!*

to hurt dolere *doh-lAY-reh*; far male *fahr mAH-leh*

husband marito *mah-rEE-toh*

hygienic igienico *ee-jee-AY-nee-koh*

I

I io *EE-oh*

ice ghiaccio *ghee-AH-chee-oh*; **ice cream** gelato *jeh-lAH-toh*; **ice cubes** cubetti di ghiaccio *koo-bAYt-tee dee ghee-AH-chee-oh*; **ice water** acqua ghiacciata *AH-koo-ah ghee-ah-chee-AH-tah*

identification card carta d'identità *kAHr-tah dee-dehn-tee-tAH*

if se *seh*

ignition accensione *ah-chehn-see-OH-neh*

illness malattia *mah-laht-tEE-ah*

imagination fantasia *fahn-tah-sEE-ah*

important importante *eem-pohr-tAHn-teh*

impossible impossibile *eem-pohs-sEE-bee-leh*

in in *een*

included incluso *een-klOO-soh*

infection infezione *een-feh-tsee-OH-neh*

inn trattoria *traht-toh-rEE-ah*

innocent innocente *een-noh-chehn-teh*

inside dentro *dAYn-troh*

instead invece *een-vAY-cheh*

insomnia insonnia *een-sOHn-nee-ah*

instead invece *een-vAY-cheh*

insulin insulina *een-soo-lEE-nah*

insurance assicurazione *ahs-see-koo-rah-tsee-OH-neh*

international internazionale *een-tehr-nAH-tsee-oh-nAH-leh*

interesting interessante *een-teh-rehs-sAHn-teh*

interpreter interprete *een-tehr-preh-teh*

intersection incrocio *een-krOH-chee-oh*

into in *een*

iodine iodio *ee-OH-dee-oh*

iron ferro *fEHr-roh*

it esso *AYs-soh*; essa *AYs-sah*; lo *loh*; la *lah*

Italian italiano *ee-tah-lee-AH-noh*

J

jack (car) cricco *krEE-koh*; **(cards)** cavallo *kah-vAHl-loh*

jacket giacca *jee-AH-kah*

jade giada *jee-AH-dah*

jam marmellata *mahr-mehl-lAH-tah*

January gennaio *jehn-nAH-ee-oh*

Japanese giapponese *jee-ahp-poh-nAY-seh*

jar vasetto *vah-sAYt-toh*

jewel gioiello *jee-oh-ee-EHl-loh*; **jeweler** gioielliere *jee-oh-ee-EHl-lee-EH-reh*; **jewelry shop** gioielleria *jee-oh-eeEHl-leh-rEE-ah*

Jewish ebreo *ay-brEH-oh*; israeliano *ees-rah-eh-lee-AH-noh*

juice succo *sOO-koh*

July luglio *lOO-ly-ee-oh*

June giugno *jee-OO-ny-oh*

K

to keep tenere *tay-nAY-reh*; **keep off the grass** non calpestare le aiuole *nohn kahl-pays-tAH-reh leh ah-ee-ooOH-leh*

key chiave *key-AH-veh*

kick calcio *kAHl-chee-oh*; **kick off** calcio d'inizio *kAHl-chee-oh dee-nEE-tsee-oh*

kidney rognone *roh-ny-OH-neh*

kilogram chilo *kEE-loh*; chilogrammo *key-loh-grAHm-moh*

kilometer chilometro *key-lOH-meh-troh*

king re *ray*

to kiss baciare *bah-chee-AH-reh*

kiss bacio *bAH-chee-oh*

kitchen cucina *koo-chEE-nah*

knee ginocchio *jee-nOH-key-oh*

knife coltello *kohl-tEHl-loh*

knight (chess) alfiere *ahl-feeEH-reh*

to know (facts) sapere *sah-pAY-reh*; **to know (people)** conoscere *koh-nOH-shay-reh*

L

lace merletto *mehr-lEHt-toh*; pizzo *pEE-tsoh*

laces (shoe) lacci *lAH-chee*

lady signora *see-ny-OH-rah*; **ladies' room** bagno per signora *bAH-ny-oh pehr see-ny-OH-rah*

lake lago *lAH-goh*

lamb agnello *ah-ny-EHl-loh*

lamp lampada *lAHm-pah-dah*

land terra *tEHr-rah*

landscape panorama

language lingua *lEEn-goo-ah*

large grande *grAHn-deh*; **larger** più grande *pee-OO grAHn-deh*

to last durare *doo-rAH-reh*

last ultimo *OOl-tee-moh*

late tardi *tAHr-dee*; **the train is late** il treno è in ritardo *eel trEH-noh EH een ree-tAHr-doh*; **later** più tardi *pee-OO tAHr-dee*; **at the latest** al più tardi *ahl pee-OO tAHr-dee*

lateness ritardo *ree-tAHr-doh*

to laugh ridere *rEE-deh-reh*

laundry biancheria *beeAHn-keh-rEE-ah*

lawyer avvocato *ahv-voh-kAH-toh*

laxative lassativo *lahs-sah-tEE-voh*

to leak perdere acqua *pEHr-deh-reh AH-koo-ah*

to learn apprendere *ahp-prAYn-deh-reh*

leather pelle *pEHl-leh*

to leave lasciare *lah-sheeAH-reh*; partire; *pahr-tEE-reh*

left sinistro *see-nEEs-troh*; **to the left** a sinistra *ah see-nEEs-trah*

leg gamba *gAHm-bah*

lemon limone *lee-mOH-neh*

lemonade limonata *lee-moh-nAH-tah*

lens lente *lEHn-teh*; **contact lenses** lenti a contatto *lEHn-teh ah kohn-tAHt-toh*

lentils lenticchie *lehn-tEE-key-eh*

letter lettera *lAYt-teh-rah*; **air mail** via aerea *vEE-ah ahEH-reh-ah*; **insured** assicurata *ahs-see-koo-rAH-tah*; **registered** raccomandata *rAH-koh-mahn-dAH-tah*; **special delivery** espresso *ehs-prehs-soh*; **with return receipt** con ricevuta di ritorno *kohn ree-chay-vOO-tah dee ree-tOHr-noh*

lettuce lattuga *laht-tOO-gah*

library biblioteca *bee-blee-oh-tEH-kah*

to lie down sdraiarsi *sdrah-eeAHr-see*; **lie down!** si sdrai! *see sdrAH-ee!*

life vita *vEE-tah*

lifeguard bagnino *bah-ny-EE-noh*

to lift alzare *ahl-tsAH-reh*

light (color) chiaro *keyAH-roh*; **(electric)** luce *lOO-cheh*; **(weight)** leggero *lay-jEH-roh*

lighter (cigarette) accendino *ah-chayn-dEE-noh*

to like piacere *pee-ah-chAY-reh*; **I like it** mi piace *mee peeAH-cheh*

lime cedro *chAY-droh*

line linea *lEE-neh-ah*

linen biancheria *beeAHn-keh-rEE-ah*; lino *lEE-noh*

lips labbra *lAHb-brah*

lipstick lipstick; rossetto *rohs-sAYt-toh*

liqueur liquore *lee-kooOH-reh*

list elenco *eh-lEHn-koh*; lista *lEEs-tah*

to listen ascoltare *ah-skohl-tAH-reh*

liter litro *lEE-troh*

little piccolo *pEE-koh-loh*

to live abitare *ah-bee-tAH-reh*

liver fegato *fAY-gah-toh*

to load caricare *kah-ree-kAH-reh*

loaf (of bread) filone di pane *fee-lOH-neh dee pAH-neh*

loan prestito *prEHs-tee-toh*

lobster aragosta *ah-rah-gOHs-tah*

local (train) locale *loh-kAH-leh*

long lungo *lOOn-goh*

to look guardare *gooAHr-dAH-reh*; **to take a look** dare un'occhiata *dAH-reh oo-noh-keyAH-tah*; **to look for** cercare *chayr-kAH-reh*

to lose perdere *pEHr-deh-reh*

lotion lozione *loh-tsee-OH-neh*;
suntan lotion lozione per
l'abbronzatura solare
*loh-tsee-OH-neh pehr
lahb-brohn-tsah-tOO-rah
soh-lAH-reh*

lots of molto *mOHl-toh*

loud forte *fOHr-teh*

love amore *ah-mOH-reh*

low basso *bAHs-soh*

lubricate lubrificare
loo-bree-fee-kAH-reh

luck fortuna *fohr-tOO-nah*; **good
luck!** buona fortuna! *booOH-nah
fohr-tOO-nah!*

luggage bagaglio *bah-gAH-ly-ce-oh*;
luggage rack portabagagli
pohr-tah-bah-gAH-ly-ee

lump (swelling) gonfiore
gohn-feeOH-reh

lunch pranzo *prAHn-tsoh*

lung polmone *pohl-mOH-neh*

M

machine macchina *mAH-key-nah*

mad pazzo *pAH-tsoh*

maid cameriera *kah-meh-reeEH-rah*

mail posta *pOHs-tah*; **mailbox**
cassetta postale *kas-sAYt-tah
pohs-tAH-leh*

main principale *preen-chee-pAH-leh*

magazine rivista *ree-vEEs-tah*

major maggiore *mah-jee-OH-reh*

to make fare *fAH-reh*

malt malto *mAHl-toh*

man uomo *oo-OH-moh*

manager direttore *dee-reht-tOH-reh*

mango mango *mAHn-goh*

manicure manicure
mah-nee-kOO-reh

many molti *mOHl-tee*

map cartina *kahr-tEE-nah*

March marzo *mAHr-tsoh*

margarine margarina
mahr-gah-rEE-nah

market mercato *mehr-kAH-toh*

married sposato *spoh-sAH-toh*

Mass Messa *mAYs-sah*

massage massaggio
mahs-sAH-jee-oh; **(hair)** frizione
free-tsee-OH-neh

match fiammifero
fee-ahm-mEE-feh-roh

to matter importare
eem-pohr-tAH-reh; **what's the
matter with you?** ma che
cos'ha? *mah kay koh-sAH?*

mattress fnaterasso
mah-teh-rAHs-soh

May maggio *mAH-jee-oh*

maybe forse *fOHr-seh*

me me *may*

meal pasto *pAHs-toh*

to mean significare
see-ny-ee-fee-kAHreh; **what does
this mean?** che cosa significa
questo? *kay kOH-sah
see-ny-EE-fee-kah koo-AYs-toh?*

means mezzo *mEH-tsoh*

measurements misura
mee-sOO-rah

meat carne *kAHr-neh*

meatball polpetta *pohl-pAYt-tah*

mechanic meccanico
meh-kAH-nee-koh

medical medico *mEH-dee-koh*

medicine medicina
meh-dee-chEE-nah

to meet incontrare
een-kohn-trAH-reh

melon melone *may-lOH-neh*

men uomini *oo-OH-mee-nee*; **men's
room** bagno per uomini (signore)
*bAH-ny-oh pehr oo-OH-mee-nee
(see-ny-OH-reh)*; gabinetto *gah-bee-
nAYt-toh*

to mend rammendare *rahm-mehn-dAH-reh*

menu menu *meh-nOO*

message messaggio *mehs-sAH-jee-oh*

meter (length) metro *mEH-troh*

Mexican messicano *mehs-see-kAH-noh*

middle mezzo *mEH-tsoh*

midnight mezzanotte *mEH-tsah-nOHt-teh*

mileage chilometraggio *key-loh-meh-trAH-jee-oh*; **unlimited mileage** chilometraggio illimitato *key-loh-meh-trAH-jee-oh EEl-lee-mee-tAH-toh*

mild leggero *lay-jEH-roh*

milk latte *lAHt-teh*

million milione *mee-lee-OH-neh*

mind mente *mEHn-teh*; **do you mind?** le dispiace? *lay dees-peeAH-cheh?*

mineral water acqua minerale *AHkoo-ah mee-neh-rAH-leh*

minister ministro *mee-nEEs-troh*

minute minuto *mee-nOO-toh*

mirror specchio *spEH-key-oh*

Miss signorina *see-ny-oh-rEE-nah*

to miss mancare *mahn-kAH-reh*; **I miss you** mi manchi *mee mAHn-key*

mistake sbaglio *sbAH-ly-ee-oh*

moment momento *moh-mEHn-toh*

Monday lunedì *loo-nay-dEE*

money denaro *day-nAH-roh*; soldi *sOHl-dee*; **money order** vaglia *vAH-ly-ee-ah*

month mese *mAY-seh*

moped motorino *moh-toh-rEE-noh*

more più *peeOO*

morning mattino *maht-tEE-noh*

mosque moschea *mohs-kEH-ah*

mother madre *mAH-dreh*

motor motore *moh-tOH-reh*; **motor coach** autopullman *AHoo-toh-pOOl-mahn*; **motor scooter** lambretta *lahm-brAYt-tah*; vespa *vEHs-pah*

motorcycle moto *mOH-toh*

mountain montagna *mohn-tAH-ny-ah*

moustache baffi *bAHf-fee*

mouth bocca *bOH-kah*; **mouthwash** disinfettante per la bocca *dee-seen-feht-tAHn-teh pehr lah bOH-kah*

to move muovere *mooOH-vay-reh*

movie cinema *chEE-neh-mah*; **movie camera** cinepresa *chee-neh-prAY-sah*

Mr. signore *see-ny-OH-reh*

Mrs. signora *see-ny-OH-rah*

much molto *mOHl-toh*; **how much is it?** quanto costa? *koo-AHn-toh kOHs-tah?*

museum museo *moo-sEH-oh*

mussels cozze *kOH-tseh*

music musica *mOO-see-kah*

must dovere *doh-vAY-reh*; **I must go** debbo andarmene *dAYb-boh ahn-dAHr-meh-neh*

mustard senape *sEH-nah-peh* mostarda *moh-stAHr-dah*

mutton montone *mohn-tOH-neh*

my mio *mEE-oh*; miei *meeAY-ee*; mia *mEEah*; mie *mEEeh*

mystery mistero *mees-tEH-roh*; **it's a mystery!** è un giallo! *EH oon jeeAHl-loh!*

N

nail unghia *OOn-ghee-ah*; **nail clippers** tagliaunghie *tAH-ly-ee-ah-OOn-ghee-eh*; **nail polish** smalto per le unghie *smAHl-toh pehr leh OOn-ghee-eh*; **polish remover** acetone *ah-chay-tOH-neh*

name nome *nOH-meh*; **last name** cognome *koh-ny-OH-meh*; **my name is . . .** mi chiamo *mee keyAH-moh*

napkin tovagliolo *toh-vah-ly-ee-OH-loh*; **sanitary napkins** assorbenti igienici *ahs-sohr-bEHn-tee ee-jeeEH-nee-chee*

nationality nazionalità *nah-tsee-oh-nah-lee-tAH*

near accanto *ah-kAHn-toh*

necessary necessario *neh-chEHs-sAH-ree-oh*

necklace catenina *kah-tay-nEE-nah*; collana *kohl-lAH-nah*; monile *moh-nEE-leh*

necktie cravatta *krah-vAHt-tah*

to need avere bisogno di *ah-vAY-reh bee-sOH-ny-oh dee*; **I need help** ho bisogno d'aiuto *oh bee-sOH-ny-oh dah-eeOO-toh*

needle ago *AH-goh*

new nuovo *nooOH-voh*

newspaper giornale *jee-ohr-nAH-leh*

newsstand edicola *ay-dEE-koh-lah*; giornalaio *jee-ohr-nah-lAH-ee-oh*

next to accanto *ah-kAHn-toh*

night club night club *nAHeet klOOb*

nine nove *nOH-veh*

nineteen diciannove *dee-chee-ahn-nOH-veh*

ninety novanta *noh-vAHn-tah*

ninth nono *nOH-noh*

nonsense! sciocchezze! *shee-oh-kAY-tseh!*; ma che! *mah kAY!*

noon mezzogiorno *mEH-tsoh-jee-OHr-noh*

normal normale *nohr-mAH-leh*

north nord *nord*

nose naso *nAH-soh*

not non *nOHn*

notebook taccuino *tah-kooEE-noh*; block-notes *blOHk-nOH-tays*

nothing niente *neeEHn-tay*

now adesso *ah-dEHs-soh*; ora *OH-rah*

nuisance seccatura *say-kah-tOO-rah*

number numero *nOO-meh-roh*; **numbered** numerato *noo-meh-rAH-toh*

nut (fruit) noce *nOH-chay*; **(mechanical)** dado *dAH-doh*

nylon nylon

O

to observe osservare *ohs-sehr-vAH-reh*

to obstruct ostruire *ohs-trooEE-reh*

to obtain ottenere *oht-tay-nAY-reh*

occupied occupato *oh-koo-pAH-toh*

ocean oceano *oh-chEH-ah-noh*

October ottobre *oht-tOH-breh*

octopus polipo *pOH-lee-poh*

oculist oculista *oh-koo-lEEs-tah*

of di *dee*

office ufficio *oof-fEE-chee-oh*

often spesso *spAYs-soh*

oil olio *OH-lee-oh*

omelet frittata *freet-tAH-tah*

on sopra *sOH-prah*; su *soo*

once una volta *OO-nah vOHl-tah*

one un *oon*; uno *OO-noh*; una *OO-nah*; un' *oon*; **one way** senso unico *sEHn-soh OO-nee-koh*

onion cipolla *chee-pOHl-lah*

only solamente *soh-lah-mEHn-teh*

onyx onice *OH-nee-cheh*

to open aprire *ah-prEE-reh*

open aperto *ah-pEHr-toh*

opera opera *OH-peh-rah*; **operetta** operetta *oh-peh-rAYt-tah*

opposite contrario *kohn-trAH-ree-oh*

optician ottico *OHt-tee-koh*

or o *oh*

orange (fruit) arancia *ah-rAHn-chee-ah*; **(tree)** arancio *ah-rAHn-chee-oh*

orangeade aranciata *ah-rahn-cheeAH-tah*

orchestra orchestra *ohr-kEHs-trah*; **(group) section** platea *plah-tEH-ah*

to order ordinare *ohr-dee-nAH-reh*

other altro *AHl-troh*

ouch! ahi! *AHee!*

outcome risultato *ree-sool-tAH-toh*

outside fuori *fooOH-ree*

oven forno *fOHr-noh*

overcoat soprabito *soh-prAH-bee-toh*

to overheat surriscaldare *soor-rEEs-kahl-dAH-reh*

own proprio *prOH-pree-oh*

oyster ostrica *OHs-tree-kah*

P

package pacchetto *pah-kAYt-toh*

pantyhose collant *kOHl-lahnt*

pair paio *pAH-ee-oh*

palace palazzo *pah-lAH-tsoh*

panorama panorama

panties mutandine *moo-tahn-dEE-neh*

pants pantaloni *pahn-tah-lOH-nee*

paper carta *kAHr-tah*

parcel pacco *pAH-koh*

to park parcheggiare *pahr-kay-jeeAH-reh*; **no parking** divieto di sosta *dee-veeAY-toh dee sOHs-tah*; **park (garden)** parco *pAHr-koh*

partridge pernice *payr-nEE-cheh*

parts (car) pezzi di ricambio *pEH-tsee dee ree-kAHm-bee-oh*

to pass passare *pahs-sAH-reh*

passport passaporto *pahs-sah-pOHr-toh*

pastry pasticceria *pahs-tee-cheh-rEE-ah*

pathway sentiero *sayn-teeAY-roh*

to pay pagare *pah-gAH-reh*

peas piselli *pee-sEHl-lee*

peach pesca *pAYs-kah*

pear pera *pAY-rah*

pedestrian pedone *peh-dOH-neh*

pen penna *pAYn-nah*; **ball-point pen** penna a sfera *pAYh-nah ah sfEH-rah*

pencil matita *mah-tEE-tah*; **pencil sharpener** temperamatite *tEHm-peh-rah-mah-tEE-teh*

penicillin penicillina *pay-nee-cheel-lEE-nah*

perfume profumo *proh-fOO-moh*

perhaps forse *fOHr-seh*

period periodo *payr-EEoh-doh*

to permit permettere *pehr-mEHt-teh-reh*

permit (license) patente *pah-tEHn-teh*

pharmacy farmacia *fahr-mah-chEE-ah*

pheasant fagiano *fah-jeeAH-noh*

to photograph fotografare *foh-toh-grah-fAH-reh*

photograph (picture) fotografia *foh-toh-grah-fEE-ah*

piece pezzo *pEH-tsoh*

pig (pork) maiale *mah-eeAH-leh*

pill pillola *pEEl-loh-lah*

pillow cuscino *koo-shEE-noh*

pin spilla *spEEl-lah*

pineapple ananasso *ah-nah-nAHs-soh*

place posto *pOHs-toh*; località *loh-kah-lee-tAH*

plate piatto *pee-AHt-toh*

plant pianta *peeAHn-tah*

plastic plastica *plAHs-tee-kah*

platform piattaforma *peeAHt-tah-fOHr-mah*

platinum platino *plAH-tee-noh*

to play giocare *jeeOH-kAH-reh*

playground zona giochi *tsOH-nah jeeOH-key*

please per favore *pehr fah-vOH-reh*; per piacere *pehr pee-ah-chAY-reh*

pliers pinze *pEEn-tseh*

plug: electric spina per la corrente *spEE-nah pehr lah kohr-rEHn-teh*; **spark plug** candela *kahn-dAY-lah*

plum susina *soo-sEE-nah*; prugna *prOO-ny-ah*

poker poker *pOH-kehr*

police polizia *poh-lee-tsEE-ah*; **police station** stazione di polizia *stah-tsee-OH-neh dee pohlee-tsEE-ah*; Commissariato *kOHm-mees-sah-reeAH-toh*; caserma dei carabinieri *kah-sEHr-mah dAY-ee kah-rah-bee-neeAY-ree*

Polish polacco *poh-lAH-koh*

pond stagno *stAH-ny-oh*

pork maiale *mah-eeAH-leh*

portable portatile *pohr-tAH-tee-leh*

porter portabagagli *pOHr-tah-bah-gAH-ly-ee*

portion porzione *pohr-tsee-OH-nay*

Portuguese portoghese *pohr-toh-ghAY-say*

possible possibile *pohs-sEE-bee-leh*

post office ufficio postale *oof-fEE-chee-oh pohs-tAH-leh*

postage affrancatura *ahf-frahn-kah-tOO-rah*

postcard cartolina postale *kahr-toh-lEE-nah pohs-tAH-leh*; **picture post-card** cartolina illustrata *kahr-toh-lEE-nah EEl-loos-trAH-tah*

poster poster; manifesto *mah-nee-fEHs-toh*

potable potabile *poh-tAH-bee-leh*

potato patata *pah-tAH-tah*

prayer preghiera *pray-gheeEH-rah*

to prefer preferire *preh-fay-rEE-reh*

pregnant incinta *EEn-chEEn-tah*

to prepare preparare *preh-pah-rAH-reh*

prescription ricetta *ree-chEHt-tah*

to present presentare *preh-sayn-tAH-reh*

present (gift) regalo *ray-gAH-loh*

price prezzo *prEH-tsoh*

priest prete *prEH-teh*

print (photo) copia *kOH-pee-ah*

private privato *pree-vAH-toh*

profession professione *proh-fehs-seeOH-neh*

prophylactics profilattici *proh-fee-lAHt-tee-chee*; preservativi *preh-sehr-vah-tEE-vee*

program programma *proh-grAHm-mah*

Protestant protestante *proh-tays-tAHn-tay*

to prove provare *pro-vAH-reh*

pudding budino *boo-dEE-noh*

to pull tirare *tee-rAH-reh*

pump pompa *pOHm-pah*; **fuel pump** pompa della benzina *pOHmpah dAYl-lah behn-tsEE-nah*

to purchase comprare *kohm-prAH-reh*

purse borsetta *bohr-sAYt-tah*

to push spingere *spEEn-jay-reh*

to put mettere *mAYt-tay-reh*

Q

quarter quarto *kooAHr-toh*
queen (cards) donna *dOHn-nah*
question domanda *doh-mAHn-dah*
quick presto *prEHs-toh*

R

rabbi rabbino *rahb-bEE-noh*
rabbit coniglio *koh-nEE-ly-ee-oh*
racetrack ippodromo
eep-pOH-droh-moh
racquet racchetta *rah-kAYt-tah*
radiator (car) radiatore
rah-dee-ah-tOH-reh
radish ravanello *rah-vah-nEHl-loh*
railroad ferrovia *fehr-roh-vEE-ah*;
railroad station stazione
ferroviaria *stah-tsee-OH-neh
fEHr-ro-veeAH-ree-ah*
to rain piovere *pee-OH-veh-reh*
raincoat impermeabile
eem-pehr-mayAH-bee-leh
raspberry lampone *lahm-pOH-neh*
razor rasoio *rah-sOH-ee-oh*; **razor
blades** lamette *lah-mAYt-teh*
to reach raggiungere
rah-jeeOOn-jay-reh; arrivare
ahr-ree-vAH-reh
to read leggere *lEH-jeh-reh*
ready pronto *prOHn-toh*
receipt ricevuta *ree-chay-vOO-tah*
to receive ricevere
ree-chAY-vay-reh
receiver (telephone) destinatario
days-tee-nah-tAH-ree-oh
to recommend consigliare
kohn-see-ly-ee-AH-reh;
raccomandare
rAH-koh-mahn-dAH-reh

record (phonograph) disco
dEEs-koh; **record player**
giradischi *jEE-rah-dEEs-kee*
reduced ridotto *ree-dOHt-toh*
red rosso *rOHs-soh*
referee arbitro *AHr-bee-troh*
refund rimborso *reem-bOHr-soh*
religious religioso
ray-lee-jeeOH-soh
to remain restare *rays-tAH-reh*
to rent (car) noleggiare
noh-lay-jeeAH-reh; **(house)**
affittare *ahf-feet-tAH-reh*
to repair aggiustare
ah-jee-oos-tAH-reh; riparare
ree-pah-rAH-reh
repair shop officina meccanica
ohf-fee-chEE-nah may-kAH-nee-kah
to repeat ripetere *ree-pEH-teh-reh*
reservation prenotazione
preh-noh-tah-tsee-OH-neh
reserved riservato
ree-sehr-vAH-toh; prenotato
preh-noh-tAH-toh
to reside risiedere
ree-seeAY-deh-reh
to rest riposare *ree-poh-sAH-reh*
rest room gabinetto
gah-bee-nAYt-toh; bagno
bAH-ny-oh; toilette *tooAH-lEHt*
restaurant ristorante
rEEs-toh-rAHn-teh
result risultato *ree-sool-tAH-toh*
to return ritornare
ree-tohr-nAH-reh
rice riso *rEE-soh*
right destro *dEHs-troh*; **that's all
right** va bene *vah bEH-neh*;
right away subito *sOO-bee-toh*
ring anello *ah-nEHl-loh*
river fiume *feeOO-meh*
road via *vEE-ah*; strada *strAH-dah*;
road map cartina stradale
kahr-tEE-nah strah-dAH-leh

roast arrosto *ahr-rOHs-toh*

robe accappatoio
ah-kAHp-pah-tOH-ee-oh

roll (film) rullino *rool-lEE-noh*

room camera *kAH-meh-rah*;
  bedroom camera da letto
  kAH-meh-rah dah lEHt-toh

rose rosa *rOH-sah*

rouge rossetto *rohs-sAYt-toh*

row (theater) fila *fEE-lah*

ruler riga *rEE-gah*

Rumanian rumeno *roo-mAY-noh*

to run correre *kOHr-ray-reh*;
  running water acqua corrente
  AH-koo-ah kohr-rEHn-tay

Russian russo *rOOs-soh*

rye segala *sAY-gah-lah*

S

saccharin saccarina
  sah-kah-rEE-nah; dolcificante
  dohl-chee-fee-kAHn-teh

salad insalata *een-sah-lAH-tah*

salami salame *sah-lah-meh*

sale svendita *svAYn-dee-tah*

salmon salmone *sahl-mOH-neh*

salt sale *sAH-leh*; **salty** salato
  sah-lAH-toh

same stesso *stAYs-soh*

sand sabbia *sAHb-bee-ah*

sandwich panino (imbottito)
  pah-nEE-noh (eem-boht-tEE-toh)

sapphire zaffiro *tsahf-fEE-roh*

sardine sardina *sahr-dEE-nah*

Saturday sabato *sAH-bah-toh*

sauce salsa *sAHl-sah*

saucer piattino *pee-aht-tEE-noh*

to say dire *dEE-reh*

schedule orario *oh-rAH-ree-oh*; **on
  schedule** in orario *een
  oh-rAH-ree-oh*

science fiction fantascienza
  fAHn-tah-shee-EHn-tsah

scissors forbici *fOHr-bee-chee*

score punteggio *poon-tAY-jee-oh*

Scotch tape nastro adesivo
  nAHs-troh ah-day-sEE-voh

scram! si tolga dai piedi! *see
  tOH-lgah dAHee pee-EH-dee!*

screw vite *vEE-teh*

sea mare *mAH-reh*

seasickness mal di mare *mAHl dee
  mAH-reh*

second secondo *say-kOHn-doh*

sedative sedativo *say-dah-tEE-voh*

to see vedere *vay-dAY-reh*

selection selezione
  say-leh-tsee-OH-neh

to sell vendere *vAYn-day-reh*

to send mandare *mahn-dAH-reh*;
  spedire *spay-dEE-reh*

September settembre
  seht-tEHm-breh

series serie *sEH-ree-eh*

to serve servire *sayr-vEE-reh*

service servizio *sayr-vEE-tsee-oh*

seven sette *sEHt-teh*; **seven
  hundred** settecento *sEHt-teh
  chEHn-toh*

seventeen diciassette
  dEE-chee-ahs-sEHt-teh

seventh settimo *sEHt-tee-moh*

seventy settanta *sEHt-tAHn-tah*

to sew cucire *koo-chEE-reh*

shade ombra *OHm-brah*;
  (window) tendina *tehn-dEE-nah*

to shave oneself farsi la barba
  fAHr-see lah bAHr-bah;
  after-shave dopobarba
  dOH-poh-bAHr-bah

shaving cream crema per la barba
  krEH-mah pehr lah bAHr-bah

she lei *lEH-ee*; ella *AYl-lah*; essa
  AYs-sah

sherry sherry

to shine shoes lucidare le scarpe
loo-chee-dAH-reh leh skAHr-peh

ship nave *nAH-veh*

shirt camicia *kah-mEE-chee-ah*;
man's shirt camicia da uomo
kah-mEE-chee-ah dah ooOH-moh

shoe scarpa *skAHr-pah*; **shoe
store** calzaturificio
kahl-tsah-too-ree-fEE-chee-oh

shoelaces lacci per le scarpe
lAH-chee pehr leh skAHr-peh

shoemaker calzolaio
kahl-tsoh-lAH-ee-oh

shop negozio *nay-gOH-tsee-oh*;
shop window vetrina
vay-trEE-nah

short corto *kOHr-toh*; **(person)**
basso(a) *bAHs-soh(ah)*; **short
story** novella *noh-vEHl-lah*

shorts pantaloncini
pahn-tah-lohn-chEE-nee

shoulder spalla *spAHl-lah*

to show indicare *een-dee-kAH-reh*

shower doccia *dOH-chee-ah*

shrimps gamberetti
gahm-bay-rAYt-tee

to shuffle mischiare
mees-key-AH-reh

shut up! zitto! *tsEEt-toh!*

sick malato *mah-lAH-toh*

side (body) fianco *feeAHn-koh*

sidewalk marciapiede
mAHr-chee-ah-pee-EH-deh

to sign firmare *feer-mAH-reh*

signature firma *fEEr-mah*

silence silenzio *see-lEHn-tsee-oh*

silk seta *sAY-tah*

silly sciocco *sheeOH-koh*; **silliness**
sciocchezza *shee-oh-kAH-tsah*

silver argento *ahr-jEHn-toh*

sin peccato *peh-kAH-toh*

since siccome *see-kOHm-eh*

to sing cantare *kahn-tAH-reh*

single (room) camera a un letto
kAH-may-rah ah oon lEHt-toh

sister sorella *soh-rEHl-lah*

to sit sedersi *say-dAYr-see*

site località *loh-kah-lee-tAH*

six sei *sEH-ee*; **six hundred**
seicento *sEH-ee-chEHn-toh*

sixteen sedici *sAY-dee-chee*

sixth sesto *sEHs-toh*

sixty sessanta *says-sAHn-tah*

size misura *mee-sOO-rah*; taglia
tAH-ly-ee-ah

to ski sciare *shee-AH-reh*

ski boots scarponi da sci
skahr-pOH-nee dah shEE; **lifts**
sciovie *shee-oh-vEE-eh*; **slopes**
piste (per sciare) *pEEs-teh (pehr
sheeAH-reh)*

skiing (water skiing) sci
acquatico *shEE ah-kooAH-tee-koh*

skin pelle *pEHl-leh*

skirt gonna *gOHn-nah*

to sleep dormire *dohr-mEE-reh*

sleeping car (train) vagone letto
vah-gOH-neh lEHt-toh

sleeve manica *mAH-nee-kah*

slice fetta *fAYt-tah*; **sliced**
affettato *ahf-fayt-tAH-toh*

slip sottoveste *soht-toh-vEHs-teh*

slippers pantofole
pahn-tOH-foh-leh; ciabatte
chee-ah-bAHt-teh

slowly lentamente
layn-tah-mEHn-teh; piano
pee-AH-noh

small piccolo *pEE-koh-loh*;
smaller più piccolo *pee-OO
pEE-koh-loh*

to smile sorridere
sohr-rEE-day-reh; fare un sorriso
fAH-reh oon sohr-rEE-soh; **smile!**
sorrida! *sohr-rEE-dah!*

to smoke fumare *foo-mAH-reh*; **no
smoking** vietato fumare
vee-ay-tAH-toh foo-mAH-reh

smoker fumatore *foo-mah-tOH-reh*

to snatch scippare *sheep-pAH-reh*

to snow nevicare *nay-vee-kAH-reh*

snow neve *nAY-veh*

so cosí *koh-sEE*

soap sapone *sah-pOH-neh*;
saponetta *sah-poh-nAYt-tah*

soccer calcio *kAHl-chee-oh*; **soccer game** partita di calcio *OO-nah pahr-tEE-tah dee kAHl-chee-oh*

socks calzini *kahl-tsEE-nee*;
calzettini *kahl-tsayt-tEE-nee*

soft drink bibita analcolica *bEE-bee-tah ah-nahl-koh-lEE-kah*

sole (fish) sogliola *sOH-ly-ee-oh-lah*

soles (shoes) suole *soo-OH-leh*; **half-soles** mezze suole *mEH-tseh soo-OH-leh*

solid color tinta unita *tEEn-tah oo-nEE-tah*

some alcuni *ahl-kOO-nee*; qualche *koo-AHl-keh*; **someone** qualcuno *koo-ahl-kOO-noh*; **something** qualche cosa *koo-AHl-keh kOH-sah*; **sometimes** qualche volta *koo-AHl-keh vOHl-tah*

son figlio *fEE-ly-ee-oh*

soon presto *prEHs-toh*; **as soon as possible** appena possibile *ahp-pAY-nah pohs-sEE-bee-leh*

soprano soprano

sorry (to be sorry) dispiacere *dees-pee-ah-chAY-reh*; **I'm sorry** mi dispiace *mee dees-peeAH-cheh*

soup minestra *mee-nEHs-trah*

south sud *sood*

spades (cards) picche *pEE-keh*

Spanish spagnolo *spah-ny-OH-loh*

spare tire la ruota di scorta *lah roo-OH-tah dee skOHr-tah*

spark plug candela *kahn-dAY-lah*

sparkling wine spumante *spoo-mAHn-teh*

to speak parlare *pahr-lAH-reh*

special speciale *spay-chee-AH-leh*

specialty specialità *spEH-chee-ah-lee-tAH*

to spend (money) spendere *spEHn-deh-reh*; **(time)** passare *pahs-sAH-reh*

spinach spinaci *spee-nAH-chee*

sponge spugna *spOO-ny-ah*

spoon cucchiaio *koo-keyAH-ee-oh*; **teaspoon** cucchiaino *koo-key-ah-EE-noh*

sports car macchina sportiva *mAH-key-nah spohr-tEE-vah*

spot posto *pOHs-toh*

to sprain slogare *sloh-gAH-reh*

sprain (injury) slogatura *sloh-gah-tOO-rah*

spring molla *mOHl-lah*; **(season)** primavera *pree-mah-vEH-rah*

squab (pigeon) piccioncino *pEE-chee-ohn-chEE-noh*

square piazza *peeAH-tsah*

squid calamari *kah-lah-mAH-ree*

stadium stadio *stAH-dee-oh*

stairs scale *skAH-leh*

stamp francobollo *frahn-koh-bOHl-loh*

to stand stare in piedi *stAH-reh een peeEH-dee*

to start cominciare *koh-meen-chee-AH-reh*; **(car)** avviare *ahv-vee-AH-reh*

station stazione *stah-tsee-OHn-neh*

to steal rubare *roo-bAH-reh*

steel acciaio *ah-chee-AH-ee-oh*; **stainless steel** acciaio inossidabile *ah-chee-AH-ee-oh een-OHs-see-dAH-bee-leh*

steering wheel volante *voh-lAHn-teh*

still ancora *ahn-kOH-rah*

stocking calza *kAHl-tsah*

stomach stomaco *stOH-mah-coh*

stone pietra *pee-EH-trah*; **precious stone** pietra preziosa *pee-EH-trah pray-tsee-OH-sah*

to stop fermare *fayr-mAH-reh*

stop fermata *fayr-mAH-tah*; **bus stop** fermata del bus *fayr-mAH-tah dayl-boos*

store negozio *nay-gOH-tsee-oh*

stories racconti *rah-kOHn-tee*; storie *stOH-ree-eh*

straight diritto *dee-rEEt-toh*

stream ruscello *roo-shEHl-loh*

street strada *strAH-dah*; via *vEE-ah*

streetcar tram *trAHm*; tranvai *trahn-vAH-ee*

string beans fagiolini *fah-jee-oh-lEE-nee*

strong forte *fOHr-teh*; **stronger** più forte *pee-OO fOHr-teh*

stuck bloccato *bloh-kAH-toh*

stupid stupido *stOO-pee-doh*; **don't be stupid** non fare lo stupido *nohn fAH-reh loh stOO-pee-doh*

subtitle sottotitolo *sOHt-toh-tEE-toh-loh*

subway metropolitana *mEH-troh-poh-lee-tAH-nah*

suede (leather) renna *rAYn-nah*; pelle scamosciata *pEHl-lay skah-moh-shee-AH-tah*

sugar zucchero *tsOO-keh-roh*; **sugar substitute** dolcificante *dohl-chee-fee-kAHn-teh*

suit abito *AH-bee-toh*; vestito *vays-tEE-toh*

suitcase valigia *vah-lEE-jee-ah*

summer estate *ehs-tAH-teh*

sun sole *sOH-leh*

sunburn scottatura solare *skoht-tah-tOO-rah soh-lAH-reh*

Sunday domenica *doh-mAY-nee-kah*

sunglasses occhiali da sole *oh-key-AH-lee dah sOH-leh*

supermarket supermercato *sOO-pehr-mehr-kAH-toh*

supper cena *chAY-nah*; **to have supper** cenare *chay-nAH-reh*

sweater maglia *mAH-ly-ee-ah*

Swedish svedese *svay-dAY-say*

sweet dolce *dOHl-cheh*

swelling gonfiore *gohn-fee-OH-reh*

to swim nuotare *nOO-oh-tAH-reh*

swimming pool piscina *pee-shEE-nah*; **(indoor)** piscina coperta *pee-shEE-nah koh-pEHr-tah*; **(outdoor)** piscina scoperta *pee-shEE-nah skoh-pEHr-tah*

Swiss svizzero *svEE-tsay-roh*

switch interruttore *een-tehr-root-tOH-reh*

swollen gonfio *gOHn-fee-oh*

synagogue sinagoga *see-nah-gOH-gah*

synthetic poliestere *poh-lee-EHs-tay-reh*; sintetico *seen-tEH-tee-koh*

syrup sciroppo *shee-rOHp-poh*

system sistema *sees-tEH-mah*

T

table tavola *tAH-voh-lah*

tablecloth tovaglia *toh-vAH-ly-ee-ah*

tablet pasticca *pahs-tEE-kah*

tag cartellino *kahr-tayl-lEE-noh*

tailor sarto *sAHr-toh*

to take (to a place) portare *pohr-tAH-reh*; prendere *prayn-dAY-reh*; **to take off (airplane)** decollare *day-kohl-lAH-reh*

taken (occupied) occupato *oh-koo-pAH-toh*

talcum powder talco *tAHl-koh*

tall alto *AHl-toh*

to talk parlare *pahr-lAH-reh*

tampons tamponi igienici
tahm-pOH-nee EE-jeeEH-nee-chee

tangerine mandarino
mahn-dah-rEE-noh

tariff tariffa *tah-rEEf-fah*

tavern trattoria *traht-toh-rEE-ah*

tax tassa *tAHs-sah*; imposta
eem-pOH-stah

taxi tassì *tahs-sEE*

tea tè *tEH*

team squadra *skoo-AH-drah*

telegram telegramma
teh-leh-grAHm-mah

to telephone telefonare
teh-leh-foh-nAH-reh; **I want to
make a phone call** voglio fare
una telefonata *vOH-ly-ee-oh
fAH-reh OO-nah
teh-leh-foh-nAH-tah*; **local call**
urbana *oor-bAH-nah*; **long
distance** in teleselezione, *een
teh-leh-say-leh-tsee-OH-neh*;
interurbana *een-tayr-oor-bAH-nah*;
person to person con
preavviso *kohn prEH-ahv-vEE-soh*;
reverse charge riversibile
ree-vehr-sEE-bee-leh

telephone telefono
teh-lEH-foh-noh; **public
telephone** telefono pubblico
teh-lEH-foh-noh pOOb-blee-koh

television televisione
teh-leh-vee-see-OH-neh

to tell dire *dEE-reh*; **tell me** mi
dica *mee dEE-kah*

temperature temperatura
tehm-peh-rah-tOO-rah

temporarily provvisoriamente
prohv-vee-sOH-ree-ah-mEHn-teh

ten dieci *dee-EH-chee*

tennis tennis

tenor tenore *teh-nOH-reh*

tenth decimo *dEH-chee-moh*

terminal (bus, tram, auto)
capolinea *kah-poh-lEE-neh-ah*

terrace terrazza *tehr-rAH-tsah*

terrible terribile *tehr-rEE-bee-leh*

thanks grazie *grAH-tsee-eh*;
thank-you very much molte
grazie *mOHl-teh grAH-tsee-eh*

that che *kay*; **that one** quello
koo-AYl-loh

the il *eel*; lo *loh*; la *lah*; i *ee*; gli
ly-ee; le *leh*

theater teatro *teh-AH-troh*

their loro *lOH-roh*

them li *lee*; le *lay*; loro *lOH-roh*

there lì *lEE*; là *lAH*; **there are** ci
sono *chee sOH-noh*; **there is** c'è
chEH

thermometer termometro
tehr-mOH-meh-troh

these questi *koo-AYs-tee*; queste
koo-AYs-tay

they essi *AYs-see*; esse *AYs-say*;
loro *lOH-roh*

thief ladro *lAH-droh*

thigh coscia *kOH-shee-ah*

thin sottile *soht-tEE-leh*

thing cosa *kOH-sah*

to think pensare *pehn-sAH-reh*

third terzo *tEHr-tsoh*

thirsty assetato *ahs-say-tAH-toh*

thirteen tredici *trAY-dee-chee*

thirty trenta *trEHn-tah*

this questo *koo-AYs-toh*; questa
koo-AYs-tah

those quelli *koo-AYl-lee*; quelle
koo-AYl-leh

thousand mille *mEEl-leh*

thread filo *fEE-loh*

three tre *tray*

throat gola *gOH-lah*

thumb pollice *pOHl-lee-cheh*

Thursday giovedì *jee-oh-vay-dEE*

ticket biglietto *bee-ly-ee-AYt-toh*; **a one-way ticket** un biglietto di andata *oon bee-ly-ee-AYt-toh dee ahn-dAH-tah*; **a round-trip ticket** un biglietto di andata e ritorno *oon bee-ly-ee-AYt-toh dee ahn-dAH-tah ay ree-tOHr-noh*; **ticket office** biglietteria *bee-ly-ee-AYt-tay-rEE-ah*

to tighten stringere *strEEn-jay-reh*

time tempo *tEHm-poh*; **timetable** orario *oh-rAH-ree-oh*

tip mancia *mAHn-chee-ah*

tire pneumatico *pneh-oo-mAH-tee-koh*; **flat tire** gomma bucata *gOHm-mah boo-kAH-tah*

tired stanco *stAHn-koh*

to a *ah*

to toast brindare *breen-dAH-reh*

tobacco tabacco *tah-bAH-koh*; **tobacco shop** tabaccheria *tah-bAH-kay-rEE-ah*; **snuff tobacco** tabacco a fiuto *tah-bAH-koh dah fee-OO-toh*

today oggi *OH-jee*

toe alluce *AHl-loo-cheh*

together insieme *een-see-EH-meh*

toilet gabinetto *gah-bee-nAYt-toh*; toilette *too-ah-lEHt*; bagno *bAH-ny-oh*; **toilet paper** carta igienica *kAHr-tah ee-jeeEH-nee-kah*

token gettone *jayt-tOH-nay*

tomato pomodoro *poh-moh-dOH-roh*

tomorrow domani *doh-mAH-nee*; **the day after tomorrow** dopodomani *dOH-poh-doh-mAH-nee*; **see you tomorrow** a domani *ah doh-mAH-nee*

tonic tonico *tOH-nee-koh*

tonight stasera *stah-sAY-rah*

tonsils tonsille *tohn-sEEl-leh*

too anche *AHn-keh*

tools attrezzi *aht-trAY-tsee*

tooth dente *dEHn-tah*; **toothache** mal di denti *mAHl dee dEHn-tee*; **toothbrush** spazzolino per i denti *spah-tsoh-lEE-noh pehr ee dehn-tee*; **toothpaste** dentifricio *dehn-tee-frEE-chee-oh*

top cima *chEE-mah*

topaz topazio *toh-pAH-tsee-oh*

to touch toccare *toh-kAH-reh*

tourist (for tourists) turistico *too-rEEs-tee-koh*

tow truck carroattrezzi *kAHr-roh-aht-trAY-tsee*

towel asciugamano *ah-shee-OO-gah-mAH-noh*

toy store negozio di giocattoli *nay-gOH-tsee-oh dee jee-oh-kAHt-toh-lee*

track (train) binario *bee-nAH-ree-oh*

traffic light semaforo *seh-mAH-foh-roh*

train treno *treh-noh*

training allenamento *ah-lay-nah-mehn-toh*

transit transito *trAHn-see-toh*

travel viaggio *vee-AH-jee-oh*; **travel agency** agenzia di viaggi *ah-jehn-tsEE-ah dee vee-AH-jee*

traveler's check traveler's check

tree albero *AHl-beh-roh*

to trim (hair) spuntare *spoon-tAH-reh*

trip viaggio *vee-AH-jee-oh*; gita *jEE-tah*

trouble fastidio *fahs-tEE-dee-oh*

trout trota *trOH-tah*

true vero *vEH-roh*

to try provare *proh-vAH-reh*

Tuesday martedì *mahr-teh-dEE*

tuna tonno *tOHn-noh*

turkey tacchino *tah-kEE-noh*

Turkish turco *tOOr-koh*

to turn girare *jee-rAH-reh;* **it's your turn** tocca a lei *tOH-kah ah lEH-ee*

turquoise turchese *toor-kAY-seh*

tweezers pinzette *peen-tsAYt-teh*

twelve dodici *dOH-dee-cheé*

twenty venti *vAYn-tee;* **twenty-one** ventuno *vayn-tOO-noh;* **twenty-two** ventidue *vAYn-tee-dOO-eh*

two due *dOO-eh;* **two hundred** duecento *doo-eh-chEHn-toh*

typing paper carta per battere a macchina *kAHr-tah payr bAHt-teh-reh ah mAH-kee-nah*

U

umbrella ombrello *ohm-brEH-loh*

uncle zio *tsEE-oh*

under sotto *sOHt-toh*

undershirt canottiera *kah-noht-teeEH-rah*

to understand capire *kah-pEE-reh*

underwear biancheria intima *bee-AHn-kay-rEE-ah EEn-tee-mah*

university università *oo-nee-vayr-see-tAH*

unless a meno che *ah mAY-noh keh*

until fino a *fEE-noh ah*

us ci *chee*

to use usare *oo-sAH-reh*

usher (theater) maschera *mAHs-keh-rah*

V

very molto *mohl-toh*

view panorama

village villaggio *veel-lAH-jee-oh*

vinegar aceto *ah-chAY-toh*

to visit visitare *vee-see-tAH-reh*

W

to wait aspettare *ahs-peht-tAH-reh*

waiter cameriere *kah-meh-ree-EH-reh*

waitress cameriera *kah-meh-ree-EH-rah*

to wake up svegliare *svay-ly-ee-AH-reh*

to walk camminare *kahm-mee-nAH-reh*

to want volere *voh-lAY-reh*

warm caldo *kAHl-doh*

to wash lavare *lah-vAH-reh*

to watch guardare *goo-ahr-dAH-reh*

watch orologio *oh-roh-lOH-jee-oh;* **wrist watch** orologio da polso *oh-roh-lOH-jee-oh dah pOHl-soh;* **watchmaker** orologiaio *oh-roh-loh-jee-AH-ee-oh*

water acqua *AH-koo-ah;* **drinkable water** acqua potabile *AH-koo-ah poh-tAH-bee-leh;* **running water** acqua corrente *AH-koo-ah kohr-rehn-teh*

waterfall cascata *kahs-kAH-tah*

watermelon cocomero *koh-kOH-may-roh;* anguria *ahn-gOO-ree-ah*

wave onda *OHn-dah*

wavy hair capelli ondulati *kah-pAYl-lee ohn-doo-lAH-tee*

we noi *nOH-ee*

weak debole *dAY-boh-leh*

to wear portare *pohr-tAH-reh;* indossare *een-dohs-sAH-reh*

weather tempo *tehm-poh*

Wednesday mercoledì *mehr-koh-lay-dEE*

week settimana *sayt-tee-mAH-nah*

well bene *beh-neh*

west ovest *OH-vehst*

what che *kay;* che cosa *kay kOH-sah*

wheel ruota *roo-OH-tah*

when quando *koo-AHn-doh*

where dove *dOH-veh*; **where is it?** dov'è? *doh-vEH?*

which quale *koo-AH-leh*

whiskers baffi *bAHf-fee*

while mentre *mEHn-treh*

white bianco *bee-AHn-koh*

who chi *key*; che *kay*

why perché *payr-kAY*

wide largo *lAHr-goh*

wife moglie *mOH-ly-ee-eh*

to win vincere *vEEn-chay-reh*

window finestra *fee-nehs-trah*

wine vino *vEE-noh*; **wineshop** enoteca *AY-noh-teh-kah*; rivendita di vini *ree-vAYn-dee-tah dee vEE-nee*

wing ala *AH-lah*

winter inverno *een-vEHr-noh*

to wish desiderare *day-see-deh-rAH-reh*

with con *kohn*; **within** dentro *dEHn-troh*; **without** senza *sEHn-tsah*

woman donna *dOHn-nah*

wonderful fantastico *fahn-tAH-stee-koh*; stupendo *stoo-pEHn-doh*

wool lana *lAH-nah*

word parola *pah-rOH-lah*

to work lavorare *lah-voh-rAH-reh*; **(machineries)** funzionare *foon-tsee-oh-nAH-reh*

to worship adorare *ah-doh-rAH-reh*

wound ferita *fay-rEE-tah*

wow! eh! *AY!*

to wrap incartare *een-kahr-tAH-reh*

to write scrivere *skrEE-veh-reh*

writing pad blocchetto di carta *bloh-kAYt-toh dee kAHr-tah*

Y

yard iarda *ee-AHr-dah*

year anno *AHn-noh*

yellow giallo *jee-AHl-loh*

yes sì *sEE*

yesterday ieri *ee-AY-ree*

you tu *too*; lei *lEH-ee*; voi *vOH-ee*; te *tay*; loro *lOH-roh*

young giovane *jee-OH-vAH-neh*; **young lady** signorina *see-ny-oh-rEE-nah*; **young man** giovanotto *jee-oh-vah-nOHt-toh*

your suo *sOO-oh*; sua *sOO-ah*; vostro *vOH-stroh*; loro *lOH-roh*; tuo *tOO-oh*; tua *tOO-ah*

youth gioventù *jee-oh-vayn-tOO*; **youth hostel** ostello della gioventù *ohs-tEHl-loh dAYl-lah jee-oh-vayn-tOO*

Yugoslav jugoslavo *ee-OO-gohs-lAH-voh*

Z

zero zero *tsEH-roh*

zipper cerniera *chayr-nee-EH-rah*

zoo zoo *tsOH-oh*

ITALIAN-ENGLISH DICTIONARY

The following Italian words are presented here with accent marks to aid pronunciation. As there are actually very few accents used in Italian, you will find most of these words without accents when used in context.

A

a to, at, in

abbàcchio lamb, spring lamb

abbagliànti headlights

abbastànza enough

abbronazatúra suntan

abitàre to live

àbito dress, suit; _____ **da séra** evening gown

accànto next to, near

accappatòio robe for man

accèndere to light

accendíno cigarette lighter

accensióne ignition

accettàre to accept

acciàio steel; _____ **inossidàbile** stainless steel

acciúga anchovy

accónto deposit, partial payment

accorciatòia shortcut

acéto vinegar

acetóne nail polish remover

àcqua water; _____ **corrènte** running water; _____ **potàbile** drinkable water

acquamarína aquamarine

adèsso now

adoràre to adore, to worship

aèreo airplane

aeropòrto airport

affàre business

affettàto sliced; **affettàti** cold cuts

affittàre to rent; **si affítta** for rent

affrancatúra postage

agenzía agency; _____ **d'informazioni** information office; _____ **di viaggi** travel agency

aggiustàre to fix, to repair

àglio garlic

agnèllo lamb

àgo needle

agósto August

ahi! ouch!

aiuòla flower bed, garden, grass

aiutàre to help

aiúto help

àla wing

albèrgo hotel, inn

àlbero tree

albicòcca apricot

àlbum album

àlcool alcohol

alcúni a few, some

alfière knight

allenaménto training, practice

allèrgico allergic

àlluce big toe

àlto high

àltro other; **un àltro** another

alzàre to lift, to raise; _____ il màzzo to cut cards

amàlgama amalgam

ambulatòrio first aid station, doctor's office

americàno(a) American

ametísta amethyst

amíco(a) friend

amóre love; **per l'amòr del cièlo!** my goodness!

analcòlico nonalcoholic; **bíbita analcòlica** soft drink

ananàsso pineapple

ancòra still

andàre to go; **andiàmo** let's go!

andàta one-way trip; **andàta e ritórno** round trip

anèllo ring

àngolo corner; **all'àngolo** at the corner

anguílla eel

angùria watermelon

ànitra duck

ànno year

antiàcido antacid

antibiòtico antibiotic

antícipo advance

antipàsto appetizers, hors d'oeuvre

antisèttico antiseptic

aperitívo aperitif

apèrto open

appartamènto apartment

appéna as soon as

appendicíte appendicitis

apprèndere to learn, to come to know of

appuntaménto appointment

apríle April

apríre to open; **è apèrto?** is it open?

aragósta lobster

arància(a) orange tree (fruit)

aranciáta orangeade

àrbitro referee

argènto silver

ària air; _____ condizionàta air-conditioning

arínga herring

arrivàre to reach, to get to a place

arrivedérci goodbye

arròsto roast

artícolo item, article

ascensóre elevator (lift)

ascèsso abscess

asciugacapélli hairdryer

asciugamàno towel

ascoltàre to listen

àsma asthma

aspàragi asparagus

aspettàre to wait; **aspètti!** wait!

aspirína aspirin

àsso ace

asségno check

assicurazióne insurance

assístere to assist, to help

assorbènti igiènici sanitary napkins

attàcco cardíaco heart attack

attènto(a) attentive, careful; **attènto!** watch out!

attenzióne attention; **stía attènto(a)!** be careful!

atterràre to land

attórno around, roundabout

attravèrso across, through

attrazióne attraction

attrézzi tools

àuto car; **mal d'àuto** travel sickness

autoambulànza ambulance

àutobus bus

automàtico automatic

autopúllman (motor-)coach

autoriméssa garage

autóre author

autostràda highway

autúnno fall

avére to have; **ma che còsa ha?** what's the matter with you?

avànti forward; **avànti!** come in!

avventúra adventure; **avventúre poliziésche** detective stories

avviàre to start

avvocàto lawyer

azzúrro blue

B

baciàre to kiss

bacíno pelvis; basin

bàcio kiss

bàffi moustache

bagníno lifeguard

bàgno bathroom

balcóne balcony

ballàre to dance

ballétto ballet

bàllo dance

bambíno child, kid, baby

bàmbola doll

banàna banana

bànca bank

banconòta banknote

bàrba beard, shave

barbería barbershop

barítono baritone

bàsso low, short, bass voice

bàsta enough; **bàsta (cosí)!** that's enough!

battería battery

bellézza beauty; **salóne di ____** beauty parlor

bèl, bèllo(a) beautiful, handsome, nice

bène well; **va bène** that's all right

benzína gasoline (petrol)

bére to drink

bianchería linen, laundry; **bianchería íntima** underwear

biànco(a) white

bíbita drink

bibliotèca library

bicchière drinking glass

biciclétta bicycle

bigliettería ticket office

bigliétto ticket, banknote; **un bigliétto da mílle líre** a 1000-lire bill; **un bigliétto di andàta e ritórno** a round-trip ticket

bióndo (chiàro) (light) blond

bírra beer

biscòtto cookie

bisognàre to be necessary, to have to

bisógno need

bistécca beefsteak

bloccàto(a) stuck

blocchétto (di càrta) writing pad

blu blue

blúsa blouse

bócca mouth; **in ____ al lùpo!** good luck!

boccóne bite; **mangiàre un ____** to have a bite

bollíto boiled

bórsa handbag

botànico botanic

botteghíno (theater) box office

bottíglia bottle

bottóne button

bowling bowling

bracciàle armlet, bangle, bracelet

bràccio arm

branzíno bass (fish)

brívido shiver, chills

bròdo broth

bruciàto burnt

brúna dark-haired woman, brunette

budíno pudding

bullóne bolt

bugía lie; **è una _____!** it's a lie!

buòno(a) good

búrro butter

bústa envelope

C

cabína cabin; **_____ telefònica** phone booth

cachèt color rinse

cadére to fall; **sono cadùto(a) I** have fallen

caffè coffee; **_____ corrètto** with liquor

calamàri squid

càlcio kick, soccer; **il _____ d'inìzio** the kick off; **una partita di _____** a soccer game

càldo warm, hot

callìfugo corn plaster

calpestàre to crush under foot; **è vietàto _____ l'èrba.** keep off the grass.

càlza stocking

calzaturifício shoe store

calzíni socks

calzolàio shoemaker

cambiàre to change, to exchange

càmbio change; **l'ufficio di _____** (money) exchange office

càmera room; **_____ da lètto** bedroom

camerièra maid, waitress

camerière waiter

camícia shirt; **_____ da uòmo** man's shirt

campàgna countryside

campéggio camping

càmpo field; **_____ di golf** golf course

cancellàre to erase

candéla spark plug, candle

canottièra man's undershirt

cantàre to sing

capélli hair; **un tàglio di _____** a haircut

capíre to understand; **io capísco I** understand

càpo head

capolínea (bus) terminal

cappèllo hat

càpperi! man alive!

cappóne capon

caprétto baby goat

caramèlla candy

carburatóre carburetor

cariàto decayed; rotten

caricàre to load

càrne meat

caròta carrot

carroattrézzi tow truck

carròzza railroad car; **in _____!** all aboard!; **_____ ristorànte** dining car

càrta paper, map; **_____ di crèdito** credit card; **_____ d'identità** identification card; **_____ stradàle** road map; **_____ da giuòco** playing card; **_____ igiènica** toilet paper; **_____ da imballàggio** wrapping paper; **_____ per bàttere a màcchina** typing paper

cartellíno chart, tag

cartolína card; **_____ illustràta** picture postcard; **_____ postàle** postcard

cartúccia cartridge

càsa house

cascàta waterfall

che who, that; _____ **còsa?** what?

chi who; _____ **è?** who is it?

chiamàre to call; **mi chiàmo** my name is

chiàro clear, light-colored

chiàve key

chièsa church

chiffon chiffon

chílo kilogram

chilòmetro kilometer; **a chilometràggio illimitàto** unlimited mileage

chiúdere to close; **pòsso _____?** may I close?

chiúso closed

céci chickpeas

cetriólo cucumber

ciabàtte slippers

ciào hi, hello, bye

cièlo heaven, sky; **per l'amór del _____!** my goodness!

cíglia eyelash

ciliègia cherry

cínema cinema, movie house

cineprésa movie camera

cinquànta fifty

cínque five

cinquecènto five hundred

cintúra belt

cioccolàta chocolate

ciòndolo charm

cipólla onion

città city

clàcson (car) horn

clàsse class

cocktail cocktail

cocómero watermelon

còfano hood

cognóme last name

colazióne breakfast

cólla glue

còllant pantyhose

collína hill

collírio eye drops

cólpo d'aria (al pètto) (chest) cold

coltèllo knife

cóme as, how; _____ **sta?** how are you?

cominciàre to begin

commèdia comedy

commerciàle commercial

commissariàto police station

compartiménto compartment

compràre to buy

complèto complete, full

compréso included

con with

concèrto concert; **sàla da concèrti** concert hall

confermàre to confirm

coníglio rabbit

conóscere to know

consegnàre to deliver

consèrva (di pomodòro) (tomato) sauce

consigliàre to recommend, to suggest

consolàto consulate

consommé consomme

contagióso contagious

continuàre to continue, to keep (doing something)

cónto bill, check; **cónti separàti** separate checks

contórno garnish; **càrne con contórno** meat and vegetables

contracettívo contraceptive

contusióne bruise

copèrta blanket

còpia copy, print

coràllo coral

coróna crown

còrpo body

corrènte current, running

corrètto correct; caffè _____ coffee with liquor

corridòio aisle

córsa fare

cortíle courtyard

córto(a) short

còsa thing; che _____? what?

cosí so, this way; bàsta _____! that's enough!

cosmètico cosmetic

costàta rib

costàre to cost; quànto còsta? how much is it?

costóso expensive; méno _____ cheaper

costúme (da bàgno) bathing suit

cotolétta cutlet

cotóne (idròfilo) (sanitary) cotton

còtto cooked; ben còtto well-done

còzze mussels

cràmpi cramps

cravàtta necktie

crèdito credit; càrta di _____ credit card

crèma cream

crícco jack (car)

cristàllo crystal

cròcchia bun

croissànt croissant

cròsta crust

cuccétta berth

cucchiàio spoon

cucchiaíno teaspoon

cucína kitchen, cooking

cucíre to sew

cuòre heart

cúrva curve

cuscíno pillow

D

da from, by, to, at the house of, since

dàdo nut

dàma checkers

danàro money

dàre to give; mi sta dàndo he (she) is giving me; dàre le càrte to deal

dàta date; qual è la dàta di òggi? what is today's date?

dàtteri dates (fruit)

davànti before, in front of

débole weak

dècimo tenth

decollàre to take off

dènte tooth; mal di dènti toothache

dentifrício toothpaste

dentísta dentist

deodorànte deodorant

depòsito deposit

desideràre to desire

dessert dessert

destinatàrio receiver; a càrico del destinatàrio collect

deviazióne detour

diabète diabetes

dèstro right; a dèstra to the right

detergènte detergent

diamànte diamond

diapositíve slides

diarrèa diarrhea

diàvolo devil; ma che diàvolo vuòle? what the devil do you want?

dicèmbre December

dichiaràre to declare

diciannòve nineteen

diciassètte seventeen

diciòtto eighteen

dièci ten

diètro in back of, after

díre to say; **mi díca** tell me; **ha détto** he (she) has said

dirètto direct, express train

direttóre conductor, director, manager

direzióne direction; **in che direzióne?** which way?

dirítto straight; **avànti dirítto** straight ahead

dísco disk, record

discotèca discotheque

disinfettànte (per la bócca) mouthwash

dispiacére to dislike; **mi dispiàce** I'm sorry; **le dispiàce?** do you mind?

dissenterìa dysentery

disturbàre to disturb

dito finger

dóccia shower; **fàre la dóccia** to take a shower

documénto document

dódici twelve

dogàna customs; **pagàr dogàna** to pay duty

dólci sweets

dolcificànte sugar substitute

dolére to hurt; **mi duòle** it hurts

dòllaro dollar

domàni tomorrow; **a domàni** see you tomorrow

doménica Sunday

dòmino dominoes

dònna woman; queen (for card games)

dopobàrba after-shave lotion

dopodomàni the day after tomorrow

dormìre to sleep

dottóre doctor

dóve where; **dov'è?** where is it?

dovére to have to, to owe; **quànto le devo?** how much do I owe you?

dràmma drama

drìtto straight

dùbbio doubt; **sènza dúbbio** without fail

dùe two

duecènto two hundred

durànte during

duràre to last

E

e and

ècco here is (are), there is (are)

edìcola newsstand

eh! wow!

égli he

elènco list

elettricità electricity

elèttrico electric

élla she

emergènza emergency

entràre to enter; **éntri!** come in!

equipaggiaménto equipment

èrba grass

esprèsso espresso (coffee), express train, special delivery

èssere to be

estàte summer

estràrre to extract, to pull out

ètto, ettogràmmo 100 grams, hectogram

F

fàccia face

facciàle facial; **massàggio facciàle** facial massage

fagiàno pheasant

fagiòlo bean

fagiolíno green bean

fàme hunger; **ho fàme** I'm hungry

famìglia family

fanalíni (tail) lights

fantasciènza science fiction

fantasìa imagination

fantàstico imaginary, fantastic, wonderful

fàre to do, to make; **mi fàccio il bàgno** I'm taking a bath; **fa fréddo** it is cold; **fa càldo** it is warm; **fàre la fíla** to stand in line

farmacìa pharmacy, drugstore

fàscia bandage

fastìdio trouble, nuisance

fattorìa farm

favóre favor; **per favóre** please

fazzolétto handkerchief; **fazzolétto di carta** paper handkerchief, "tissue"

febbràio February

fìbbre fever, temperature; **la fébbre del fièno** hay fever

fégato liver

féltro felt

ferìta wound, cut

fermàglio brooch

fermàre to stop

fermàta stop (bus stop, etc.)

férmo (pòsta) general delivery

ferraménta hardware store

ferrovìa railroad

fétta slice

fiammìfero match

fìco (fìchi) fig(s)

fìglia daughter

fìglio son

fìla line, row

fìlo thread, wire

fìlm film

filóne long loaf

fìltro filter

finèstra window

finestrìno (train) window

fioràio florist

fióre flower; **fiòri** clubs (card)

fìrma signature

firmàre to sign, to endorse

fiùme river

flanèlla flannel

folclorìstico folkloric

fontàna fountain

fòrbici scissors

forchétta fork

forcìna hairpin

forèsta forest

formàggio cheese

fórno oven; **al fórno** baked

fórse perhaps, maybe

fòrte strong; **più fòrte!** faster!

fortúna fortune; **buòna fortúna!** good luck!

fòrza! go!

fotografìa photograph

fòto-òttica camera store

fra between, among

fràgole strawberries

francobòllo postage stamp

fràngia bang(s)

fratèllo brother

frattúra fracture

fréccia direction indicator

fréddo cold

fréno brake

frésco cool, fresh

frétta hurry; **ho frétta** I'm in a hurry

frittàta omelet

frítto fried; **frítto místo** fish fry

frizióne tonic, massage, clutch

frónte front, forehead

frullàto (di làtte) (milk) shake

frullatóre blender

frútto(a) fruit

fumàre to smoke

fumatóre smoker

fúngo mushroom, fungus

funzionàre to work

fuòco fire; **al fuoco!** fire!

fuòri outside; **fuòri!** get out!

G

gabardíne gabardine

gabinétto toilet, rest room

gàmba leg

gàmberi prawns, shrimp

gas gas

gassàta with gas; **àcqua gassàta** carbonated water

gelatería ice cream store

gelàto ice cream

gengíve gums

gennàio January

gettóne token

ghiacciàto iced; **àcqua ghiacciàta** ice water

ghiàccio ice; **cubétti di ghiàccio** ice cubes

ghiàndole glands

giàcca jacket

giàda jade

giàllo yellow; **è un giàllo** it's a mystery

giàra jar

ginòcchio knee

giocattoleria toy store

gioielleria jewelry store

giornàle newspaper

giórno day; **buòn giórno** good morning

giovanòtto young man

giovedì Thursday

gioventù youth

giradíschi record player

giràre to turn; **giràre un asségno** to endorse a check; **mi gíra la tèsta** I'm dizzy

gíta trip, tour

giúgno June

giocàre to play (games)

gli the, to him

góla throat; **mal di góla** sore throat

gómito elbow

gómma eraser; **gómma bucáta** flat tire

gónfio swollen

gonfióre swelling, lump

gónna skirt

gràmmo gram

grànchio crab

grànde large, big; **più grànde** larger

gràzie thanks; **mólte gràzie** thank-you very much

grígio gray

grúcce dress hangers

guància cheek

guànto glove

guardàre to look at, to watch

guardaròba check room

guàsto breakdown, trouble

guàva guava

guída guide, guidebook

guidàre to drive

H

hambúrger hamburger

hotèl hotel

I

identità identity; **càrta d'identità** identification card

iàrda yard

ièri yesterday

igiénico hygienic; **un ròtolo di càrta igiènica** a roll of toilet paper

impaccàre to wrap up, to pack

impermeàbile raincoat

impiegàto clerk

importàre to matter; **non impòrta** it doesn't matter

importànte important

impossíbile impossible

impòsta tax

in into, in

incartàre to wrap in paper

incínta pregnant

inclúso(a) included

incominciàre to start

incontràre to meet

incrócio crossing, crossroad

indicàre to show, to point out

indiètro back, backward(s)

indirízzo address

indossàre to wear

infezióne infection

influènza flu

inglèse English

ingranàggio (del càmbio) gearshift

ingrèsso entrance

iniziàre to start

innamoràto(a) lover, sweetheart (girlfriend)

innocènte innocent

insalàta salad

insième together

insònnia insomnia

insulína insulin

intagliàto carved

interessànte interesting

internazionàle international

interpretàre to interpret

intèrprete interpreter

interròmpere to cut off (telephone)

interruttóre (electric light) switch

interurbàna long distance call

intórno around

invéce instead

investíto(a) run over (by a car)

inviàre to send

io I; **io stésso** myself

iòdio iodine

ippòdromo racetrack

L

la the, her, you

là there

làbbra lips

làcca hair spray

làcci (da scàrpe) shoelaces

làdro thief

làgo lake

lamétta blade

lambrétta motor scooter

làmpada lamp

lampóne raspberry

làna wool

lancétta hand (of a watch)

lasciàre to leave; **mi làsci in pàce!** don't bother me!

lassatívo laxative

làto side

làtte milk

lattúga lettuce

lavàggio wash; **lavàggio a sécco** dry cleaner

lavàre to wash; **lavàre a sécco** to dry-clean

le the, them, to her, to you

leggèro light, mild

lèi she, her, you

lentaménte slowly

lènte lens; **lènte a contàtto** contact lens

lentícchie lentils

lèpre hare

lèttera letter; **per vía aèrea** air mail; **assicuràta** insured; **raccomandàta** registered; **esprèsso** special delivery; **con ricevùta di ritórno** with return receipt

lètto bed

li them

lì there

líbero free, not occupied; **il líbero** halfback (soccer player)

librería bookstore

líbro book

lièto happy

limétta (per le únghie) (nail) file

limóne lemon

línea line

língua tongue

líno linen

liquóre liqueur

lísta list

lítro liter

locàle place

località site, place

lontàno distant, far away

lóro their, theirs; **a lóro** to them

lozióne lotion; **lozióne per l'abbronzatùra** suntan lotion

lubrificàre to lubricate, to grease, to oil

lúce light

lucidàre to shine (shoes)

lùglio July

lùi he, him

lunedí Monday

lúngo long

M

ma but, yet, however; **ma che!** nonsense!

màcchina machine, automobile

macedònia fresh-fruit salad

macellería butcher shop

màdre mother

magazzíno department store

mággio May

màglia sweater

magnífico great

maiàle pig

màle ill, sickness; **màl d'àuto** travel sickness

maledizióne malediction, curse; **maledizióne!** darn it!

màlto malt

mancàre to be lacking, to be missing; **tu mi mànchi** I miss you

mància tip

mandàre to send

mandaríno tangerine

màndorle almonds

mangiàre to eat

màngo mango

mànica sleeve

manicúra manicure

manifésto poster

maníglia doorknob

màno hand; **mi día una màno** give me a hand

mànzo beef

màrca brand

màrcia gear (car)

marciapiède sidewalk

màre sea; **che dà sul màre** facing the sea

margarína margarine

maríto husband

marróne brown

martedí Tuesday

martèllo hammer

màrzo March

màschera usher (theater)

masticàre to chew

materàsso mattress

matíta pencil; _____ **per il trùcco** eyeliner

màzze (da golf) (golf) clubs

màzzo (di càrte) deck (of cards)

me me

meccànico mechanic

medicína medicine

mèdico doctor

mèglio better

méla apple

melanzàna eggplant (aubergine)

melóne melon

menù menu

meraviglióso wonderful

mercàto market; **a buòn mercàto** cheap

mercoledí Wednesday

merlétto lace

merlúzzo codfish

mése month

Méssa Mass

messàggio message

metà half

mètro meter

metropolitàna subway

méttere to put

mezzanótte midnight

mèzzo half, means

mezzogiórno midday, noon

mía my

mi me

miéi my

miglióre better; **il miglióre** the best

milióne million

mílle one thousand

mineràle mineral

minéstra soup

mínimo minimum

minístro minister

minúto minute

mío my

mischiàre to shuffle

misúra measurement, size

mobiliàto furnished

mòdulo blank, form

mòglie wife

mòlla spring

mólto much, a lot

moménto moment

moníle necklace

montàgna mountain

montatúra frame

montóne mutton

moschèa mosque

mostràre to show; **mi mòstri** show me

motociclétta motorcycle

motoríno moped; **motoríno d'avviamènto** starter

muòvere to move

musèo museum

mùsica music; _____ **clàssica** classical music; _____ **modèrna** modern music

mutànde shorts, underwear

mutandíne panties

N

nàscita birth; **dàta di nàscita** birth date

nasèllo hake (fish)

nàso nose

nàstro (adesívo) Scotch tape

Natàle Christmas

naturalménte! of course!

nàve ship

nazionalità nationality

ne of (something)

necessàrio necessary

negòzio store; **negòzio d'abbigliaménto** clothing store

néro black

néve snow

nevicàre to snow

niènte nothing

night club nightclub

no no

nocciolíne hazelnuts

nóce (di còcco) (coco)nut

nói we, us

noleggiàre to rent

nóme name

non not

nòno ninth

normàle normal

nòstro(a) our, ours

nòtte night; **buòna nòtte** good night

novànta ninety

nòve nine

novecènto nine hundred

novèlla short story

novèmbre November

núlla nothing

numeràto numbered

número number

nuotàre to swim

nuòvo new

nylon nylon

O

o or

òca goose

occhiàli eyeglasses; **occhiàli da sóle** sunglasses

occhiàta look; **dàre un'occhiàta** to take a look

òcchio eye

occórrere to be necessary; **mi occórrono** I need (them)

occupàto taken, busy

ocèano ocean

oculísta oculist, eye doctor

officína meccànica repair shop

oggètti preziósi jewelry

òggi today

òlio oil

ómbra shade

ombrétto eye shadow

ónda wave

ondulàto wavy; **capélli onduláti** wavy hair

ònice onyx

òpera opera

operétta operetta

óra hour, now; **a che óra?** at what time?

oràrio timetable; **in oràrio** on schedule

ordinàre to order

orecchíno earring

òro gold; **d'òro massíccio** solid gold; **d'òro placcàto** gold plated

orologiàio watchmaker

orològio watch, clock; **orològio da pólso** wristwatch

òrzo barley

osservàre to observe, to watch

ostèllo (délla gioventù) (youth) hostel

ostería wineshop, tavern

òstrica oyster

ostruíre to obstruct, to block up

ottànta eighty

ottenére to obtain

òttico optician

òtto eight

ottocènto eight hundred

ottòbre October

otturàre to fill (a tooth)

P

pacchétto packet, small parcel, small package

pàcco package, parcel

pàdre father

paése village, town

pagàre to pay

pàio pair

palàzzo palace

pàlla ball

pallíni dots

pancétta bacon

pàne bread; **pàne tostàto** toasted bread

panettería bakery

paníno roll

pànna cream

pànno cloth

pannolíno linen cloth, diaper, sanitary napkin; **pannolíni ùsa e gètta** disposable diapers

panoràma view, panorama, landscape

pantalóni (a pair of) trousers, slacks, pants

pantòfola slipper

pantaloncíni shorts

paraúrti bumper

parcheggiàre to park

parchéggio parking

pàrco park

paréggio draw, tie (sport)

parlàre to speak, to talk

parrucchière hairdresser

pàrte part, section, area

partíre to depart, to leave

partíta game

passàggio passage, crossing; **divièto di passàggio** no crossing

passapòrto passport

passàre to pass, to go by

pàsta pasta, pastry

pastícca (per la tósse) (cough) drop

pàsto meal

pastóre pastor

patènte di guída driver's license

pàzzo mad, crazy; **mi sta facèndo uscíre pàzzo** it's driving me crazy

peccàto sin; **che peccàto!** what a shame!

pedóne pedestrian; pawn (chess)

pèlle skin, leather

penicillína penicillin

pénna pen; _____ **a sfèra** ball-point pen

pensàre to think

pensióne private residence, usually with meals; **pensióne complèta** room with 3 meals a day

pépe pepper

péra pear

per for, through, about

perché why, what, because

pèrdere to lose

perícolo danger; **pericolóso** dangerous

período period

pèrla pearl

permésso permitted, permit; **con permésso! permésso!** excuse me!

perméttere to permit, to allow

pernìce partridge

personàggio character

personàle personal

pesànte heavy

pèsca peach

pietrína flint

pèttine comb

pèzzo piece; _____ **di ricàmbio** spare part

piacére pleasure; **per piacére** please; **con piacére** with pleasure

piacére to please, to like, to be fond of; **mi piàce** I like him/her

piànta plant, tree, map

piàtto plate, dish

piattíno saucer

pícche spades (cards)

picción̄e (implùme) squab (pigeon)

píccolo small; **più píccolo** smaller

piède foot; **andare a pièdi** to walk

pièno full

piètra preziósa (precious) stone

píllola pill

pínze pliers

pinzétta tweezers

piòvere to rain

piscína swimming pool

pisèlli peas

písta dance floor; **le píste per sciàre** ski slopes

più more

pízzo lace; pointed beard

plàstica plastic

platèa orchestra (theater)

plàtino platinum

pneumàtico tire; **un materassíno pneumàtico** an air mattress

pòco little

pòker poker

polièstere synthetic

polizía police; **stazióne di polizía** police station

pòllice thumb, inch

póllo chicken

polmóne lung

polpétta meatball

pólipo octopus

pólso wrist

pólvere dust, powder

pomeríggio afternoon

pomodòro tomato

pómpa pump; **pómpa della benzína** fuel pump

pompèlmo grapefruit

pónte bridge

pòrta door, gate

portabagàgli luggage rack, porter

portacénere ashtray

portafòglio wallet

portàre to bring; **mi pòrti** bring me; **dove pòrta quésta stràda?** where does this road lead to?

portàta course (meal)

pòrto port, harbor

porzióne portion

possíbile possible

pòsta mail

postàle postal; **vàglia postàle** money order; **pòste e telègrafi** postal and telegraph services

posteggiàre to park

postéggio parking

pósto place, spot, seat

potàbile potable, drinkable

potére to be able to, can
pranzàre to dine, to have dinner
prànzo dinner, lunch
preferíre to prefer
prefísso area code
preghièra prayer
prègo you're welcome
prèndere to take; **lo (la) prèndo!** I'll take it!
prenotazióne reservation
présa di corrènte electric outlet
presentàre to present
prèstito loan
prèsto early
prète priest
prèzzo price; **a prèzzo físso** fixed price
primavèra spring
prímo first
principàle main, principal
privàto private
professióne profession
profilàttici prophylactics
profúmo perfume
prónto ready; **prónto soccórso** first aid; **prónto!** hello! (telephone)
pròprio own, private
prosciútto ham
pròssimo near, next
pròtesi dentària dental prosthesis
protestànte protestant
provàre to prove, to try; **pòsso provàrmelo?** may I try it on?
prúgna plum
pulíre to clean
púllman motor coach
punch punch
puntéggio score
puntíno dot; **a puntíno** medium (of meat)

Q

qua here
quàdro picture, painting
quàdri diamonds (cards)
quàlche a few, some, any
qualcúno somebody, someone, anybody
qualità quality
quàndo when
quànto how much; **quànto còsta?** how much is it?
quarànta forty
quàrto fourth, quarter
quattórdici fourteen
quàttro four
quattrocènto four hundred
quéllo that, that one; **che cos'è quéllo?** what's that?
quésto this
qui here
quíndici fifteen
quínto fifth

R

rabbíno rabbi
racchétta racquet; **racchétte da scí** ski poles
raccommandàta registered letter
raccónti stories
ràdio portàtile portable radio
raffreddóre cold
ragàzza girl
ragàzzo boy
raggiúngere to reach, to get to, to arrive at
rammendàre to mend
rasóio razor
rattoppàre to patch up, to mend

ravanèllo radish

re king

recapitàre to deliver

regàlo gift

regalíno little present

reggiséno brassiere, bra

regína queen

registratóre tape recorder

religióso religious

rènna suede

respiràre to breathe

restàre to stay, to remain

rèsto change (from a paid bill)

rètro behind; **sul rètro** in the back

rícciolo curl

ricètta prescription

ricévere to receive

ricevúta receipt

ricreazióne recreation

ridótto reduced; **a taríffa ridótta** half-price ticket

ríga ruler; **con ríghe** with stripes

rigonfiaménto swelling

rimanére to remain, to stay

rimorchiàre to tow

riparàre to repair, to fix

riservàto reserved

risièdere to reside, to live

ríso rice

ristorànte restaurant

risultàto score, result, outcome

ritàrdo delay, lateness

ritornàre to return, to go back

ritórno return; **andàta e ritórno** round trip

rivísta magazine, periodical

rognóne kidney

romànzo love story, novel

ròsa rose, pink

rosétta small round bread, bun

rossétto rouge; _____ **per le làbbra** lipstick

rósso red

roulòtte trailer

rubàre to steal

rubinétto faucet

rubíno ruby

rullíno roll of film

ruòta wheel

ruscèllo brook, small stream

S

sàbato Saturday

sàbbia sand

saccarína saccharin

sacchétto bag

sàla large room; **la sàla da prànzo** dining room

salàto salted, salty

salàme salami

sàle salt

salmóne salmon

salóne di bellezza beauty parlor

salòtto living room

salumería delicatessen

salúte health; **salúte!** cheers!

salúti greetings

sàngue blood; **sto sanguinàndo** I'm bleeding

sapére to know; **lo so!** I know it!

saponétta small bar of soap

sardína sardine

sàrto tailor

sbagliàre to make a mistake, to go wrong in (something); **número sbagliàto** wrong number

sbigàrsi to hurry up; **si sbríghi!** hurry up!

scàcchi chess

scacchièra chessboard

scàcco chessman

scaccomàtto checkmate

scamosciàto suede

scàmpi shrimp

scàpolo bachelor

scàrpa shoe

scarpóni da sci ski boots

scàtola box

scattàre una fòto to take a picture

scéndere to go down, to get off

schièna back

scí ski; **scí acquàtico** waterskiing

sciàre to ski

sciocchézza silliness; **sciocchèzze!** nonsense!

sciòcco silly, fool

sciovíe ski lifts

scíppo bag snatching

sciròppo syrup

scottatúra solàre sunburn

scrívere to write

scúro dark

scusàre to excuse; **mi scúsi!** excuse me!

sdraiàrsi to lie down, to stretch; **si sdrài!** lie down!

seccatúra nuisance; **ma che seccatúra!** what a nuisance!

sécco dry

secóndo second

sèdano celery

sedatívo sedative

sedére to sit, to be sitting; **vòglio sedérmi** I want to sit.

sèdia chair; **sèdia a sdràio** chaise longue

sédici sixteen

ségala rye

seguíre to follow

sèi six

seicènto six hundred

selezióne selection; **telefonàta in tele-selezióne** long distance call

selvaggína game

semàforo traffic light

sémola bran; **pàne integràle** whole wheat (whole meal) bread

sentièro path, pathway

sentíre to feel, to hear; **non mi sènto bène** I don't feel well.

sènape mustard

sènza without

séppia squid

séra evening, night; **buòna séra** good evening

serbatóio fuel tank

sèrie series; **in sèrie A** major league (sport)

servíre to serve

servízio service; **servízi di traspòrti pùbblici** public transportation

sessànta sixty

séte thirst; **ho séte** I'm thirsty.

settànta seventy

sètte seven; **sètte e mèzzo** blackjack (card game)

settecènto seven hundred

settimàna week

sèttimo seventh

shampoo shampoo; **shampoo e méssa in pièga** wash and set

sherry sherry

si one, they, people, oneself, himself, herself, themselves

sí yes

sídro cider

sigarétta cigarette

sígaro cigar

significàre to mean, to signify; **che còsa signífica quésto?** what does this mean?

signóra lady, wife, Mrs.

signóre gentleman, Mr. (use *signór* when addressing the person); **Signór Róssi, come stà?** Mr. Rossi, how are you?

signoría young lady, Miss

silènzio silence

sinagòga synagogue

sinístro left, left-hand; **a sinístra** to the left

sistèma system

slip man's briefs, shorts

slogàre to sprain

smàlto enamel; **smàlto per le únghie** nail polish

smeràldo emerald

soccórso help, aid; **prónto soccórso** first aid

sògliola sole (fish)

sòldi money

sóle sun

sólo alone

sópra on, upon, upstairs

sopràbito overcoat

sopràno soprano

sorèlla sister

sorrídere to smile

sósta stop; **divièto di sósta** no parking

sottotítolo subtitle

sottovèste slip, undergarment

souvenir souvenir

spàlla shoulder

spàzzola brush

spazzolíno per i dènti toothbrush

spècchio mirror

specialità specialty

spedíre to send, to mail

spésso often

spettàcolo show

spiàggia beach

spíccioli small change

spílla brooch

spína per la corrènte electric plug

spinàci spinach

spíngere to push

splèndido wonderful

spogliàre to undress; **si spògli** undress yourself

spòrco dirty

sportèllo window (bank, post office, ticket office)

sportívo sporting; **una màcchina sportíva** a sports car

sposàto(a) married

spúgna sponge

spumànte sparkling wine

spuntàre to trim

sputàre to spit

squàdra team

stàdio stadium

stagióne season

stàgno pond

stàlla barn

stànco(a) tired; **mi sènto stànco** I'm tired

stàre to be, to stay, to remain

staséra this evening

stazióne station

stécca carton

sterlíne pounds (British pound sterling)

stésso same

stiràre to iron; **che non si stíra** permanent press

stitichézza constipation

stiyàle boot

stòmaco stomach

stórto twisted

stràda street, road

strétto tight, narrow

stríngere to tighten

stupèndo(a) wonderful

stúpido(a) stupid; **non èssere stúpido!** don't be stupid!

stuzzicadènti toothpicks

su on, upon, up, upstairs

súbito at once, right away

succèdere to happen; **che còsa succède?** what's up?

suòle soles (shoes)

supermercàto supermarket

surf (tàvola da surf) surf

surriscaldàre to overheat

susína plum

svéndita sale

svegliàre to wake up

sveníre to faint

sviluppàre to develop

T

tabacchería tobacco shop

tabàcco tobacco; _____ **da fiúto** snuff tobacco

tacchíno turkey

tàcchi heels (shoes)

taccuíno notebook

tàglia size

tagliàre to cut; **un tàglio di capélli** a haircut

tagliaúnghie nail clippers

tàlco talcum powder

tampóni igiènici sanitary tampons

tànto a lot, much

tàrdi late; **a più tàrdi** see you later; **al più tàrdi** at the latest

tariffa tariff, rate, fare

tàxi taxi

tàvola table

tàzza cup

tè tea

teàtro theater

telefonàre to telephone

telefonàta phone call; **in teleselezióne** long distance; **interurbàna** long distance; **urbàna** local; **con preavvíso** person to person; **riversíbile** reverse the charge

telèfono telephone; **cabína telefónica** telephone booth; **elènco telefónico** telephone directory

telegràmma telegram

televisióne television

temperamatíte pencil sharpener

temperatúra temperature

tèmpo time, weather

temporaneamènte temporarily

tènnis tennis

tenóre tenor

tergicristàllo windshield wiper

termòmetro thermometer

tèrra earth, land

terràzza terrace

terríbile terrible

terzíno fullback (sport)

tèrzo third

tèssera card, ticket, pass, identification card

tèsta head

ti you, yourself

tínta uníta solid color

tintoría dry cleaner

tintúra dye; **tintúra di iódio** tincture of iodine

títolo title

toccàre to touch

toilette rest room

tònico tonic

tonsílle tonsils

tónno tuna

topàzio topaz

tornàre to return, to come back

tórta cake, pie

tósse cough

tossíre to cough

tour trip, excursion

tovàglia tablecloth

tovaglìolo napkin

trànsito transit; **divièto di trànsito** no entrance

tranvài streetcar

trascórrere to spend, to pass

trasmissióne transmission

trattoría inn, tavern

traversàta crossing

tre three

trecènto three hundred

trédici thirteen

trèno train

trènta thirty

trentúno thirty-one

trentadúe thirty-two

tròta trout

trúcco makeup

tu you

turchése turquoise

túbo di scappamènto exhaust pipe

turístico for tourists

tútto(a) all, everything; **tútta l'estàte** all summer

U

uccèllo bird

uff! phew!

ufficio office; **ufficio postàle** post office

uh! ugh!

último(a) last

úndici eleven

università university

un, úno, úna, un' an, a, one

uòvo egg; **uòva sode** hard-cooked eggs; _____ **strapazzàte** scrambled eggs; _____ **alla coque** soft-boiled eggs

urbàno urban

uscíre to go out; **èsca!** get out!

uscíta exit, gate

ustióne burn

V

vacànza vacation

vàglia money order

vagóne railroad car; **vagóne lètto** sleeping car

valígia suitcase

vallàta valley

valúta currency

vaníglia vanilla

vedére to see

vellúto velvet

velóce fast; **più velóce** faster

véndere to sell

venerdí Friday

vénti twenty

ventidúe twenty-two

ventimíla twenty thousand

vènto wind; **tíra vènto** it's windy

ventàglio fan

ventúno twenty-one

vérde green

vèro true, real

vèspa motor scooter

vestàglia robe

vèste dress

vestírsi to get dressed; **si vèsta** get dressed

vestíto dress, suit

vetrína shop window

vétro glass; **vétro soffiàto** blown glass

vía street, way; **vía aèrea** air mail

viàggio trip

vicíno near, next to

vietàto forbidden; **vietàto sputàre** no spitting

villàggio village

villíno cottage

víncere to win

víno wine

vísita visit

vitamína vitamin

víte screw

vitèllo calf; **cotolétte di vitèllo** veal cutlets

volànte steering wheel

volére to want, to wish; **vorrèi** I'd like

vólo flight

vòlta time; **úna vòlta** once

vóngole clams

Z

zàffiro sapphire

zèro zero

zía aunt

zío uncle

zítto! shut up!

zóna zone, area

zòo zoo; **giardíno zoològico** zoological garden

zúcchero sugar

INDEX

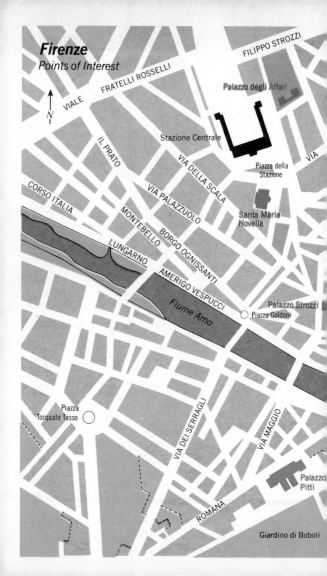